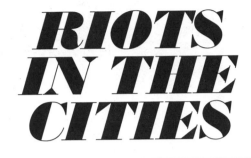

RIOTS IN THE CITIES

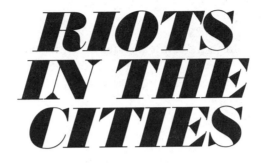

RIOTS IN THE CITIES

Popular Politics and the Urban Poor in Latin America, 1765-1910

Edited by
Silvia M. Arrom and Servando Ortoll

A Scholarly Resources Inc. Imprint
Wilmington, Delaware

Scholarly Resources Inc.
104 Greenhill Avenue
Wilmington, DE 19805-1897

Library of Congress Cataloging-in-Publication Data

Riots in the cities : popular politics and the urban poor in
  Latin America, 1765–1910 / edited by Silvia M. Arrom and
  Servando Ortoll.
        p.   cm. — (Latin American silhouettes)
    Includes bibliographical references.
    ISBN 0-8420-2580-4 (alk. paper). — ISBN 0-8420-2581-2
(pbk. : alk. paper)
      1. Riots—Latin America—History. 2. Urban poor—Latin
America—Political activity—History. 3. Cities and towns—
Latin America—History. I. Arrom, Silvia Marina, 1949–   .
II. Ortoll, Servando. III. Series.
HV6485.L29R56   1996
303.6'23'098—dc20   95-25920
                                                              CIP

⊗ The paper used in this publication meets the minimum requirements of the American National Standard for permanence of paper
for printed library materials, Z39.48, 1984.

To our children,

Christina Alexandra and Daniel David Oran

and

Servando Amir and Amnón Gabriel Ortoll-Bloch,

with the hope that they will one day comprehend

the history of our continent

Acknowledgments

The editors would like to thank the many people who have contributed to this volume. Silvia Arrom is particularly grateful to Marilyn Brooks for her cheerful assistance with the myriad last-minute details of manuscript preparation, and to David Oran for his constant support and generous sharing of his computer expertise. Servando Ortoll expresses his gratitude to Dr. Juan Manuel Durán Juárez, president of the Social Sciences and Humanities Campus at the University of Guadalajara; to Licenciado Fernando Moreno Peña, president of the University of Colima; and to Licenciado Luis Ignacio Villagarcía, director of the Instituto Colimense de Cultura, for continuously supporting his research and assisting him in the development of this project. He especially thanks Avital H. Bloch, who, with unmatched spirit, has encouraged his ideas and projects for many years. The editors are also indebted to William Beezley and the staff at Scholarly Resources for their enthusiasm and patience.

Contents

Preface

Every book has a history of its own, and this one is no exception. In the mid-1980s I started a project about city riots with Tymothy Gilfoyle, a fellow graduate student at Columbia University. We planned to publish a series of articles on urban disturbances then being studied around the world, but we abandoned the venture as we each became involved in our doctoral research.

My interest in urban riots did not diminish, however. While doing research for my dissertation on Mexican Catholic organizations during the 1920s and 1930s, I unexpectedly discovered information about two nights of rioting in my hometown of Guadalajara, Mexico, in two archives in the United States: the records of the American Board of Commissioners for Foreign Missions, then under restricted access at Harvard University, and the consular records at the National Archives in Washington, DC. Both contained the correspondence of Methodist missionaries stationed in Guadalajara who had been victims of the mob's anger, as well as reports of the American consul in Jalisco's capital and of the U.S. ambassador in Mexico City. These accounts challenged the view of Guadalajara, long propounded by local historians and antiquarians, as a conservative and peaceful city that contrasted with other rebellious areas of Mexico. I decided to look further into the events and was able to find local and national newspapers that gave me a radically different view of the city's residents.

In 1985 I returned to Mexico after a ten-year absence and presented a paper on the Guadalajara riots which I wrote with my wife, Avital H. Bloch, who also was a graduate student at Columbia University. At the Seventh Conference of Mexican and United States Historians, held in the colonial city of Oaxaca, I met historian Silvia Arrom, who was presenting a paper on the 1828 riot of the Parián. We decided to edit a volume of the most important articles written about Latin American riots. After some investigation, we realized that most of the research on popular disturbances in the region dealt with rural uprisings or military coups. We proposed to help fill this vacuum by collecting articles about urban riots that occurred before 1910, to counter the widespread belief that the political participation of the popular classes was a new phenomenon in the twentieth century. We also thought that the Latin American riots should not be studied in isolation but would benefit from the intensive research being produced by scholars in Europe and the United States on worldwide popular protests. Desiring a comparative perspective, I approached Charles Tilly, a leading expert on European collective social movements whom I had met while writing my dissertation, and he agreed to write an article for this volume. Meanwhile, several new studies of urban riots appeared and were incorporated into the collection.

Finally, after ten years of planning, the book is complete. It includes seven important studies of riots in Latin American cities written by historians and sociologists. It opens and closes with two original essays. The introductory chapter by Arrom explores the significance of these riots for understanding Latin American politics in the colonial period and the nineteenth century. The conclusion by Tilly reviews the essays and suggests directions for future research based on his knowledge of the European experience.

It is our hope that this book will change the way scholars think about Latin American cities. True, ours is a history of episodic outbreaks of violence. Taken together, however, the essays show the importance of the urban masses as political actors prior to the emergence of revolutionary and populist politics after 1910. By analyzing the underlying causes of the riots, who the rioters were, and the adversaries they faced, these essays also make theoretical contributions to understanding the conditions under which people revolt. We hope that by bringing together previously scattered articles, this collection will make this research accessible to a wide readership from several disciplines—for it has significant implications for policymakers, sociologists, and political scientists as well as for the historians who read the journals in which the case studies originally appeared. Finally, we hope that this volume will encourage more research on popular politics in Latin American cities, a subject neglected by students of the past and present conditions of our continent.

Servando Ortoll

Introduction: Rethinking Urban Politics in Latin America before the Populist Era

Silvia Marina Arrom*

Students of Latin American populism portray the political participation of the urban masses as a new phenomenon, one that emerged after 1910, and one that distinguished the twentieth century from the past when elites firmly controlled the political process.[1] Although historians never forgot the sweeping Tupac Amaru and Comunero revolts of 1780 and 1781, or the localized uprisings that accompanied the Bourbon Reforms in the 1760s,[2] these were viewed as exceptional incidents that only briefly punctuated centuries of elite dominion. Recently, however, revisionist scholars have questioned the degree of elite power prior to the twentieth century by studying the peasant rebellions and slave revolts, as well as less violent but more continuous forms of resistance, that were ubiquitous in rural areas.[3] While peasants and slaves have now been restored to their rightful place as significant political actors, the urban poor have been largely overlooked. Indeed, in his 1988 analysis of Latin American riots and rebellions during the eighteenth and nineteenth centuries, John Coatsworth lamented that he was forced to focus on rural rebellions because, "with the exception of Brazilian slave insurrections in the nineteenth century, the history of . . . urban social struggles has yet to be written."[4]

The authors of this volume contribute to the writing of that history by providing seven studies on urban riots in Latin America before the period of populist politics. These essays analyze riots in six major cities between 1765 and 1910—all of them capitals of either states (Salvador, Bahia; and Guadalajara, Jalisco), nations (Mexico City, Mexico; Rio de Janeiro, Brazil; and Bogotá, Colombia), or viceroyalties (Quito, viceroyalty of New Granada). Their populations were large: the smallest, Quito and Salvador, numbered approximately 30,000 and 66,000, respectively; the others reached the hundreds of thousands, with Rio approaching 800,000 by 1904.

*The author wishes to thank Leslie Berliant, Eugene Black, Sandra L. Graham, and Catherine LeGrand for their helpful comments on this essay.

And their riots were dramatic, involved thousands of participants, and caused major disruptions as the crowd temporarily took over sections of the cities. For that reason most of these incidents are well known in their nation's histories. Indeed, all but two (the smaller riots of Bogotá in 1893 and Guadalajara in 1910, which were "discovered" by the authors in archival records) quickly earned the nicknames by which they have been known ever since: the Rebellion of the Barrios (Quito 1765); the Parián Riot (Mexico City 1828); the Cemiterada (Salvador 1836); the Vintem Riot (Rio de Janeiro 1880); and the Revolta Contra Vacina (Rio 1904). Yet despite their renown, these incidents have received little serious scholarly attention until recently.

These studies, originally published between 1980 and 1992, were inspired by the great histories of European riots written by Eric Hobsbawm and George Rudé.[5] Beginning in the 1950s, these scholars changed the way that historians interpreted the violence of urban crowds. Unlike previous chroniclers who viewed rioters as a crazed mob, Hobsbawm and Rudé portrayed them as rational—indeed, heroic—protesters motivated by shared goals and an incipient sense of class struggle. This perspective led to a proliferation of studies on collective violence in Europe and the United States.[6] Only in the late 1970s, in the wake of the dramatic urban riots of the previous decade, did Latin American riots begin to be studied by a new generation of social historians who reacted against centuries of elite-centered histories that ignored, disparaged, or at best portrayed the popular classes as faceless victims.[7]

The essays collected in this volume show that Hobsbawm's and Rudé's interpretations of urban riots apply to Latin America in some respects. After carefully examining the conditions that led to violence, the composition of the crowds, and their demands and targets, the authors find that the Latin American rioters, like the European ones, were far from irrational. They responded to specific provocations or calls for popular mobilization in support of a given cause, and their rampages were not indiscriminate. On the whole, they attacked property rather than people. Although the violence occasionally threatened to get out of control, the crowds largely vented their rage on selected targets that symbolized hated figures or policies (such as tax administration buildings, police headquarters, import merchants' shops, or foreigners' houses). Even the one case of apparently aimless destruction (the 1904 looting of stores and smashing of streetlamps and telegraph equipment in Rio) is portrayed by Jeffrey Needell as a rational strategy to gain a tactical advantage.

The authors follow Hobsbawm and Rudé's lead in viewing the Latin American riots as an expression of broadly shared beliefs and attitudes. These studies thus help answer the question: What do the poor want? (or perhaps, What do the poor believe?)—answers largely lacking for cities in the region before 1910. The issues that engaged the urban poor in Latin America were extraordinarily diverse and cannot simply be reduced to the "economic" category emphasized by these Marxist historians. The Quito and Rio riots of 1765 and 1880, sparked by opposition to new taxes, were clearly attempts to defend the material well-being of the populace. In the other cases, the rioters were motivated by a strong sense of justice, nationalism, religion, and the right to privacy. Their grievances included opposition to a law prohibiting burials in churches (Salvador 1836) and to compulsory vaccination (Rio 1904); outrage at the news of the lynching of a Mexican in Texas (Guadalajara 1910); resentment of police repression (Bogotá 1893 and Rio 1904) and of a journalist's defamation of the city's artisans (Bogotá 1893); and xenophobic hatred of Spaniards and Protestant Yankees (Quito 1765, Mexico City 1828, and Guadalajara 1910). The rioters in Mexico City in 1828 also expressed support for politicians who opposed the government. These studies point to the need, as posited by Florencia Mallon for peasant society, to write a serious intellectual history of subordinate groups who are too often seen as "acting only on the urging of their stomachs."[8]

Such studies may find less of a "leveling instinct" than among the populace in European cities, for the Latin American rioters appear to come from a broader spectrum of society than those studied by Hobsbawm and Rudé. Our knowledge of the composition of the Latin American crowds is imprecise due to the absence or miniscule numbers of arrests following the tumults (with the notable exceptions of the 1893, 1904, and 1910 riots in Bogotá, Rio, and Guadalajara, which were severely punished). Perhaps for the same reason these studies fail to discover leaders or organizers among the rioters, if such existed (except in 1904). Yet the available evidence on the participants suggests that the Latin American crowds included not only the "honest" shopkeepers and artisans emphasized—and idealized—by Hobsbawm and Rudé as precursors of organized labor[9] but also unemployed slumdwellers and, in some cases, soldiers (Mexico City 1828), policemen and students

(Guadalajara 1910), and nuns and priests (Salvador 1836, and perhaps also Quito 1765).

Thus, the Latin American riots do not always duplicate the patterns described by Hobsbawm and Rudé. Although, as in Europe, the rioters were far from a criminal rabble, there was little lower-class solidarity or interclass conflict in the Latin American tumults. In at least three cases the riots appear to have been multiclass (Quito 1765, Salvador 1836, Guadalajara 1910, and perhaps also in Rio 1880); indeed, Anthony McFarlane labels the Quito riots "the rebellion of a community rather than a class."[10] Even when the crowd apparently represented the popular classes, the rioters did not lash out at the rich in general; on the contrary, in most cases they were closely allied with, and initially mobilized by, disgruntled elites. In fact, the 1893 riots in Bogotá are the only ones in this volume where the popular uprisings did not follow peaceful protests or coup attempts by dissident politicians or students (future elites in the Latin American context) and where the grievances of one group—the city's artisans—sparked the melee.

In the other six riots the role of elites was critical in arousing popular protest. Just how the interclass alliance worked is unclear from these studies. The elites quickly lost control of the mobilized masses, thereby showing that they were not mere tools of elite politicians. Yet a question that needs further research is the degree of independent popular consciousness. Since we cannot assume a preexisting class consciousness, as posited by the older generation of Marxist historians, we should address the questions raised by the "new social movements" theorists, who argue that group identity must be constructed.[11] We might ask, for example, whether a popular agenda was already there and merely "released" by the split among elites, as implied by the diverging grievances of lower-class rioters and elite participants in the riots of 1765 and 1904. Alternatively, a popular awareness might have been instilled by elite mobilizers, elite conflict might have provided the opportunity for the formation of group identity, or, as suggested by Sandra Lauderdale Graham, it might have developed through direct action and the appropriation of elite rhetoric. In any case, the repeated coincidence of the Latin American riots with partisan struggles indicates their linkages with elite politics. It is therefore misleading to label the urban poor as either "prepolitical," as did Hobsbawm, or as "apolitical," as did Oscar Lewis.[12]

The possible distinctiveness of Latin American popular movements is also hinted at by recent studies of bandits.[13] First, they demonstrate that the causes for banditry in the region were more often political than economic, corresponding to the weakening of centralized authority more than to the encroachment of capitalism. Thus, banditry, like urban rioting, must be understood within the context of the larger political system. Second, these studies show that it is inaccurate to portray Latin American bandits as champions of the people because so many allied themselves with powerful elites and victimized the poor connected with the other faction. Just as with the urban riots, it appears that in eighteenth- and nineteenth-century Latin America, where patron-client bonds were strong, vertical ties were at least as important as horizontal ones. Perhaps this is one reason why populism, with its multiclass base, became so appealing in the twentieth century.

When taken together, the essays in this volume help us begin to reconceptualize how Latin American politics worked in the period before the emergence of populism. They show that urban politics prior to 1910 was not a strictly elite affair, and that those who study "high politics" to the exclusion of street politics have missed the importance of the masses as political actors. Furthermore, they demonstrate that lower-class city residents held strong opinions about many political issues, that they acted on their convictions, and that their struggles had an impact (although not always the one intended) on who held power and what policies were implemented.

Indeed, the tendency of urban officials to bargain with the poor rather than repress them—at least until the end of the nineteenth century—suggests that we might want to resuscitate the notion of a "social compact" to explain how peace was maintained in Latin American cities with minimal force during the colonial period and nineteenth century. Although the existence of a social compact was frequently invoked by Spanish Americans in the early nineteenth century to justify their struggle for independence from Spain, they were thinking of a compact between themselves and the monarchy in Madrid. At its broadest this term was used to describe an unstated agreement between local communities and the central government that the state's authority would be respected in return for some local autonomy.[14] Perhaps this notion should be extended to include a compact between rich and poor—a compact that, although ratifying social inequality, established boundaries of acceptable behavior recognized by all parties.[15]

The studies in this volume support this notion in several ways. First, the riots were not entirely spontaneous reactions by an enraged populace. The authors suggest that the crowds believed that their direct action was legitimized by the concurrent protest or struggle of dissident elites or, in the 1893 case, by the orderly protest of Bogotá's largest mutual aid society. In other words, the rioters may have assumed that they had a kind of permission to disrupt the peace and, at least initially, may have thought that they were playing by the rules. Moreover, the rioters repeatedly showed that they expected to be heard by city authorities as part of their fundamental rights as citizens.[16] Indeed, it was the authorities' failure to meet with protesters in 1880 in Rio that caused a peaceful demonstration to become violent. Finally, the outcomes of the riots, prior to 1880, show that Latin American elites responded with remarkable flexibility and moderation. In fact, in three of the five cases where specific demands were made, city officials gave in to them. Thus, in 1765, 1836, and 1904 the crowd "won" when the offensive tax, law, or policy was rescinded. In the two cases where no demands were made, in 1828 and 1910, the violence quickly spent itself. Only in 1880 and 1893 did the authorities refuse to make concessions to the crowds, as both republican and colonial authorities had previously.

Although it is tempting to argue that the social compact between rich and poor was a republican innovation, born when the legitimacy of the state rested on the explicit consent of the governed, these essays suggest a different chronology, where the compact operated most successfully during the colonial and early republican periods and began unraveling toward the end of the nineteenth century. The essays on the 1828 and 1880 riots present the alliance between dissident politicians and the masses as a new development connected with republican politics. The Parián Riot resulted from the courting of the poor, not yet barred from suffrage, in a fiercely contested election and coup; the Vintem Riot likewise followed the arousal of the masses by politicians intent on discrediting the monarchy (Brazil became a republic only in 1889). Yet both the 1765 Rebellion of the Barrios and the great Mexico City riots of 1624 and 1692 show that the social compact was much older, for in these cases peace was restored only after a tacit bargain was struck with the urban populace.[17] These incidents where social order was temporarily disrupted suggest that in normal times the social compact enjoyed the active consent of the urban poor. Indeed, it worked well enough that Latin American elites in the eighteenth and early nineteenth centuries feared threats from outside their cities—whether from Indian villagers, *comuneros* march-

ing on Bogotá, or Miguel Hidalgo's "hordes" attacking Guanajuato
—much more than they feared uprisings of the populace within.

It is worth analyzing how urban peace was maintained before
the creation of professional police forces in the late eighteenth and
nineteenth centuries. In explaining why rural areas were more prone
to riot than urban ones, Eric Van Young emphasizes what we might
call the "negative" factors preventing collective action in Latin
American cities: their large size, lack of cohesiveness due to ethnic
heterogeneity, fluid and substantially migrant population, and
the relative weakness of popular organizations.[18] Alberto Flores
Galindo, in his study of colonial Lima, emphasizes the prevalence
of "domestic" violence, within the family and between masters and
servants or patrons and clients, that made state force unnecessary.[19]
Although these factors undoubtedly played a part, historians also
would do well to explore the "positive" factors that contributed to
social peace. These factors include, as Douglas Cope, Alejandra
Moreno Toscano, and Michael Scardaville suggest in recent studies, a political culture that emphasized conciliation and class har-
mony, a social reality where bonds of patronage and clientelism
united members of disparate classes, rudimentary social services
provided by municipal authorities, and the expectation of justice
from the court system.[20] In addition, the Church played a crucial
role in preserving order, with priests serving dual roles as both agitators and peacemakers in the colonial riots, as they did in the Independence Wars.[21] Indeed, the urban crowds usually sided with
ecclesiastical, rather than secular, authorities when disputes arose,
thereby reminding us of the religious basis of legitimacy of the
colonial state.[22]

These studies suggest, however, that the "positive" factors were
working less effectively by the end of the nineteenth century and
that urban peace was increasingly maintained by force instead of
by consent. The incipient organization of the urban working classes,
hinted at in the role of mutual aid societies and the syndicalist movement in the 1893 and 1904 riots, signaled a weakening of patron-
client ties as well as a parallel rise in class consciousness. The
reduced role of the Church as peacemaker is implied by the disap-
pearance of priests as agents to restore order in the republican
riots. As these traditional mechanisms of control declined, the
police took on an increasingly important function.[23] Thus, it was
only in the 1880 and 1893 riots that the crowds were brutally repressed instead of heard; in 1904, when the crowd action succeeded

in forcing the suspension of a compulsory vaccination campaign, massive force was nonetheless used to restore order as well. Moreover, the police emerged as targets of popular ire only in 1893 and 1904. It may be, then, that the populist politics of the twentieth century were necessary to restore a social compact that had become increasingly strained. The new compact eventually included the recognition and co-optation of urban labor by populist governments.

Some scholars might argue that seven riots in six cities is too small a sample from which to draw such broad conclusions; indeed, that riots were so rare that they represented the exception that proved the rule of urban passivity. Van Young implies as much when he characterizes Latin American cities as "islands in the storm," whose "quiet" contrasts sharply with the "continual sea of rural riot and rebellion."[24] Certainly, peasant villages were more prone to violence, as entire communities frequently united to protest the violation of local norms. And it is worth noting that the uprisings of Quito and Salvador, the two smallest cities, came closest to this "village" model, thus supporting Van Young's observation that urbanization is negatively correlated with widespread collective action.

Urban riots should not be discounted simply because they were rare, however; instead, the few large-scale uprisings should be seen as the tip of an iceberg. As scholars delve into the Latin American archives, smaller urban protests, often based in one neighborhood,[25] are constantly coming to light. For example, in his study of Mexico City between 1824 and 1854, Frederick Shaw documents riots in 1838, 1844, 1847, and 1849 in addition to the well-known 1828 explosion of the Parián. Although these tumults are not as dramatic as the incidents studied in this volume, Shaw concludes that, in all but one case where the crowd "failed" to achieve its objective, the riots (and, in 1840, the fear of riots) caused politicians to modify their behavior by withdrawing from elections, resigning from office, or desisting from plans to establish a dictatorship.[26] Thus, the minor incidents, like the major ones, were a vehicle for popular input into politics.

The significance of these riots further increases when we realize that violent uprisings were merely one type within a broad range of popular political action—what Charles Tilly calls a "repertoire of contention."[27] Much more frequent, and more moderate, types of urban protest in Latin America included gathering in front of municipal buildings, chanting insults outside the homes of hated foreigners or authorities, stoning shops during bread shortages, resisting forced army recruitment, storming prisons, and tearing down statues of unpopular politicians or burning them in effigy.[28] These manifestations of popular politics may be found throughout the colonial as well as republican periods. For example, J. I. Israel's study of seventeenth-century Mexico documents how on numerous occasions crowds took sides in disputes among viceregal and ecclesiastical officials and how authorities regularly considered the potential response of the populace in formulating their policies, even in planning the timing and routes of their public appearances.[29] Several recent studies of Mexico City likewise show how the urban poor successfully resisted the plans of Bourbon administrators to suppress begging, regulate alcohol consumption, impose sanitary measures, and change working conditions in the Tobacco Factory.[30] Thus, the popular classes contested the state for control of their daily lives, and they often won.

In addition to expressing protest, city residents demonstrated approval by roaming the streets and cheering, ringing church bells, or gleefully carrying popular candidates on their shoulders, sometimes against the candidates' will.[31] Urban crowds could therefore be celebratory as well as angry, a fact often overlooked by those who see only repression and resistance everywhere. And in nineteenth-century capital cities, *el pueblo* was a constant fixture in the galleries of Congress, with the people jeering or applauding to let the deputies know their views on the issues at hand. Thus, "public opinion" was not restricted to the elite circles of literate readers of newspapers and journals.[32]

Moreover, urban crowds were essential to the public assemblies that, as Emile Durkheim argues, played an important political role by reinforcing the sense of community, of social solidarity and hierarchy, and of state legitimacy.[33] These rituals (what E. P. Thompson terms the Theater of the Great)[34] included the public celebrations of religious holidays, coronations, royal weddings, and, later, national festivals; the auto-da-fé and public execution; the alms given to the poor at baptisms; and even the conspicuous displays of luxury and rank so well documented by foreign travelers.[35] Crowds were therefore an ever-present feature of both colonial and republican cities, and they were an integral part of the rituals that legitimated the social order. Indeed, some elaborate ceremonies, such as those accompanying Antonio López de Santa Anna's proclamation of the Bases Orgánicas in Mexico City in 1843—in which a day-long round of parades, processions, speeches, a Te Deum, and a bullfight were capped by filling the fountains of the Alameda park with sangría so that the poor could celebrate publicly while the wealthy held private dinners[36]—demonstrate that the urban poor were considered a part, albeit an unequal one, of the body politic.

When we stop viewing urban riots in isolation and instead see them as part of this rich tradition of political engagement, it is clear that the collective action of the urban poor was far from exceptional, even though rioting may have been.[37] To be sure, elites often did not want to recognize the degree to which the poor were political actors; hence, routine manifestations of popular politics were omitted from national histories that only noted the rare violent tumult. Yet dissident elites well understood both the potential of harnessing popular power and the dangers of enfranchising the poor in a society where stark inequalities meant that class conflict was always a possibility. Consequently, at various points in the nineteenth century, republican constitutions excluded the poor from electoral politics by severely restricting suffrage.[38] Still, if the disenfranchised masses had no formal right to participate in republican government, they continued to be involved through street politics and public assemblies, as they always had been.

Thus, the rule of elites was contested even before the period of twentieth-century populism because their options for action were circumscribed by the responses, or potential responses, of the lower classes. As Thompson puts it in describing eighteenth-century England, "A world of patricians and of plebs . . . doesn't . . . deprive the plebs of all political existence. They are one side of the necessary equation," in which "rulers and crowd needed each other, watched each other, performed theater and countertheater to each other's auditorium, [and] moderated each other's political behavior."[39] In Latin America, too, the political marginalization of the urban poor before 1910 was relative, not absolute, for the social order rested on their active compliance, not on their passivity. Following Antonio Gramsci's distinctions, then, we may conclude that Latin American elites exercised "hegemony" rather than "domination," controlling the populace more through consent than coercive force.[40]

My hope is that this volume will lead to a better understanding of the reciprocal relationship between rulers and ruled by encouraging new studies of popular politics in urban areas. Future works should look not only at major cities such as the ones analyzed here but also at mining centers and provincial towns, where we know that considerable strife existed.[41] They should go beyond the search for riots to study the full spectrum of expressions of popular politics, including public processions and assemblies as well as protest actions. In studying protest they should avoid focusing on a static genre, such as The Riot, and instead should look for changes in the mix of repertoires of contention, as Tilly has proposed;[42] for if rioting and looting have persisted to the present day, other forms of protest, such as strikes, have grown in importance.[43] When more studies of urban disturbances are available, we may be able to trace changes in the mix of motivating issues, such as the potential replacement of religion by nationalism, or in the occasions for collective violence, such as the decline in religious holidays.[44] In this way "exceptional" episodes can illuminate a great deal about the "normal" texture of society and the nature of historical change.

The authors in this volume have taken an important first step in this direction. They demonstrate that riots are an excellent source for understanding not only "social" history (popular attitudes and beliefs) but also "political" history (the nature of popular politics, the alliances among classes, and the compact that included all members of society). It is becoming increasingly clear that the isolation of "political" and "social" history in the past has led to an inaccurate understanding of how Latin American cities functioned. It is time to put together what too often have been separate studies of elite politics and mass protest and to concentrate on how the political system worked as a whole.

Notes

1. See, for example, Torcuato di Tella, "Populismo y reforma en América Latina," *Desarrollo Económico* 4 (1965): 391–425; and the essays in Michael L. Conniff, ed., *Latin American Populism in Comparative Perspective* (Albuquerque: University of New Mexico Press, 1982).

2. For detailed studies of these revolts see, for example, David Cahill, "Taxonomy of a Colonial 'Riot': The Arequipa Disturbances of 1780," in *Reform and Insurrection in Bourbon New Granada and Peru*, ed. John R. Fisher, Allan J. Kuethe, and Anthony McFarlane (Baton Rouge: Louisiana State University Press, 1991), 255–91; Alberto Flores Galindo, ed., *Tupac Amaru, 1780: Sociedad colonial y sublevaciones populares* (Lima: Retablo de Papel Ediciones, 1976); Scarlett O'Phelan Godoy, *Rebellions and Revolts in Eighteenth-Century Peru and Upper Peru* (Cologne: Böhlau Verlag Köln Wien, 1985); John L. Phelan, *The People and the King: The Comunero Revolution in Colombia, 1781* (Madison: University of Wisconsin Press, 1978); and Felipe Castro Gutiérrez, *Movimientos populares en Nueva España: Michoacán, 1766–1767* (Mexico City: UNAM, 1990).

3. The literature on Latin American peasant and slave rebellions is huge. Outstanding examples, with extensive citations to the broader literature, can be found in Anthony McFarlane, "Civil Disorders and Popular Protests in Late Colonial

New Granada," *Hispanic American Historical Review* 64, 1 (February 1984): 17–54; Friedrich Katz, *Riot, Rebellion, and Revolution: Rural Social Conflict in Mexico* (Princeton: Princeton University Press, 1988); Steve Stern, ed., *Resistance, Rebellion, and Consciousness in the Andean Peasant World, 18th to 20th Centuries* (Madison: University of Wisconsin Press, 1987); Richard Price, ed., *Maroon Societies* (Garden City: Anchor Press, 1973); Michael Craton, *Testing the Chains* (Ithaca: Cornell University Press, 1982); and João José Reis and Eduardo Silva, *Negociação e conflito: Resistência negra no Brasil escravista* (São Paulo: Companhia das Letras, 1989). On peasant participation in forging national projects in the nineteenth century see Florencia E. Mallon, *Peasant and Nation: The Making of Postcolonial Mexico and Peru* (Berkeley: University of California Press, 1995).

4. John H. Coatsworth, "Patterns of Rural Rebellion in Latin America: Mexico in Comparative Perspective," in Katz, *Riot, Rebellion, and Revolution*, 24. On the most famous of Brazil's urban slave revolts see João José Reis, *Slave Rebellion in Brazil: The Muslim Uprising of 1835 in Bahia* (Baltimore: Johns Hopkins University Press, 1993).

5. George F. Rudé, *Paris and London in the Eighteenth Century: Studies in Popular Protest* (London: Collins, 1970) and *The Crowd in History: A Study of Popular Disturbances in France and England, 1730–1848* (New York: Wiley, 1964); Eric J. Hobsbawm, *Primitive Rebels: Studies in Archaic Forms of Social Movement in the 19th and 20th Centuries* (Manchester: Manchester University Press, 1959), esp. chap. 7, on "The City Mob."

6. See, for example, the influential articles by E. P. Thompson, "The Moral Economy of the English Crowd in the Eighteenth Century," *Past and Present* 50 (February 1971): 76–136; and Charles Tilly, "Collective Violence in European Perspective," in *The History of Violence in America: Historical and Comparative Perspectives*, ed. Hugh D. Graham and Ted R. Gurr (New York: Praeger, 1969), 4–45. For excellent reviews of the literature of the past three decades, with extensive bibliographies, see Sidney Tarrow, *Struggle, Politics, and Reform: Collective Action, Social Movements, and Cycles of Protest* (Ithaca: Cornell Center for International Studies Occasional Paper No. 21, 1991); and Charles Tilly, "Contentious Repertoires in Great Britain, 1758–1834," *Social Science History* 17, 2 (Summer 1993): 253–80.

7. There were exceptions, to be sure. For example, the great Mexico City riots of 1624 and 1692 received scholarly attention before the 1970s. See Chester L. Guthrie, "Riots in Seventeenth-Century Mexico: A Study in Social History with Special Emphasis upon the Lower Classes" (Ph.D. diss., University of California, Berkeley, 1938); Guthrie, "Riots in Seventeenth-Century Mexico City: A Study of Social and Economic Conditions," in *Greater America: Essays in Honor of Herbert Eugene Bolton*, ed. Adele Ogden and Engel Sluiter (Berkeley: University of California Press, 1945), 243–58; Rosa Feijóo, "El tumulto de 1624," *Historia Mexicana* 14, 1 (1964): 42–70; and Feijóo, "El tumulto de 1692," *Historia Mexicana* 14, 4 (1965): 656–79. The best recent studies of these riots are: (1624) J. I. Israel, *Race, Class and Politics in Colonial Mexico, 1610–1670* (London: Oxford University Press, 1975), chap. 5; and (1692) R. Douglas Cope, *The Limits of Racial Domination: Plebeian Society in Colonial Mexico City, 1660–1720* (Madison: University of Wisconsin Press, 1994), chap. 7.

Recent studies of Latin American urban riots in the twentieth century include Herbert Braun, *The Assassination of Gaitán: Public Life and Urban Violence in Colombia* (Madison: University of Wisconsin Press, 1985), chap. 7, on the *bogotazo* of 1948; José A. Moisés and Verena Stolcke, "Urban Transport and

Popular Violence: The Case of Brazil," *Past and Present* 86 (February 1980): 174–92; and Daniel James, "October 17th and 18th, 1945: Mass Protest, Peronism, and the Argentine Working Class," *Journal of Social History* 21, 3 (Spring 1988): 441–61.

8. Mallon, *Peasant and Nation*, 10. The xenophobia of rioting crowds in 1765, 1828, and 1910 supports her point that nationalism has deep popular roots in Latin America and was not an ideology created and imposed by republican elites.

9. Hobsbawm and Rudé's prejudice against unemployed "marginals" seems misplaced, especially in Latin America where the "marginal" population was huge and the distinction between the employed and unemployed was far from clear cut. See Frederick Shaw, "Poverty and Politics in Mexico City, 1824–1854" (Ph.D. diss., University of Florida, 1975), esp. iv. Furthermore, the emphasis on the class composition of the crowd obscures other possible variables, such as youth and suburban residence, analyzed by James ("October 17th," 454–57), or kinship bonds, noted by Godoy (*Rebellions and Revolts*, esp. 280).

10. In this volume. For a different interpretation of this riot see Martin Minchom, *The People of Quito, 1690–1810: Change and Unrest in the Underclass* (Boulder, CO: Westview Press, 1994), chap. 8.

11. See discussions in Arturo Escobar and Sonia E. Alvarez, eds., *The Making of Social Movements in Latin America: Identity, Strategy, and Democracy* (Boulder, CO: Westview Press, 1992), esp. 3–5, 92, 319; Jeffrey Gould, *To Lead as Equals: Rural Protest and Political Consciousness in Chinandega, Nicaragua, 1912–1979* (Chapel Hill: University of North Carolina Press, 1990), esp. 5–8, 292–304; and Mallon, *Peasant and Nation*, chap. 1.

12. See especially Oscar Lewis, "The Culture of Poverty," *Scientific American* 215, 4 (October 1966): 19–25, and the critiques in Eleanor Burke Leacock, *The Culture of Poverty: A Critique* (New York: Simon and Schuster, 1971); and Wayne Cornelius, "Urbanization and Political Demand Making: Political Participation among the Migrant Poor in Latin American Cities," *American Political Science Review* 68, 3 (September 1974): 1125–46. Many scholars have also criticized Hobsbawm's categorization. James C. Scott, for instance, calls it a manifestation of "a unilinear theory of lower-class history which anticipates that every primitive form of resistance will in due course be superseded by a more progressive form until a mature Marxist-Leninist vision is reached." *Weapons of the Weak: Everyday Forms of Peasant Resistance* (New Haven: Yale University Press, 1985), 273.

13. On the debate about social banditry see, for example, Christon I. Archer, "Banditry and Revolution in New Spain, 1790–1821," *Biblioteca Americana* 1, 2 (1982): 59–90; Richard W. Slatta, ed., *Bandidos: The Variety of Latin American Banditry* (New York: Greenwood Press, 1987); Gonzalo Sánchez and Donny Meertens, *Bandoleros, gamonales y campesinos: El caso de la violencia en Colombia* (Bogotá: Ancora, 1983); Gilbert M. Joseph, "On the Trail of Latin American Bandits: A Reexamination of Peasant Resistance," *Latin American Research Review* 25, 3 (1990): 7–53; and the critiques of Joseph's article by Richard Slatta, Peter Singlemann, and Christopher Birback, along with Joseph's reply, in *Latin American Research Review* 26, 1 (1991): 145–74. See also Catherine LeGrand's review of Slatta's *Bandidos* in *American Historical Review* 93, 4 (October 1988): 1145.

14. For discussions of colonial doctrines of popular sovereignty see Richard M. Morse, "The Heritage of Latin America," in *The Founding of New Societies*, ed. Louis Hartz (New York: Harcourt, Brace and World, 1964), 151–59, 171–77; Phelan, *The People and the King*; and McFarlane, "Civil Disorders."

15. E. P. Thompson developed a similar concept, which he termed "mutual reciprocity," in his article "Patrician Society, Plebeian Culture," *Journal of Social History* 7 (1974): 382–405. In an earlier article (cited in note 6), Thompson proposed the term "moral economy" to describe the "traditional view of social norms and obligations" which bound the authorities as much as the people.

16. On this point see Mallon, *Peasant and Nation*, 4, 149.

17. In 1624 the "bargain" was to remove an unpopular viceroy who trampled community norms (Israel, *Race*, chap. 5). In 1692 the "bargain" was less clear, but the riot supports the notion of a social compact in that 1) social order disintegrated only after the "moral economy" of the crowd was violated by the denial of dialogue with the archbishop and viceroy (Cope, *Limits*, 136); and 2) one of the first measures enacted to restore order was to increase the availability of grains whose scarcity had been a precipitating factor for the incident (Feijóo, "El tumulto de 1692").

18. Eric Van Young, "Islands in the Storm: Quiet Cities and Violent Countrysides in the Mexican Independent Era," *Past and Present* 118 (February 1988): 130–55. There is still much we need to know, however, before we can conclude that Latin American urban populations were disorganized. More research is needed on the religious *cofradías* referred to by Reis; the guilds, and later mutual aid societies, referred to by Sowell; and the *capoeiras* (Afro-Brazilian gangs) referred to by Needell.

19. Flores Galindo, *Aristocracia y plebe: Lima, 1760–1830 (estructura de clases y sociedad colonial)* (Lima: Mosca Azul Editores, 1984), 232.

20. Cope, *Limits*, esp. 162–65; Alejandra Moreno Toscano, "Los trabajadores y el proyecto de industrialización, 1810–1867," in *La clase obrera en la historia de México*, ed. Enrique Florescano et al. (Mexico City: Siglo Veintiuno Editores, 1980), esp. 328–32; Michael Scardaville, "(Hapsburg) Law and (Bourbon) Order: State Authority, Popular Unrest, and the Criminal Justice System in Bourbon Mexico City," *The Americas* 50, 4 (April 1994): 501–25. See also June E. Hahner, *Poverty and Politics: The Urban Poor in Brazil, 1870–1920* (Albuquerque: University of New Mexico Press, 1986), 35–36.

21. The role of priests is especially striking in the riots of 1624 in Mexico City and of 1765 in Quito. Richard Warren also documents the role of priests as leaders of popular mobilizations in early independent Mexico, in "Vagrants and Citizens: Politics and the Poor in Mexico City, 1808–1836" (Ph.D. diss., University of Chicago, 1994), 102, 168.

22. See discussion in Eric Van Young, "Mentalities and Collectivities: A Comment," in *Patterns of Contention in Mexican History*, ed. Jaime E. Rodríguez O. (Wilmington, DE: Scholarly Resources, 1992), 338–39. The continued importance of the Church in the eighteenth century appears to distinguish it from the England analyzed by E. P. Thompson ("Patrician Society, Plebeian Culture") in that the Latin American Church still commanded the "leisure" of the poor well into the nineteenth century through its control of frequent religious holidays and rites of passage such as baptisms, first communions, weddings, and burials.

23. Thomas H. Holloway's recent book on the growth of the police in Brazil as a mechanism for enforcing order supports this hypothesis: *Policing Rio de Janeiro: Repression and Resistance in a Nineteenth-Century City* (Stanford: Stanford University Press, 1993).

24. Van Young, "Islands in the Storm," 130.

25. On the importance of the *barrio* as a unit of collective action see Minchom, *People of Quito*, chap. 8.

26. Shaw, "Poverty and Politics," chap. 7, esp. 323, 331–33. See also the smaller riots or near-riots documented for colonial Quito in Minchom, *People of Quito*, chap. 8.

27. Charles Tilly, *The Contentious French: Four Centuries of Popular Struggle* (Cambridge: Harvard University Press, 1986); and "Contentious Repertoires in Great Britain."

28. See Shaw, "Poverty and Politics," chap. 7; Christon Archer, *The Army in Bourbon Mexico, 1760–1810* (Albuquerque: University of New Mexico Press, 1977); Hahner, *Poverty and Politics*, chap. 2; as well as additional incidents referred to by Arrom, Needell, Bloch and Ortoll, and Sowell in this volume.

29. Israel, *Race*, esp. 135–60, 168, 230–40, 259, and 264–65. See also an example of the populace taking sides in a dispute within the Franciscan order in Minchom, *People of Quito*, chap. 8.

30. Silvia M. Arrom, "The Mexico City Poor House, 1774–1884: A Failed Experiment in Social Control," forthcoming in the Proceedings of the Ninth Conference of Mexican and North American Historians; Susan Deans-Smith, *Bureaucrats, Planters, and Workers: The Making of the Tobacco Monopoly in Bourbon Mexico* (Austin: University of Texas Press, 1992), chap. 7; Michael C. Scardaville, "Alcohol Abuse and Tavern Reform in Late Colonial Mexico City," *Hispanic American Historical Review* 60, 4 (November 1980): 643–71; Juan Pedro Viqueira Albán, *¿Relajados o reprimidos? Diversiones públicas y vida social en la ciudad de México durante el siglo de las luces* (Mexico City: Fondo de Cultura Económica, 1987); and Pamela Voekel, "Peeing on the Palace: Bodily Resistance to Bourbon Reforms in Mexico City," *Journal of Historical Sociology* 5, 2 (1992): 183–208.

31. See the excellent analyses of popular participation in Mexico's early electoral politics in Virginia Guedea, "El pueblo de México y la política capitalina, 1808 y 1812," *Mexican Studies/Estudios Mexicanos* 10, 1 (Winter 1994): 27–61; and Warren, "Vagrants and Citizens."

32. On this point see Fernando Escalante Gonzalbo, *Ciudadanos imaginarios: Memorial . . .* (Mexico City: El Colegio de México, 1992), 278–86.

33. See the excellent discussion in Robert J. Holton, "The Crowd in History: Some Problems of Theory and Method," *Social History* 3, 2 (May 1978): 219–33.

34. Thompson, "Patrician Society, Plebeian Culture."

35. For an excellent start at interpreting public rituals in Latin America see *Rituals of Rule, Rituals of Resistance: Public Celebrations and Popular Culture in Mexico*, ed. William H. Beezley, Cheryl English Martin, and William E. French (Wilmington, DE: Scholarly Resources, 1994). On Carnaval in Rio see Sandra Lauderdale Graham, *House and Street: The Domestic World of Servants and Masters in Nineteenth-Century Rio de Janeiro* (Cambridge: Cambridge University Press, 1988), 66–71; and Roberto DaMatta, *Carnivals, Rogues, and Heroes: An Interpretation of the Brazilian Dilemma* (1979; trans. John Drury, Notre Dame, IN: University of Notre Dame Press, 1991).

36. José Ramón Malo, *Diario de sucesos notables*, ed. Mariano Cuevas (Mexico City: Editorial Patria, 1948), entry for June 12, 1843, vol. 1, 226–27. See also vol. 1, 384–85; and vol. 2, 468.

37. I am here extending to Latin American cities the point about rural protests made by Anthony McFarlane in his critique of Phelan's *The People and the King*. See McFarlane's review in "Riot and Rebellion in Colonial Spanish America," *Latin American Research Review* 17, 2 (1982): 216.

38. See, for example, Warren, "Vagrants and Citizens," chap. 5; and María Ligia Coelho Prado, "Mora y Echeverría: Dos visiones sobre la soberanía popular en el siglo XIX," *Secuencia* 22 (January–April 1992): 55–65.

39. Thompson, "Patrician Society, Plebeian Culture," 395–96.

40. See Antonio Gramsci, *Selections from the Prison Notebooks*, ed. and trans. Quintin Hoare and Geoffrey N. Smith (New York: International Publishers, 1971), esp. xiv and Part II; and the discussion in Joseph V. Femia, *Gramsci's Political Thought* (Oxford: Clarendon Press, 1981), 24–25, 47–49; and Mallon, *Peasant and Nation*, 6–7, 20, 333 fn. 10.

41. See, for example, the excellent studies of riots in small urban centers by Mercedes Chen Daley, "The Watermelon Riot: Cultural Encounters in Panama City, April 15, 1856," *Hispanic American Historical Review* 70, 1 (February 1990): 85–108; and Rebecca Earle Mond, "Indian Rebellion and Bourbon Reform in New Granada: Riots in Pasto, 1780–1800," *Hispanic American Historical Review* 73, 1 (February 1993): 99–124. On conflicts in mining areas, including what Doris M. Ladd claims is the first strike in North America, see her *The Making of a Strike: Mexican Silver Workers' Struggles in Real del Monte, 1766–1775* (Lincoln: University of Nebraska Press, 1988).

42. Tilly, "Contentious Repertoires."

43. See Teresa Meade, " 'Living Worse and Costing More': Resistance and Riot in Rio de Janeiro, 1890–1917," *Journal of Latin American Studies* 21 (May 1989): 241–66.

44. See suggestions, based on rural riots, in Van Young, "Mentalities and Collectivities," 338–40.

1

The "Rebellion of the Barrios": Urban Insurrection in Bourbon Quito, 1765

Anthony McFarlane

Anthony McFarlane is a senior lecturer in Latin American history at the University of Warwick, England. He has devoted much of his career to studying popular contention in colonial Latin America, especially in the viceroyalty of New Granada (today's Colombia, Ecuador, and Venezuela). His numerous articles analyze riots, rebellions, slave resistance, and independence movements. Professor McFarlane's books include Reform and Insurrection in Bourbon New Granada and Peru *(coedited with John R. Fisher and Allan J. Kuethe, 1991),* Colombia before Independence: Economy, Society, and Politics under Bourbon Rule *(1993), and* The British in the Americas, 1480–1815 *(1994).*

This detailed study of the Rebellion of the Barrios is based on unusually rich surviving documentation. It explores the complex causes and significance of two riots spaced only one month apart. McFarlane shows that the incidents must be understood on many levels, for they expressed the overlapping grievances of several groups in the viceregal capital. They also reveal what E. P. Thompson calls the "moral economy" of the community, which believed that the colonial power had violated the unspoken rules of proper governance when it imposed tax reforms. Yet the rebellion remained what Eric Hobsbawm labels a "Church and King" movement for, despite their xenophobia, the rioters accepted the overall legitimacy of the colonial system whose policies they protested.*

In 1765, one of the longest, largest, and most formidable urban insurrections of eighteenth-century Spanish America occurred in Quito. Throughout that year, the city was affected by a conflict which touched virtually every level of its society, shook the

From *Hispanic American Historical Review* 69, no. 2 (May 1989): 283–330. © 1989 by Duke University Press. Reprinted by permission.

*E. P. Thompson, "The Moral Economy of the English Crowd in the Eighteenth Century," *Past and Present* 50 (February 1971): 76–136; Eric J. Hobsbawm, foundations of government, and eventually required a military expedition fully to restore royal authority. It was not the only challenge to government authority to occur in the Audiencia of Quito during the eighteenth century: there were other incidents of civil disorder of varying proportions and potency, mainly from among the large Indian population of the Ecuadorian highlands.[1] But in terms of its scale, duration, and the directness of the challenge that it presented to the colonial government, the insurrection of the capital city was without precedent or parallel. The Quito rebellion was, moreover, a significant episode in the history of late colonial Spanish America, for it was the first of the major insurrections provoked by the Caroline reforms of the later eighteenth century and one which, in some respects, prefigured the later rebellions of the Comuneros in New Granada and Tupac Amaru in Peru.

Yet, like much else in the history of Ecuador, the Quito rebellion has attracted relatively little attention from historians. In Ecuadorian historiography—where it has become known as the "rebellion of the barrios" and is regarded as an early avatar of independence—the events of 1765 have never been fully reconstructed, and analysis of their significance has been confined within a national framework.[2] The only recent work has been that of Joseph Pérez, a French historian. Drawing on the rich and previously unused documentation in the Archivo de Indias, Pérez provided both a more detailed account of the rebellion and a broader interpretation of its significance, linking it to the other major rebellions of the later eighteenth century.[3]

There is, however, considerable scope for enhancing and revising our view of Quito's "rebellion of the barrios." First, the nature of its causes has yet to be adequately explored. A view commonly taken at the time, and one that has been echoed by historians since, was that the city's poverty, brought on by economic decline, goaded its people to react fiercely to the threat of more taxation. This explanation is, however, inadequate in two respects. It fails to show why changes in the excise brought such a powerful and widespread rejection in 1765, when previous changes—such as the introduction of the aguardiente *estanco* years earlier—had been made without evoking a similar response. It also fails to show why the reforms provoked such widespread antagonism, ranging across a social spec-

---

Primitive Rebels: Studies in Archaic Forms of Social Movement in the 19th and 20th Centuries (Manchester: Manchester University Press, 1959), 116–21.

trum that reached from the urban patriciate to the plebeians of the city's popular barrios.

Another aspect of the rebellion which deserves reexamination concerns the political culture within which it emerged and developed. While identification of economic discontent and material interests is a necessary condition for explaining the rebellion, it is not sufficient. Economic grievances and social resentments were not new to Quito: it required the interaction of other elements to channel them into sustained insurrection against the colonial government. Here an element hitherto absent from analysis of the rebellion is that of ideology. What were the ideas, beliefs, and attitudes by which the rebels understood and justified their actions? Can we detect any coherent ideology behind their behavior and, if so, where did it come from? How did ideas and aims vary between social groups, and how did they emerge and develop during the course of the rebellion?

Like any large-scale rebellion, that of Quito was based on a mobilization of elements of the lower classes. And yet the popular dimension of the rebellion has been virtually ignored. To the official mind, searching for scapegoats, only one explanation seemed possible: that there was a hidden agency behind the popular uprising, composed of creole conspirators who sought to manipulate mob violence when they failed to achieve their political objectives by peaceful means. However, this judgment—although it has appealed to historians of the Quito rebellion—is far from adequate. It simply reflects contemporary social prejudices which perceived the plebeians of Quito as an ignorant and manipulable mass, stirred by spontaneous passions and without independent ideas or organization. To reexamine this position requires a closer focus on the "people of the barrios," on their behavior and their goals, and, thus, on the values and beliefs which shaped their actions.

What, then, stood at the heart of the Quito rebellion, and what was its significance? Did it present a precocious challenge to Spanish sovereignty, or were its aims more limited? Was it one movement, in which an entire community stood together to defend its interests against new taxation, or was it several, expressing social conflicts within the community? What held it together, and what did it ultimately achieve? To examine these issues, this essay will draw on contemporary accounts of the rebellion to reconstruct its history, and, by blending a narrative of its development with an analysis of its content, seek to throw some fresh light on its character and comparative significance.[4]

Patrician Politics: The Conflict of Words

The outbreak of violent action that was to mark the beginning of
rebellion in Quito occurred on May 22, 1765, when a crowd of
rioters stormed and ransacked the royal sales tax administration
and aguardiente distillery. The rioters' targets reflect the immediate cause of the disturbance: the efforts of Viceroy Pedro Messía
de la Cerda to reform Quito's excise administration.

Since the reestablishment of the Viceroyalty of New Granada
in 1739, the Audiencia of Quito had come under the fiscal and military jurisdiction of the viceroys in Bogotá, and, as a result, Quito
was exposed to the process of administrative revision and reform
that was affecting New Granada itself. And, in Quito as elsewhere,
the viceroys' main concern was with enlarging the flows of revenues available to meet their rising expenditures. Indeed, in the
field of crown finance, Quito was an area of special interest for the
viceroys, since its revenues provided the subsidies vital for maintaining the military establishment of Cartagena de Indias, New
Granada's principal port and bastion for coastal defense. The reas-
sessment of Quito's fiscal organization began during the 1750s,
when Viceroy Solís investigated irregularities in Quito's treasury
and made a preliminary, apparently unsuccessful effort to remedy
them.[5] However, after his successor Pedro Messía de la Cerda took
office in 1760, the reform of the Quito treasury was to begin in
earnest.

On investigating the fiscal affairs of Quito, Messía de la Cerda
discovered that much of its revenue was kept by the tax-farmers
who collected it, in a fiscal administration already undermined by
widespread and habitual tax evasion.[6] The aguardiente monopoly
and the alcabalas collected in the city of Quito seemed to show
particularly obvious signs of mismanagement, since they yielded
only a third of the revenues generated by their counterparts in Santa
Fe de Bogotá, a city of comparable size. Hence, apparently acting
on his own initiative rather than on direct instructions from Spain,
Viceroy Messía de la Cerda ordered that both the state monopoly
of aguardiente sales and the alcabala tax in the city and its province be removed from administration by private tax-farmers and
passed into direct management by royal officials.[7] To carry out this
task, the viceroy appointed Juan Díaz de Herrera, a peninsular Spaniard who had successfully operated a similar administration in
Bogotá. Díaz de Herrera was ordered to go first to the city of
Popayán, to put its *estanco* and alcabala administrations under di-

rect crown management and then, having carried out this task, to move on to Quito, to repeat the exercise. This, in the view of the viceroy, was to be an important step toward improving royal revenues in Quito, a source of income which had assumed a new importance as the viceregal government sought to sustain and expand military expenditure.[8]

It was, however, easier to plan reform than to implement it. When Díaz de Herrera set about his work in Quito, he met stiff opposition. Any change in taxation was likely to be a delicate and difficult matter, for, as one contemporary was later to comment, "there is no American who does not reject any novelty whatsoever in the management of taxation."[9] And the viceroy's reforms in Quito touched two particularly sensitive and potentially controversial areas of taxation. Both the *estanco de aguardiente* and the alcabala affected large sectors of the city's population, as producers, traders, and consumers alike. Thus, the proposed changes had repercussions which crossed class lines. But, if reforms in these areas were generally disliked, each of them encountered its greatest opposition among different social groups. The proposed reorganization of the *estanco* appears to have excited antagonism primarily among the hacendados who produced the sugar from which aguardiente was distilled, while the alcabala reform provoked most intense hostility among the small householders and traders of the city's popular barrios. As we shall see, this difference helps to explain both how peaceful protest, originating in patrician political circles, was transformed into rebellion and how, once launched, the rebellion was able to merge disparate groups in a common endeavor.

The Mobilization of the Elites

Of the two elements of fiscal reform, it was the reorganization of the aguardiente monopoly which provoked the first wave of opposition, leading to a confrontation between Quito's urban patriciate and colonial government. This was not surprising, as the monopoly had already aroused dissension and discord long before the viceroy's reform. In 1752, the cabildo had sought to have it extinguished and when this attempt to end the monopoly failed, dispute shifted to the question of who should control it. Indeed, in March 1764, at the very time that the viceroy decided on reform, a quarrel over control of the monopoly administration was already in progress, generating conflict within the Quito patriciate.[10] Two men—one acting

for the cabildo and the other in his personal capacity—claimed that
the recent leasing of the *estanco* administration had been fraudu-
lently organized, and was contrary to both the public interest and
the interests of the hacendados who produced sugarcane. The
cabildo's representative alleged that the successful contractor, Don
Melchor de Rivadeneira, was an impoverished lawyer whose bid
was simply a front for other interests, probably those of the town
of Ibarra, whose hacendados wanted to take over supplying the
estanco in Quito, to the great detriment of Quito's landowners.[11]
The other complainant also alleged a conspiracy to take control of
the *estanco*, but argued that Rivadeneira was the creature of the
fiscal José de Cistué and his ally, the previous contractor, Don Antonio de la Sala.[12] It seems that Sala, backed by Cistué and Oidor
Félix de Llano, sought to prevent the monopoly from passing into
new hands.[13] Whatever the truth of the matter, it is clear that the
aguardiente monopoly and its management already stood high on
the local political agenda, and was an issue capable of generating
friction both between the Quito patriciate and government and
within the ranks of each.

As soon as Díaz de Herrera arrived in Quito in late October
1764 to begin reorganizing the city's excise taxes, he encountered
stirrings of creole dissent. This was first publicly expressed within
the cabildo of Quito, the political instrument of the creole patriciate and a body which had long played a part in conflicts between
peninsular and American factions in the city.[14] At the end of October, Regidor Luis de la Cuesta complained to the viceroy that
Francisco de Borja was arousing opposition to the projected reform, on the "affected pretext that it would be harmful to the common interest."[15] He also called for Borja's expulsion from the
cabildo, on the ground that his recent co-optation to it contravened
municipal law. Borja, however, remained an active and very effective member of the cabildo, and, in the months that followed, he
stood at the center of a vigorous campaign against the viceroy's
reform, seeking by various methods to delay and ultimately to prevent its implementation.[16]

Borja's recruitment to the cabildo signals the start of the first
phase of Quiteño resistance, a phase in which the urban elites formed
an alliance to reverse the reforms through a coordinated political
campaign. For Borja—who had been brought into the cabildo as a
substitute for his father-in-law, Alférez Real Juan de Chiriboga—
was to act as the representative and spokesman for an important

section of the creole patriciate. Through his family ties, Borja formed part of a network of rich and noble families which dominated Quito's economy and society. His connections included some of the most illustrious and aristocratic names in the city, such as the marquises of Villa Orellano, of Villarocha, of Lices, and of Solanda, all members of a creole oligarchy that had built its fortunes on the ownership of great estates and, in some cases, investments in textile workshops and hat factories.[17] Furthermore, his interest in the aguardiente economy was very direct, as his father-in-law was one of the largest producers of sugarcane in the region.[18] Thus, while he posed as the spokesman for the "común" or community of Quito, Borja was the mouthpiece for both a family with a strong interest in the aguardiente economy and an aristocratic landowning elite of which he was a prominent member.

As opposition took shape in the secular ranks of the urban elites, it also spread to their ecclesiastical wing. On November 14, 1764, the prelates of the city's clerical establishment petitioned the municipal council to convene a *cabildo abierto* in order to discuss the proposed reform.[19] For the cabildo, this move by the leaders of the clergy must have been doubly reassuring. Not only did it signal the allegiance of an influential section of city society, but it also enabled the cabildo to present its case as a matter of public, rather than purely private, interest. The petition was accordingly welcomed by the cabildo, whose *procurador general* duly passed it to the Audiencia for a decision. The Audiencia responded favorably and, on November 22, named the time, place, and membership for a *cabildo abierto*.[20] The stage was thus set for creole opposition to move into a new arena, away from the relatively narrow institutional base afforded by the city council, into the wider setting of a more general congress that purported to represent the interests of the whole community.

Why, when the proposal for a *cabildo abierto* seemed to strengthen the cabildo's challenge to the viceroy's policy, did the Audiencia agree to permit it? The fiscal, José de Cistué, advised the Audiencia that, provided it was presided over by an oidor who would support the viceroy's policy, a *cabildo abierto* should be permitted. To refuse, he argued, would not only convey the misleading impression that the viceroy was seeking to impose new taxes, but would also ignore precedent and deny to the Quiteños the "facilities for defense permitted by divine and human law in representation to superiors."[21] Clearly, there was a case in both law and

politics to allow open discussion of the viceroy's plans. It is unlikely, however, that the Audiencia was swayed by these considerations alone.

For a number of reasons, the Audiencia had little cause to welcome the viceroy's reformist initiative. Indeed, there was at least
as much scope for conflict as there was for cooperation between
the viceroy and the oidores of Quito. Composed of four oidores
(one of whom acted as president) and a fiscal, the Audiencia also
included one supernumerary oidor in 1764–65, and it had a majority of creole judges.[22] Of the six serving ministers, four were Americans: Luis de Santa Cruz, Gregorio Ignacio Hurtado de Mendoza,
and Félix de Llano were all from Lima, while Juan Romualdo
Navarro was from Quito itself. All had initially purchased their
positions as supernumeraries, and all—except Félix de Llano—had
served in Quito for long periods, ranging from 15 to 19 years. The
two peninsular Spaniards were Manuel Rubio de Arévalo and José
de Cistué, respectively the most senior and junior members of the
Audiencia. Rubio de Arévalo was an established member of Quito's
patrician society, having spent his entire career in the city, and, as
senior oidor, he had also been its acting president since the death of
the Marqués de Selva Alegre in 1761. He had first been appointed
in 1720 and, though suspended and heavily fined for professional
misconduct in 1747, had remained in Quito and been granted a dis-
pensation to hold property there.[23] The other peninsular Spaniard—
José de Cistué—had spent less time in Quito, though, with 7 years
as fiscal, he was also well established in the city's social and political life.

Thus, all but one member of the Audiencia—Félix de Llano—
had served for long periods in Quito and were very familiar with, if
not sympathetic to, the preoccupations and interests of the local
upper class. For this reason, the viceroy in Bogotá did not regard
these ministers as reliable instruments for implementing his policy
innovations. Indeed, he was later to blame them for the breakdown
of order in Quito, because the oidores' overriding aim was "to promote their private interests and to avoid displeasing the *vecindario*
because of the friendships and relationships which they have with
its distinguished individuals."[24] Messía de la Cerda did not consult
them about his new policy, nor adequately inform them of the manner in which they were to proceed. Instead, he made his decision in
consultation with the Tribunal de Cuentas in Bogotá, and gave the
power to implement it to his commissioner, Juan Díaz de Herrera.
The latter was responsible directly to the viceroy and, in turn, did

not display any great respect for the Audiencia, nor make an effort to engage the oidores' support. Indeed, he portrayed the Audiencia as a major obstruction to the process of reform, and identified two of its ministers as his main enemies.

One of these was the oidor Félix de Llano, who, having been appointed as *juez conservador* of the new *estanco* administration, struggled to be relieved of the post and regaled the viceroy with arguments against the reform. The reform, he asserted, would not only be damaging to the hacendados of the area; it would also threaten public order by provoking disorder among the students, friars, and plebeians of the city, already notorious for their turbulent dispositions.[25] Llano's companion in opposition to reform was the fiscal, José de Cistué. According to Díaz de Herrera, these men prevailed on the Audiencia to obstruct the alcabala reform because they feared that more rigorous collection would uncover the "interests which the fiscal and Llano (who are those that direct and dominate the others) manage by means of *cajeros*, servants, household members, and followers," as well as revealing smuggling of prohibited goods from Lima.[26] Díaz was less specific in his condemnation of the other judges, though no less dismissive. They were, he told the viceroy, arrogant and conceited men, anxious for flattery and unable to tolerate contrary opinions.[27]

Such allegations do not mean that the ministers of the Audiencia were disloyal to the crown: supplementing a salary with earnings from local business interests was not unusual among colonial officials, and it was also common for Audiencia judges to form strong local ties during long periods of office in a particular capital. However, in this case the existence of such private interests and local ties was to have important repercussions, because it impeded the progress of reform and opened up divisions in the highest ranks of colonial government. While the viceroy and his administrator were determined to push ahead, the judges of the Audiencia put up obstacles, apparently in the hope that, by slowing reform, they might eventually stop it. At the very least, as Díaz de Herrera observed, the Audiencia's tactics gave the creole opposition led by Borja time to organize a strong resistance.[28] And, at most, it provided that opposition with the encouragement of knowing that they had allies within the upper tiers of government. Certainly their equivocations on the issues confronting them helped to create an atmosphere of division and indecision at the apex of government which, in turn, undermined authority and thus contributed to widening the political path that was ultimately to lead to open rebellion.

It was against this background that the main currents of opposition converged in the *cabildo abierto* of December 7, 1764. Under the chairmanship of the senior oidor, Manuel Rubio de Arévalo,
this meeting convoked deputies to speak on behalf of all sections
of the community. The *protector de indios* was to speak for the
Indian population, deputies from the ecclesiastical cabildo were to
represent the secular clergy, various prelates were to speak for the
monastic orders, while members of the cabildo, together with deputies for agricultural and commercial interests, were to present the
opinions of civil society. When the *cabildo abierto* took place, it
was brief, restrained, and contained little that was spontaneous or
improvised. The meeting consisted of a succession of short speeches
from clerics, denouncing the evils of aguardiente drinking, especially among the Indians, and pronouncing support for the petition
previously presented to the meeting by Francisco de Borja. Their
recommendation was unanimous, and so was the decision of the
meeting. It called for an end to the *estanco* and agreed that a representative should be dispatched to intervene with the viceroy, and
sent to Spain if necessary.[29]

As Francisco de Borja, with his strong connections to the
landowning elite, played a central part in organizing and orches-
trating the *cabildo abierto*, and given that this meeting had concentrated on the issue of the aguardiente monopoly, it seems that it
was the hacendados involved with sugar production who were the
driving force behind opposition to the viceroy's plans. It would be
a mistake, however, to regard the developing protest as simply the
defense of a narrow, upper-class economic interest, camouflaged
as an issue of public concern. Other sectors of city society were
also involved because of their connections, direct and indirect, with
the aguardiente economy. These included the small traders—the
tenderos and the *pulperos*—and the monasteries, as both groups
were engaged in distilling and selling aguardiente.[30] Indeed, according to Oidor Llano, the city was filled with bootleggers, as
virtually everyone was involved in distilling aguardiente "without
exception of person, class, or estate, including even monasteries
and leading families."[31] Consumers of aguardiente might also have
regarded stricter regulation of distilling and distribution with suspicion, since restriction threatened to increase prices. And, as the
main group of consumers was, according to a contemporary, the
"craftsmen, Indians, and mestizos of all trades," these represented
a potentially formidable source of dissent.[32] Thus, the proposed reform of the monopoly was itself enough to call up a broad spec-

trum of opposition, spanning the city's social classes. In early December, the publication of pasquinades in the city's barrios gave warning of clandestine efforts to mobilize this opposition.[33] Initially, however, the initiative was taken by members of the city's creole elite led by Francisco de Borja, and opposition concentrated on negotiation rather than intimidation. For the moment, opposition met in the *cabildo abierto* rather than on the streets.

Elite Economic Grievances

Behind the objections set forth during the meeting of the *cabildo abierto* lay a series of petitions from the different groups represented, and it is in these, rather than in the peremptory verbal statements made at the meeting, that the main arguments against the reform were rehearsed. Each group representative advanced a detailed account of the group's objections to the reform, in written submissions supposedly based on prior canvassing of opinion. The careful attention to detail in the submissions reflects a degree of political sophistication, and an expectation that reasoned argument would produce results. Rather than simply make sweeping objections, they were at pains to show why the new measures were not only damaging to the economic interests and welfare of their groups, but were also unworkable and counterproductive to the very royal purposes which they were supposed to serve. There was, moreover, one common theme running through all the presentations: the problems of the economy of the Audiencia of Quito in general, and the poverty and misery of the inhabitants of the city of Quito in particular.

The first petition submitted to the *cabildo abierto* was that of Francisco de Borja, the spokesman designated for the "vecindad" or the "común." Drawn up and circulated before the *cabildo abierto*, Borja's petition was evidently intended to serve as a manifesto, deliberately, if discreetly, designed to rally all sections of elite opinion against the viceroy's plans.[34] Directed against the aguardiente monopoly, it was clearly concerned primarily with defending the threatened interests of the urban elites.

In his presentation, Borja sought first to impugn the legitimacy of the viceroy's intention to bring the aguardiente monopoly under direct crown administration. He recalled that the monopoly had been introduced as a purely temporary measure, to cover the costs of rebuilding the Audiencia palace, and that it had outlived this purpose. Though the monopoly thus was not new, Borja argued that its reorganization was tantamount to imposing a new tax on the city, since it aimed to increase net revenues. This assault on the legality of the viceroy's policy was buttressed by an attack on its morality. The monopoly, Borja asserted, was indefensible in law because, by encouraging the spread of drunkenness, with its attendant vices, it promoted sin and scandal. It would also be counterproductive to royal interests because of its impact on the local society and economy. Heavy drinking among the Indians increased their mortality and thereby damaged royal revenues from tribute. The monopoly would damage the province's agriculture, because it was ill adapted to the conditions of local sugar production and threatened to reduce the price paid for sugar products. Finally, Borja pleaded the poverty of the province, stating that the depression of the textile trade caused by competition from European imports in Peruvian markets had deprived its people of their sole reliable source of income.

The themes raised by Borja were echoed by the other petitions presented to the *cabildo abierto*, in which the other representatives supported his contentions without reserve. The economic arguments were taken up by the representatives of civil society, testifying to the province's economic depression and outlining their own particular difficulties. The vecinos of Latacunga opposed reform both of the alcabala and of the *estanco* on the grounds that it would impose intolerable burdens on an economy whose agriculture had been afflicted by volcanic eruptions and earthquakes (the most recent in the area of Quito had been in 1757), and where many *obrajes* had been ruined by competition from imported English cloth.[35] The landowners and sugar producers argued that the aguardiente monopoly would send agriculture into a spiral of decline that would ruin all who depended on the land for their living and even affect the dead, since damage to agriculture would undermine the chantries devoted to prayer for departed souls.[36] The merchants of Quito joined this chorus, arguing that the reorganization of taxes would aggravate the already chronic shortage of specie that resulted from the decline of Quito's textile exports to Peru.[37]

Borja's denunciation of social and spiritual corruption, on the other hand, provided an appropriate theme for the clergy. The leaders of the city's ecclesiastical establishment detailed the pathology of aguardiente, warned that drink led to damnation, and duly called for the aguardiente monopoly to be suppressed in the interests of public health, both physical and moral.[38] However, despite their denunciation of drink, the clergy called for suppression of the state monopoly, not for a ban on private production, much less consumption, of aguardiente. Clearly, there was more at stake than the sturdy values of temperance. Although they did not admit it, the clergy had a strong material interest in sugar and aguardiente production, both as owners and holders of mortgages on haciendas, and as distributors and consumers of aguardiente.[39]

Thus, under the leadership of Francisco de Borja, a united front was formed in Quito to oppose reform, composed of all the leading sectors of its society, enjoying the sympathy of some members of the Audiencia, and claiming to speak for the whole community. Behind the rhetoric about public interest, there was certainly some special pleading by patrician and clerical economic interests. Long sheltered from efficient taxation, these interests, together with those who profited from the private administration of the excise taxes, were naturally opposed to any fiscal innovation that threatened to interfere with their business. But their pleas of poverty cannot simply be dismissed as specious rhetoric. Resentment at fiscal reorganization was undoubtedly sharpened by the experience of economic decline, associated primarily with the problems of the textile industry.

This decline had begun many years before, with demographic crisis in Quito during the 1690s.[40] But the industry's problems had grown worse during the eighteenth century, as it was increasingly affected by competition from Spanish and foreign contraband imports. This competition had intensified around midcentury, causing the number and output of Quito's *obrajes* to fall considerably.[41] The recent contraction stemmed from changes in commercial policy which, by opening Cape Horn, permitted direct maritime contact between Peru and Spain, and thereby made it more difficult for Quito textiles to compete in Peruvian markets. Furthermore, the problems caused by the redirection of transatlantic trade were particularly acute at the very time that the viceroy was pursuing his reforms. For, having been severely disrupted by war in 1762 and 1763, Spanish transatlantic commerce increased sharply in 1764 and 1765 to restock markets depleted by war.[42] Thus, in the years before the rebellion, prospects for the Quiteño economy looked especially bleak, and Quiteños could attribute this decline to recent modifications in crown policy. In such conditions, fiscal innovations which threatened to increase the real burden of taxation heaped insult on top of injury. Indeed, in such depressing economic circumstances, the Quiteños were looking to the crown for policies that would provide economic relief rather than fiscal rigor. And, if they had good cause to criticize crown economic policy, such criticism interacted with, and was reinforced by, a set of political ideas which helped both to inspire and to shape resistance to reform.

Political Issues and Constitutional Conflict

In opposing reform, the Quiteño elites evidently sought to protect their economic interests. But the means by which they did so, the arguments which they deployed, and the alliance which they formed suggest that their campaign also involved issues of a political order. Their conflict with the viceroy was precipitated by fiscal reform, but it was not simply about reorganization of the aguardiente monopoly. For, as they mobilized in defense of their economic interests, the creole elites of Quito also drew on a set of political ideas which, though not set out in any systematic formulation, clearly influenced their attitudes toward reform and justified their campaign of resistance.

From the start of this campaign, the Quiteño patriciate claimed a right to participate in government as the representative of the community as a whole. To exercise this claim, the creole leadership had called for the convocation of a *cabildo abierto*, an institution which, by its very nature, embodied notions of urban autonomy and corporate representation.[43] Like its Spanish medieval predecessors, Quito's *cabildo abierto* reflected the belief that the community might represent its interests directly to the crown, and thereby share in the deliberations of government when they touched on matters of pressing local concern. By setting itself to deliberate on "the public good, on justice, on the Christian and natural law, applying itself to find the means of invigorating the life of a moribund republic," the *cabildo abierto* in Quito appealed to a concept of government by negotiation, and implicitly rejected the arbitrary exercise of royal power.[44] It also claimed to represent the whole community, invoking the concepts of the "común," the "bien común," or the "bien público." And, to fortify this claim, the *cabildo abierto* rested on a representative principle, derived from the medieval practice of representing the estates or orders of a society through delegates chosen from their most distinguished members, duly adjusted to suit colonial circumstances.[45] Thus, while the clergy, the hacendados, and the merchants were represented by leading members of each group, the delegate for the Indians was the *protector de indios*, and the mestizos and common people in general were also represented indirectly, through the patrician Francisco de Borja who was deputed to speak for the *común*. Last but not least, the *cabildo abierto* included the leading member of royal government in the city: it was both convoked and moderated by the president of the Audiencia.

If, as an institution, the *cabildo abierto* implicitly embodied a traditional view of government—in which leading members of the community might represent the "public good" in order to influence royal policy—that view was advanced explicitly in the arguments that were raised against reform. These sought to identify the limits of governmental power in various ways. First, in attacking the aguardiente monopoly. Francisco de Borja claimed that the king's ministers should suspend any royal order which might, under certain conditions, lead to sin or scandal.[46] The notion that laws which encouraged offenses against morality were indefensible was unexceptionable enough. More interesting is the implicit argument that local authorities had a responsibility to change royal orders in accord with local circumstances, a line of reasoning that was most clearly adduced by the *procurador* of the Quito cabildo, Lasso de la Vega. He contended that laws had to be clearly promulgated if they were to command obedience. Thus, he not only sought to defend refusal to comply with the new excise arrangements on the ground that they had not been explained to the public, but, by stating that the government had to explain its measures, he also implied that it must justify them to its citizens. Finally, he advanced the argument that when formulating policy the crown should take account of local practices and customs. Calling attention to the differences between Bogotá and Quito "in styles, manners, and customs," as well as in physical and climatic environment, Lasso de la Vega argued that a law that was beneficial in the viceregal capital might be harmful in Quito. Indeed, he elevated the customs of the province of Quito to the level of established laws or entrenched privileges, likening them to the *fueros* of the Basques and Aragonese, the *ordenanzas* of Peru, and the municipal laws of the Indies.[47]

This was not an unorthodox reading of the law. It was also stated with great clarity by a senior oidor of the Quito audiencia, Luis de Santa Cruz, to support his opposition to viceregal reform. Early in 1765, Santa Cruz refused to publish the proclamation announcing the reform of the alcabala administration, arguing that it was essential to modify these plans in accord with "the circumstances in which we find ourselves and the deplorable state of this province."[48] He also claimed that local officials like himself were better acquainted with the province and the customs of its inhabitants, and that their advice should be heeded to ensure that policy was suitable to local conditions. There was no law, he asserted, that was universally applicable: even in the same country, there were laws which could not be applied in all cases, at least not without risk of perpetrating injustice and promoting disorder. On these premises, Oidor Santa Cruz raised several specific objections to the viceroy's project. He pointed to the injustice of taxing landowners without regard for their ability to pay, to the problem of levying taxes on ecclesiastical property, and to the threat of violent reactions from a plebeian society renowned for its insolent manners. The significance of these statements deserves emphasis. Behind these practical points lay an organizing notion of what constituted good and just government. Appealing to the authority of the seventeenth-century jurist Juan de Solórzano, to all the most celebrated political theorists (*regnícolas*) who had interpreted the public law of the Spanish kingdoms, to the ancient laws of the Siete Partidas, and to canon law, Santa Cruz concluded that the law had to be adapted to the needs of specific societies and to the customs and welfare of their peoples. Thus, like the petitioners for the *cabildo abierto*, the oidor appealed to a traditional theory of the state, in which monarch and subject were joined by mutual obligations and in which the monarch's interests were identified with the preservation and prosperity of his subjects.

There was, then, an important political dimension to the conflict over fiscal reform in Quito, embracing constitutional claims whereby leading members of the local social and political hierarchy asserted the right to consultation in the decisions of royal government, and called for local approval of new taxation. In this sense, the dispute in Quito was a striking example of that "indigenous tradition of no taxation without bureaucratic representation" which John Phelan found at the heart of a later rebellion in the viceroyalty, that of the Comuneros of New Granada in 1781.[49] Like the Comunero leadership nearly two decades later, the Quiteño patriciate drew on an ideological tradition fed by the concepts and conventions of Hispanic political theory in the Golden Age, rather than by the new ideological currents emanating from the European Enlightenment.[50] For the creole elites, the viceroy's fiscal reform not only threatened their economic interests; it also challenged their right to negotiation and consultation within the colonial bureaucracy. And such opposition was not confined to the creoles; it also included the political establishment of the colony, the judges of the Audiencia, who saw their own authority and role as power brokers being threatened by the viceroy's intervention, and who accordingly tried to defend their traditional autonomy. This was not a defiance of the crown's authority; it was rather an attempt to use and defend an existing system of government, inherited from Hapsburg practice, against Bourbon innovation. Only when this aim was frustrated, by a viceroy determined to pursue his plans, was negotiation superseded by rebellion.

Plebeian Insurrection: The Conflict of Arms

Initially, it seemed that negotiation would bear fruit, as the petitions of the *cabildo abierto* were passed on to Bogotá for the viceroy's consideration. But, unknown to the Quiteños, Viceroy Messía de la Cerda never had any intention of abandoning his scheme. By February 1765, he had already decided to take a tough line. If necessary, he was ready to enforce obedience to his orders, and he called on the metropolitan government to provide for a contingent of two hundred troops to be drawn from the cities of Quito, Cuenca, and Guayaquil.[51] As for the deliberations of the *cabildo abierto* and the arguments of the Quito oidores, the viceroy refused to take them seriously. There was a lapse of five months before he announced his opinion, and, when he did so, he gave short shrift to the arguments emanating from Quito. He scornfully dismissed the proposal that the aguardiente monopoly be abolished, observing that pious condemnation of the evils of alcohol was a flimsy cover for unwillingness to pay taxes. The subsidiary proposal—that Quito might send a representative to plead its case in Madrid—was conceded, though not without a snub. The cabildo's favorite candidate, Francisco de Borja, was specifically barred from holding this commission.[52]

When the viceroy made his pronouncement, he was probably persuaded that the opposition in Quito had weakened. Certainly, there were signs that it had slackened after the flurry of antireform activity in late November and early December of the previous year, when Díaz de Herrera had been threatened with violence and the clergy and the Audiencia had hindered his efforts to prepare the new excise administration.[53] In the new year, opposition seems to have receded, as the Audiencia temporized by placing petty procedural difficulties in Díaz de Herrera's way, and the patriciate awaited the viceroy's response to the *cabildo abierto*.[54] In the early months

of 1765, the first steps toward the new administration went ahead
until, on March 1, Díaz de Herrera opened the aguardiente monopoly and its distillery.

At first, sales were slow, as rumors circulated that the aguardiente was adulterated and the Audiencia still refused to cooperate
with its administrator.[55] However, presented with this fait accompli,
opposition seems to have faltered. Early in May, Oidor Juan
Romualdo Navarro replaced Félix de Llano as *juez conservador* of
the aguardiente *estanco*, thus removing a leading opponent from
the workings of its administration.[56] In mid-May, Díaz de Herrera
confidently reported that the new arrangements were working
smoothly, with cooperation from prominent hacendados and no signs
of the predicted popular uprising. Quito, he concluded, had no stom-
ach for rebellion.[57] However, as soon as Díaz de Herrera proceeded
to reform the administration of the sales tax, he was proved wrong.

The Entry of the Plebs

On May 22, the long-anticipated popular reaction against the viceroy's reform finally began. The protests of the elites, expressed
through petitions and meetings, were now superseded by direct and
forceful action. After failing to achieve their goals by peaceful
persuasion, the Quito patricians now found allies among the plebeians who joined in the riot that began the first phase of Quito's
rebellion.

While Quito's elites opposed the aguardiente monopoly, plebeian antagonism was triggered by reform of the sales tax administration. Following his success with installing the aguardiente
administration, Díaz de Herrera had moved to reform the alcabala
and almost immediately aroused popular anger. On May 15, he set
up a new machinery for assessing and collecting the sales tax; on
May 20, he published a proclamation outlining the penalties for
evasion; on May 21, his subordinates registered all plots of land in
the parish of San Roque for tax purposes, and began the same task
in the parish of San Sebastián. They imposed a tax of four pesos
per solar, in spite of protests that these lands were inadequate, even
for domestic uses. The tax collectors also began to enforce alcabala
payment in areas previously exempt. Payment of tax was demanded
from clerics, on foodstuffs which the latter regarded as alms and
gifts. The Indians who came to the city market were also forced to
pay taxes on small quantities of salt, vegetables, peppers, eggs, and
other provisions, and their goods were confiscated if they did not

pay. Popular remonstration with the tax collectors evoked an unsympathetic response, with threats to erect a gibbet in each parish to deal with complaints. Such official intransigence no doubt encouraged the circulation of wild rumors among the populace during these days before the riot. It was said that there were plans to impose high land taxes; tribute on children in the womb; taxes on the river stones used by washerwomen; and to create government monopolies on salt, tobacco, potatoes, sugar, and maize.[58]

The circulation of such rumors suggests that the reform of the sales tax evoked strong feelings among several lower-class groups and created a fertile recruiting ground for riot. The assessment of small plots of land for tax was first carried out in the predominantly plebeian barrios of San Roque and San Sebastián, which housed concentrations of mestizo artisans and Indian weavers and which were to play a leading role in the rebellion.[59] For such people, new taxation was bound to be a potent source of disaffection. More rigorous collection of taxes on sales would affect the products of their workshops and their plots of land, aggravating the problems already present in a city where the main industry was in decline. It would likewise have antagonized the petty traders, mestizo and Indian, who ran small liquor stores and retailed foodstuffs in city markets.

The authorities were ill prepared when the riot broke out on the night of May 22.[60] Although the city had a population of about 30,000, Quito, like most colonial cities, lacked any strong policing apparatus. Without a regular army garrison—a feature of urban society still mainly confined to ports on strategic coastlines—for public order government relied on the usual municipal officials and the support of the white citizenry. When the riot began, it was soon apparent that the government was without such support, and was, accordingly, virtually defenseless.

The riot began at about eight in the evening, when the concerted ringing of parish bells sounded the alarm in the barrios of San Blas, San Sebastián, and San Roque, and brought their people into darkened streets. The riot focused on the *plazuela* of Santa Bárbara, where crowds from the barrios converged to concentrate around an attack on the royal excise office and aguardiente distillery. Faced with this tumult, the Audiencia, together with the corregidor and *alguacil mayor* of Quito, sought to restore order with the only means at their disposal. They sent a small force of about two dozen men to confront the rioters, gathered arms for the defense of the Plaza Mayor, and appealed to the vecinos for support, calling on them to take up arms and to illuminate the streets by lighting their doorways, windows, and balconies. However, none of these measures produced the desired effect. The vecinos failed to cooperate, while the rioters proved uncontrollable. The patrols, led by Oidor Hurtado de Mendoza and by the fiscal Cistué, were showered with stones and forced to retreat. Both men reported that they gave orders to fire on the crowd, but were disregarded and deserted by their men.[61] Oidor Romualdo Navarro, accompanied by the Conde de Selva Florida, tried to parley with the rioters, but these overtures were rejected, and they, like the other ministers, were forced to retreat to the Audiencia palace.[62]

Having failed to quell the riot with a show of force, the Audiencia called on the leaders of Quito's religious communities to deal with the rioters. Jesuit intermediaries were sent to the Plaza de Santa Bárbara, and, though they were too late to prevent the rioters from breaking into the excise office, spilling its stores of aguardiente in the streets, and destroying its contents, including the sales tax records, they did eventually succeed in establishing a dialogue with the crowd. In their efforts to restore order, and presumably in response to the demands of the rioters, the clerics promised that a general pardon would be granted if the crowd dispersed. The crowd then insisted that Oidor Romualdo Navarro and the Conde de Selva Florida publicly ratify this promise. Navarro duly appeared before the rioting crowd, which he estimated at around eight thousand men, armed with lances, sticks, stones, and other weapons, and promised them a pardon in the king's name. Finally, the crowd dispersed in the early hours of the morning, after warning Navarro and his companions that failure to honor the promised pardon would cost them their property and their lives.[63]

The end of the riot and the promise of pardon did not immediately restore public order. Having failed to impose its authority by force, the Audiencia now had to submit to a humiliating process of negotiation with a turbulent populace, in an atmosphere charged with excitement, fear, and suspicion. The destruction of the excise office, begun on the night of the riot, continued on the following day until it had been completely demolished, stone by stone. Although this demolition was later attributed to the "Indians," in order to acquit the people of the barrios of any accusation of wanton vandalism, the act clearly had great symbolic importance for the rioters and signalled popular determination to see an end to the new administration.[64] At the same time, the city's parishes remained in such an agitated state that the Audiencia feared another uprising, this time in confederation with the largely Indian villages of the city's hinterland.[65]

To forestall further disturbances, the leaders of the religious communities, together with the bishop of Quito, toured the parishes in order to reassure the populace that neither the king nor the viceroy wished to harm common interests. But the barrios remained distrustful, and demanded that the clerics persuade the Audiencia to give solemn and official assurances that the new fiscal plans would be abandoned and a general pardon extended to all the rioters.[66] The Audiencia was reluctant to meet these terms, but agreed to publish an *auto de perdón*. This was initially couched in vague and ambiguous terms, as the Audiencia tried to win time while leaving the way open for later punishment of the rioters.[67] This failed to deceive the rebels, who pressured the oidores to make real concessions. It was agreed that the bishop should go to the barrio of San Roque—described as the most populous of the city's parishes—and talk with the rioters. After preaching a sermon of peace and reconciliation, the bishop conferred with the assembled people and relayed their message to the Audiencia. This called for a general public meeting in the city's main square, the Plaza Mayor, where they would declare their loyalty to the king in return for clear ratification of the general pardon and of the abolition of the new fiscal administration.

To meet this demand, the judges of the Audiencia assembled in the courtyard of their palace, together with an armed escort and flanked by artillery primed to fire. In their presence, the bishop went forward with Oidor Romualdo Navarro to confront the "multitude of people" congregated in the square. They announced a general pardon and suspended the aguardiente monopoly and the new alcabala administration. When told that this decision needed viceregal confirmation, the crowd was distinctly displeased. However, after Romualdo Navarro insisted that the Audiencia had gone to the limits of its power, the assembled people dispersed and returned to their homes.[68] An uneasy calm now settled on the city.

The Crowd and Its Composition

The riot had opened a new phase in the protest against the viceroy's fiscal reforms, in which patrician negotiation gave way to popular action and new actors entered the political arena. However, the numbers involved in the riot cannot be accurately gauged: estimates vary from a credible 3–4,000 to an improbable 16–18,000;

contemporary estimates indicate only that the crowds were impressively large. The social identity of the rioters is also difficult to determine, as contemporary descriptions are vague, and we have no trial records to provide even a sample of those who took part. In describing the rioters, contemporaries refer to the "plebeians" or to the "people of the barrios," but, as these terms are not clearly defined, the composition of the crowds remains rather blurred.

Contemporary commentators agreed that the riot was the work of more than one social group. The Audiencia stated that "the conspiracy was general among all classes and orders."[69] The corregidor of Quito, Manuel Sánchez Osorio, was equally convinced that leading citizens were responsible for the riot. He not only denounced Francisco de Borja and other cabildo members for stirring up popular feeling with their campaign against the monopoly, but he also alleged that "people of the better sort" must have been implicated in the riot, as the rabble was incapable of such organized action.[70] Contemporary references to a secret investigation of the riot, conducted by Oidor Hurtado de Mendoza, also suggest that prominent members of Quiteño society had been involved, although, as no action was ever taken against any such individuals, these allegations remained unproven.[71]

Whatever its leadership, the main body of the rioting crowd was drawn from various segments of the city's population. The riot started in the slaughterhouse district, and according to Juan de Velasco it was started by a group of some 60 butchers. When they attacked the excise house, they were then joined by some three to four thousand people from other barrios.[72] The "plebeians" who rioted were also joined by Indians who, on the following day, dismantled the excise building and carried away its materials. The riot itself, however, seems to have been mainly the work of "plebeians," so called because they were mestizos and poor whites rather than Indians.[73]

The riot was not, then, simply the work of a disorganized rabble drawn from the lowest ranks of city society. While a *lumpenproletariat* of transient workers, vagabonds, and beggars may have been drawn into the riot, its driving force came from the artisans, small tradesmen, and shopkeepers who were the bedrock of the city's business.[74] These were the people who felt most threatened by the viceroy's projected reforms, particularly that of the sales tax, since they promised to place new burdens on the most common forms of exchange. And, because they were associated in guilds and confraternities, and in daily contact through their economic activities, such groups had an organizational basis which could be mobilized for political ends when necessary.

The plebeians who rioted must also have been aware that they enjoyed widespread sympathy among the city's population. Certainly, the behavior of Quiteños during the riot indicates a broad basis of support for the rioters' objectives. During the riot, few complied with the Audiencia's orders to illuminate the streets by lighting their houses, and, from a white population of several thousand, only about 20 prominent vecinos rallied to the Audiencia's call for aid. This indifference persisted afterward. Though measures were taken to raise militia companies in the days after the riot, militiamen failed to stay at their posts, while merchants and traders evaded enlistment by closing their shops and going into hiding, showing a disloyal attitude which, the Audiencia averred, was shared by the clergy and many private citizens.[75] However, although officials were eager to show that there was elite involvement in the riot, their presumption that the plebeians were simply the instruments of a conspiracy within the creole "nobility" should not be taken at face value. The plebeians were not simply the manipulable instrument of upper-class cliques. They were, instead, part of an alliance between social groups, and though they may have been influenced by patrician patronage, they had their own grievances and objectives. This was reflected both in the timing of the first riot and in the subsequent movement toward rebellion when patrician objectives were overtaken by other issues and demands.

It is not entirely clear how these different social groups were brought together. The role attributed to the city's butchers in promoting the riot suggests that petty tradesmen were the vital intermediary group, mobilizing and leading a popular tumult which linked with the patrician campaign against the aguardiente monopoly. Certainly the parish of Santa Bárbara—where the butchers had their shops and where the riot took place—had a greater social mixture than the more popular and more mestizo barrios of San Roque and San Sebastián, and was, accordingly, more open to creole political influence.

It is also possible that plebeian defiance of the authorities was legitimated, even promoted, by sections of the clergy, particularly the regular clergy who enjoyed close relations with lay society. When the Audiencia referred to the participation of all classes in the riot, it did not exclude the clergy, and there were strong suspicions that clerics, particularly from the monastic houses, were involved. As we have seen, elements of Quito's large clerical

population had strong motives for disliking the aguardiente monopoly reform, and their leaders had actively opposed the viceroy's
plan, disguising their material interest by appealing to moral considerations. Indeed, on the very day of the riot, the bishop issued
orders to the abbesses of Quito's convents, stating that under no
circumstances should they participate in the now-illegal private trade
in aguardiente.[76] And if the monasteries were opposed to reform,
the secular clergy, led by the bishop of Quito, were also involved at
this time in a conflict with government, due to the efforts of the
fiscal José de Cistué to curb clerical exploitation of the Indians.[77]

We have no direct reports on the role of the parish clergy or the
monasteries in the popular uprising. But both, and particularly the
monasteries, had abundant opportunities for spreading dissent to a
wider population. Juan and Ulloa's account of the Quiteño clergy
suggests that the regulars, particularly the Franciscans, were inti-
mately involved in the city's social and political life. Not only did
they have an essentially secular life-style, often living outside their
monasteries, maintaining mistresses and fathering children, but they
were also organizers of the "fandangos" which brought them together with lay men and women in dissolute drinking parties.[78] Such
social contact was paralleled by the overlap of civil and ecclesiastical politics. It was common, Juan and Ulloa observed, for disputes between clerical factions—often between Europeans and
Americans—to spread outward into the lay population, arousing
and dividing it into competing groups and creating discord.[79] Indeed, there was a major instance of such discord in 1747–48, when
the plebeians of the barrio of San Roque mobilized behind a
Franciscan faction in a protracted series of popular disturbances,
the most serious to occur in eighteenth-century Quito before those
of 1765.[80] Thus, given the interest of monastic houses in the production and sale of aguardiente and their close links with different
social groups in Quito, the regular clergy had both a purpose for
encouraging opposition to reform and a position from which they
might link those groups in a common movement.

The timing of the May riot certainly strengthens speculation
about clerical involvement, for it fell within the period of preparation for the great festival of Corpus Christi, a time when the urban
confraternities came together to organize and celebrate a major ritual
event under the auspices of the clergy.[81] In the days which followed
the riot, popular preparation for this festival (which occurred on
June 5 in 1765) could have provided an associational structure for
extending and continuing the political organization of the popu-

lace in opposition to the authorities. It is clear that the organization behind the May riot did not dissolve with the suspension of the reformed aguardiente monopoly and alcabala administrations. For the riot had released emotions which were difficult to control, and the popular barrios remained in a volatile state. In the words of a contemporary observer, "The heat of victory gave off a smoke which filled their eyes and blinded them to the enormity of their crime."[82]

Repercussions of the Riot

Recognizing the instability of the situation and aware of its isolation, the Audiencia proceeded cautiously in the weeks which followed the riot. After issuing the general pardon, it suspended all the usual demonstrations of government authority in the city. Street patrols were canceled, the new excise was inoperative, and Díaz de Herrera and his subordinates remained in hiding.[83] Such caution was dictated by circumstances, for the barrios were still restive and threatening. On May 26, there was a commotion in the barrio of San Blas; this was followed by a general mobilization of all the barrios on May 29, when threats to stone or burn down the houses of officials were averted only by the intervention of clerics on both that and the following day.[84] One of those threatened was Oidor Hurtado de Mendoza, whose efforts to conduct an enquiry into the riot met with intimidation of witnesses and threats to raze his house.[85]

This did not mean that order had broken down completely in Quito. On the contrary, the barrios called for the resumption of patrols to deal with petty crime, and were quite prepared to countenance the arrest of common criminals. This respect for the law was reflected in an incident which occurred in the parish of San Blas, when an alcalde arrested a local criminal. His brother, seeking to take advantage of the unstable political conditions, sounded the tocsin and called up a tumult in the barrio. However, the parishes of San Sebastián and San Roque offered to come to the magistrate's aid, and when the people of San Blas discovered why the tocsin had been sounded, they not only restored order but also handed over the individual who had sounded the alarm.[86] Thus, the barrios were ready to maintain order and were capable of doing so in an organized manner.

A consensus against common criminality did not extend, however, to government treatment of rioters as criminals. The rapidity with which the barrios assembled to the sound of the alarm indicates that they remained on their guard, ready to oppose any reprisal against the rioters of May 22, or other unwanted interference. There were other incidents, too, which mirrored this state of popular agitation. On June 8, pasquinades calling for the expulsion of peninsular Spaniards appeared in the city, followed by demands on June 14 for a proclamation announcing this expulsion.[87] On June 18, a crowd from San Blas careered through the streets to demonstrate in front of the bishop's palace, demanding a parish priest of their choice and refusing to disperse until the bishop acceded. On June 19, to the sound of bells and fireworks, San Blas rose again, and launched an abortive attack on the jail to try to release a prisoner recently taken into custody. This was prevented by Oidor Romualdo Navarro, who defended the jail with a heavily armed patrol and, after several hours of confrontation, forced the rioters to disband without achieving their objective.[88]

The increasingly agitated state of the barrios in mid-June suggests an incipient radicalization of the movement born in protest at fiscal reform. For, with the weakness of government revealed by the May riot, new issues were drawn in and anti-Spanish feelings were starting to surface. But the troubles of June must also be seen in the context of the city's social and religious calendar. For the disturbances of mid-June occurred during the approach to a major festival, St. John's Day, on June 24. An important date in both the secular and ecclesiastical calendar, and a time when the Indians paid a half-yearly installment of tribute, St. John's Day was associated with a period of celebration which, under normal circumstances, would have called for more intensive policing in the city. However, in the aftermath of the May riot, any official show of force risked a strong response from barrios which had already shown their suspicion that policing would bring reprisals for the May riot. Thus, when, on the night of June 23, the corregidor of Quito conducted a patrol through the parishes of San Roque and San Sebastián, his behavior stimulated further agitation. The patrol rounded up dozens of prisoners and took them to the city jail, where fines were levied and whippings administered.[89] At least one of those whipped by the corregidor was a creole, which seems to have aroused considerable anger and to have fueled the suspicion that the authorities were planning retribution for the May riot. The people of the barrios now began to mobilize once more, aided no doubt by the occasion of the festival. On St. John's night itself rioting again broke out, in a major recrudescence of urban disorder. With it went all hopes for a gradual restoration of royal authority, and Quito now entered a more serious phase of rebellion.

The *"Noche de San Juan"*

The first signs of renewed rebelliousness appeared on the morning of June 24, when pasquinades posted in San Roque called for a union of all the barrios against the corregidor of Quito, and threatened to burn down his house. Throughout the day, rumors of a popular uprising swept through the city, facilitated no doubt by the drinking and carousing of a public holiday. In the late afternoon, the president of the Audiencia was warned of this danger, but was told by representatives from the barrios of San Roque and San Sebastián that the fears were exaggerated. He took no action until some hours later, when the corregidor arrived in alarm to inform him that about three hundred men from San Sebastián were moving to join forces with those of San Roque. Rubio de Arévalo ordered a cannon shot to be fired, as a prearranged signal for citizens to rally to the defense of the city. About a hundred men, including all the available peninsular Spaniards resident in Quito and many prominent creoles, assembled at the Audiencia palace. However, deciding that the tumult was no more than a rowdy affray like those of preceding nights, the majority decided to return to their homes.[90]

Had the matter been left there, nothing further might have happened. But among those who remained was an aggressive group of peninsular Spaniards, led by the corregidor Sánchez Osorio, who insisted that a patrol should be sent out into the city. Oidores Romualdo Navarro, Santa Cruz, and Hurtado de Mendoza argued against this, sensibly seeking to avoid confrontation. But the corregidor insisted that there was a riot in the barrio of San Sebastián, and prevailed on the Audiencia president to dispatch an armed patrol to contain it. Thus, at about 10:00 P.M., the corregidor led his Spanish friends and allies to sally out toward San Sebastián. En route, they attempted to make some arrests, and when they encountered resistance, they opened fire on a crowd, killing two of its members. From this moment, events moved toward a swift and violent climax.[91]

After fighting with the crowd, the patrol was forced to retreat and headed for the protection of the Audiencia palace. Now popular anti-Spanish feeling, already apparent before this riot, came into the open. The rioters first turned their attention to the house of Angel Izquierdo, a Cádiz merchant reputed to have been one of those who had fired on the crowd. When Izquierdo learned of the danger to his home, he rushed a group of some 15 men and a mortar to defend his family and property. After a protracted fight with several hundred rioters who had seized his house, Izquierdo and his party were driven back by weight of numbers, losing their mortar in the process and leaving the crowd to ransack the house, destroying Izquierdo's belongings, but allowing his wife and child to escape unharmed.[92]

By now, the main scene of battle had moved to the Plaza Mayor, and centered on the palace of the Audiencia and its small guard of officials, soldiers, and volunteers, most of whom were peninsular Spaniards. The rioters launched determined attacks on the Audiencia palace, dividing their forces in separate actions against its two entrances. The Audiencia later estimated that this attack involved ten thousand men, armed not only with sticks and stones, but with lances, swords, and some firearms. This figure was doubtless exaggerated, as the Audiencia, after its defeat, had every reason to overestimate the forces which it had confronted. Nonetheless, all contemporary reports indicate that the size of the mobs was very large, and far outnumbered the forces seeking to restrain them. Their attacks continued from around 11:00 P.M. until 4:00 A.M., leaving many dead among the rebels and several wounded among the besieged defending force.[93] Near dawn, various bands renewed the assault and killed two of the defenders before retreating among their own dead and wounded. By now, the size of the rebel force had swelled still more, with groups of rebels spread all over the city and reinforcements coming in from the neighboring villages.

In the day that followed the "noche de San Juan," there was a lull in the fighting. But the rising was not yet over, and its consequences had yet fully to be felt. The small force of 150 defenders in the Audiencia palace had managed to fend off repeated attacks, but, exhausted and facing overwhelming numbers, its position could not be sustained. Attempts were made to negotiate with the rebels, using clerical intermediaries. The bishop and other leading ecclesiastics went to the barrios of San Roque, San Sebastián, and San Blas, where they sought to persuade some "more rational" plebeians to mollify the fury of mobs which "moved by depraved designs . . . wanted to make the whole city the spoil of their ambition."[94] But efforts at peacemaking failed. By the close of the day, the Audiencia was told that more than 500 Indians had joined

the ranks of the rebels in San Blas, that the entrances and aque-
ducts of the city were occupied, blocking food and water supplies,
and that another great rising was being organized in the barrios.
Deciding that their position was hopeless, the officials and their
allies went into hiding, seeking sanctuary in churches, monasteries, and convents, and placing the royal treasury funds in the care
of the Jesuits. At nightfall, crowds advanced again into the city
center and, meeting no opposition, celebrated their victory.

The St. John's night riot was, in one sense, simply an extension
of the protest expressed in the first riot in May. It stemmed from
the official efforts to reimpose the social discipline that had been
broken in the May riot, and thus rekindled earlier antagonisms toward government. When the corregidor's patrol provoked a street
incident, the people of the barrios—still on their guard against reprisals for the earlier tumult—were quick to respond. But this second riot was also qualitatively different, for now the rioters were
no longer just protesting against fiscal reform. The June riot was a
more spontaneous and more violent outburst, born in different circumstances and with different aims. The corregidor's draconian
methods of reasserting his authority confirmed rumors that the
Europeans planned to punish a populace that they despised, and
fueled popular animosity toward them.[95] Furthermore, while the
occasion of a public festival provided a rationale for resuming strong
policing in the streets, such a festival also provided a cultural context for expressing popular antagonism toward authority.[96] In such
an atmosphere of public suspicion and excitement, the corregidor's
tactics had the opposite of their intended effect. Far from dampening disorder, they provoked an incident which sparked a great riot,
and drew disaster on the government.

Directed initially against the members of the patrol involved in
the street clash, popular retaliation moved into a more general assault on the bastions of authority. As the European Spaniards, who
had attacked the crowd in the name of authority and justice, sought
refuge behind the shield of government, so the crowds, attacking
the Spaniards in search of their own retributory justice, were drawn
into an attack on government itself. Thus, Quito's second great riot
was not only more violent than the first; it was also anti-European
and antigovernment, and, born in the popular barrios themselves,
was laced with the enmity of the poor toward the wealthy. When
the riot subsided, the damage done was not easily repaired. A major urban insurrection was under way, with a dynamic of its own,
and it was to be some months before order was fully restored.

From Riot to Rebellion

Following the riot, the balance of power in the city changed dramatically. Gangs attacked the property of some of the Spaniards who had gone into hiding, and the authorities were unable to intervene.[97] The Audiencia, defeated and bereft of authority, had no alternative but to negotiate. On the morning of June 26, the ministers convened a meeting with the bishop, only to have their weakness fully revealed. Soon after they arrived in the palace, a large crowd, estimated at more than two thousand people, surrounded the building and began to insult and threaten them. Francisco de Borja then appeared, together with two Jesuits, to mediate between the crowd and the ministers. The crowd demanded the surrender of firearms held in the royal stores. Eventually, a compromise was reached, after the oidores present had personally pleaded with the assembled people. It was agreed that clerics should conduct these arms to the monastery of Santo Domingo, and hold them there. It was also said that other demands were conceded, including the release of prisoners from jail, the exchange of prisoners taken by the crowds for those under sentence of death, and the removal of troops from the city.[98] However, while the priests were allowed to carry off some small arms, the crowd soon broke its side of the bargain and carried off the cannons to the barrios.

The situation now became still more confused and volatile. Several observers reported that large numbers of Indians from the surrounding villages started to move into the city, and that even larger numbers were assembled in the neighboring Valley of Anaquito. Oidor Hurtado, who stated that more than three thousand Indians had entered the city on June 26, feared that they would also rebel, refusing to pay tribute and killing the whites.[99] While it is likely that large numbers of Indians came into the city at this time—St. John's Day being both an important festival and the time for a half-yearly payment of tribute—it is not clear if there was any real threat that the disorders in Quito would encourage an Indian rebellion in its rural hinterland, or lead to an alliance between urban plebeians and indigenous peasants. Talk of such a threat may have been no more than an attempt by the authorities and their allies to distract the Quito rebels. Certainly, the Audiencia tried to use fears of an Indian invasion and rebellion in order to bring the urban populace back to order. Using parish priests as intermediaries, it sought to manipulate ethnic divisions, playing on the mestizos' dislike of the Indians to persuade them that the Indians were a danger to all.[100] But this failed to win the barrios over, or to convince them to return stolen arms. Indeed, it was said that the cannons were used to fortify the main entrances to the city in order to keep the Indians at bay.[101]

After the violence and excitement had subsided, the implications of the June riot became clearer. The city was in the hands of armed rebels who had effectively overturned the political hierarchy and who, because their power rested on the force of popular action, implicitly threatened the stability of the social order. But how serious was the challenge to the constituted political and social order? Was Spanish sovereignty in danger? Did the entry of the plebeians radicalize the rebellion, or introduce any sense of incipient social revolution?

Fernando de Echandía, a peninsular who had been in Quito throughout the period of the riots and stayed until July 2, took a very somber view of the events. He reported that government had been completely subverted and replaced by the rule of the people. The people, he said, "have made themselves magistrates, ordering gibbets to be built in various places, dealing with disputes, giving freedom to slaves and freeing the Indians from tribute; and, what is more, swearing allegiance to a new king." It seems that they had attempted to persuade the creole aristocrat, Conde de Selva Florida, to become their king, and, though he emphatically refused, they went on to depose "all which bore resemblance to royal justice," replacing it with their own proclamations and laws, and showing disrespect even for the Holy Sacrament.[102]

This was almost certainly an exaggerated version of events. It was written by a man who had been among the Spaniards expelled from the city by the rebels, and who had every reason to view the rebellion in a dramatic light, colored by his personal experience of anti-Spanish feeling in the city. Nonetheless, other accounts also suggest that the antitax movement which had begun in May did take on a more subversive tone after the St. John's night riot, as underlying social tensions came to the surface. Effective government had passed into the hands of local tribunes who enjoyed popular trust and acclaim. The Audiencia, clinging to the tattered shreds of its dignity, could do no more than bend with the prevailing political winds. On June 27, it was forced to divorce itself from the cause of the European Spaniards, and to order their expulsion from the city within a week.[103] It was also forced to accede to demands for another general pardon, this time for the insurrection that was still under way.

The only concession that the Audiencia was able to obtain was that the expulsion order should not include those peninsulars who were married and permanently resident in the city. Otherwise its surrender was complete. It was, moreover, conveyed in full public gaze on June 28, in an extraordinary ceremony in the Plaza Mayor, in front of the Audiencia palace. A ceremonial bench was placed on its balcony, and the oidores, the dean of the cathedral chapter, the ecclesiastical cabildo, the prelates of the regular orders, some city councillors, and "vecinos nobles" were arraigned on it, looking out over the four or five thousand people from the barrios who filled the main square. A singular spectacle then took place. The president of the Audiencia called out "Long live the king," bringing an enthusiastic response from the crowd. A speech from one of the ministers followed, pardoning the rebels, before the bishop gave them absolution, which they received on their knees. Finally, the crowd dispersed peacefully, amid a mood of reconciliation and with promises of future good behavior.[104]

This affirmation of loyalty to the crown did not, however, immediately restore order in Quito. For at least two months after the St. John's night riot, the authority of colonial government in Quito was essentially titular, and the Audiencia lived in fear of further disturbances. In the immediate aftermath of the riot, anger focused on those who had fought with the crowds and who were thought to oppose the barrios. Oidor Hurtado de Mendoza went into hiding, in fear of the mob, as did Corregidor Sánchez Osorio, and the *alguacil mayor*, Antonio de Salas.[105] The fiscal Cistué also took religious sanctuary, before fleeing the city in early July, seeking to escape to Bogotá.[106] The nonresident peninsulars were also forced to leave, in accord with the agreement made between the rebels and the Audiencia. Government now passed into the hands of men acceptable to the barrios, who enjoyed an uneasy and conditional authority over the populace.

To restore its own authority, the Audiencia turned to the creole patriciate and the religious communities, particularly the Jesuits. The Audiencia chose prominent creoles to act as "captains" or "deputies," giving them the right to police the city, and sent a Jesuit mission into the parishes of San Roque, San Sebastián, San Blas, and Santa Bárbara.[107] By July 2, the captains of the barrios were in position, and, organized by the Conde de Selva Florida, they were instrumental in persuading the barrios to return stolen arms to the officers of the crown.[108] On July 3, President Rubio de Arévalo also reported on the captains' activity in the barrios, stating that their presence promised the possibility of negotiations and so gave reason for hope.[109] Within a short time, this hope was fulfilled. On July 4, people from all the barrios convened once again in the Plaza Mayor and, amid protestations of fidelity and repentance, handed over the captured arms.[110] The oidores were forced to restate the pardon which they had granted, and the arms were then solemnly returned, with much public clamor.[111] Finally, as a symbol of the city's loyalty, the royal standard was raised on the balcony of the Audiencia palace, to be kept illuminated for three days and nights.[112] Thus, in the aftermath of the St. John's night riot, an informal government emerged in the city, as the Audiencia was forced to rely on creole notables to sustain royal authority.[113]

This "aristocratic government"—as it was called by the Audiencia's president, Rubio de Arévalo—was the only effective force in the city for the remainder of the year. The Audiencia was unable to do much more than tolerate popular demands, while secretly encouraging the efforts of the creole elites to restrain such demands. For, despite the Audiencia's initial optimism after the ceremony of July 4, the rebellion was still far from over. The people of the barrios continued to assert themselves, amid official fears that open insurrection might flare up again in the city, and that rebellion might spread to the provinces. Reports emanating from the city throughout August testify to these anxieties and the continuing problems facing the Audiencia. At the beginning of the month, treasury officials reported that they were having great difficulty in collecting taxes. Not only had revenues from the alcabala declined considerably within the city, but, due to the threat of violent rejection, they were unable to find tax-farmers for the rural hinterland and had been forced to suspend alcabala collection there.[114] Toward the end of the month, the Audiencia reported that the city was quiet, partly as a result of an epidemic which had affected most homes. However, it confirmed the earlier report of a virtual breakdown in the taxation system, stating that the Quiteño plebeians had sent many emissaries out to the Indian villages, inciting them to refuse tribute, and that, as a consequence, the collection of taxes in the area of Quito, Latacunga, and Ambato was difficult and risky.[115]

Plebeian rebelliousness was, then, expressed mainly by refusal to pay taxes or to tolerate assertions of authority by European Spaniards; it showed few signs of seeking fundamental changes in the political and social order. There were, however, some signs that an incoherent lower-class radicalism had found space to develop in the aftermath of the June riot. For reluctance to pay taxes was not the only sign of continuing popular insubordination. The informal government headed by the creole captains also found it difficult to overcome popular disregard for other aspects of the law, and popular resentments were being openly expressed through delinquency and disobedience.

The captains reported a great increase in crime after the June riot which, as magistrates, they tried to combat by creating district militias to maintain day and night patrols. This was not welcomed by the plebeians, who, having "thrown off the yoke of Justice and broken the reins of Obedience," threatened the lives and property of the captains, and challenged their decisions as magistrates. That the resentment of the poor underpinned this defiance is reflected in the comment of the barrio captains that it was difficult to convince all the plebeians "that being poor was not a safe-conduct for crimes, nor a passport for excesses."[116] Such popular inversion of the official version of justice was no doubt helped by the takeover of minor posts in municipal government by plebeian leaders, and the recognition that all such positions were "at the behest of the barrios."[117] Moreover, these barrio leaders sought to control the movement of Europeans in and out of the city, claiming the right to give licenses to peninsular merchants for specified periods, limited to the time necessary for their business.[118] Differences over how Europeans should be treated were beginning to divide the rebels, however. In mid-September, Francisco de Borja and other leading captains had to order the "delegates and leading citizens of all the barrios" to help transfer the corregidor from the convent of San Francisco to the cabildo, as his life was being threatened.[119]

If plebeian autonomy within Quito was a major worry for the Audiencia, its anxiety was aggravated by the fear that the city's example would be imitated in the provinces, spreading rebellion throughout the highlands. At the end of May and in early June, there were riots against the aguardiente monopoly and alcabalas in Ibarra, Otavalo, and Cuenca, all of them imitating the action taken by Quito's barrios.[120] Such action naturally aroused fears of a general rebellion in the provinces, and, to avert this danger, the Audiencia instructed all corregidores and *justicias mayores* to proceed with special caution, to avoid recourse to arms unless life and property were endangered, and to suspend the aguardiente monopoly, if it were necessary to preserve order.[121]

This conciliatory policy seems to have worked well, although, as the riots of Quito developed into rebellion, fears of a more general insurrection were not easily dispelled. Information gathered by the fiscal Cistué suggests that there were still some reasons for apprehension later in the year. In mid-September, he reported that in Riobamba popular solidarity with the Quito barrios had led to attacks on a tax official exiled there from Quito; unrest had also spread into ecclesiastical politics, when the convocation of the Franciscan chapter led to a popular riot in favor of a candidate related to the parish priest of San Blas in Quito. The town of Ibarra was said to have risen against European Spaniards, refusing them entry, while popular antagonism toward the aguardiente monopoly was creating insecurity in Cuenca.[122] Thus, there were still grounds for official concern about the situation not only in the capital city, but also in the provinces.

The Restoration of Royal Government

In any event, insurrection in Quito did not spread to other areas of the Audiencia and become a great regional rebellion. Apart from the early imitative rioting in provincial towns, the Quito rebellion remained confined to its urban precinct and did not lead to serious disorder even in the surrounding rural hinterland of the "five leagues." The Indian villagers of this zone around Quito did not strike up an alliance with the urban plebeians, and, rather than uniting the poor of town and countryside against the social groups which dominated them, the rebellion remained one of community rather than class.

The reasons for the rebellion's truncated development may be explained by two factors. First, there seems to have been limited potential for solidarity between urban plebeians and Indian peasants. This was partly because many, if not most, plebeians were mestizos, who would have considered themselves both different from and superior to the Indian peasantry. Equally, the city's Indian population did not necessarily identify with the native people of the rural hinterland. While some were no doubt recent migrants who retained close contacts with nearby rural areas, others were long-established members of the city's population, absorbed into its economy and society as artisans and tradesmen. That there were tensions between town and country was attested by the efforts of the Audiencia to exploit urban fears of an Indian invasion, as a means of controlling the rebellion and encouraging the rebels back to order, and by the report that Indian peasants were kept out of the city by the people of the barrios.

The potential for developing radical political ideas in Quito barrios was limited by the nature of local political culture. The plebeians, when joined in collective action, behaved like the classic urban mob in contemporary Europe. Indeed, the Quito crowd seems to fit the definition which E. J. Hobsbawm has given to the "city mob."[123] For, like the European "city mob," the crowd in Quito was a "movement of all classes of the urban poor for the achievement of economic or political change by direct action—that is, by riot or rebellion—but as a movement which was as yet inspired by no specific ideology; or, if it found expression for its aspirations at all, in terms of traditionalism and conservatism."[124] However, as Hobsbawm has explained, for such a movement to be "prepolitical" does not mean that it is without ideas about politics. Typically, by its direct action, the urban mob makes a claim to participate in politics, tends to be directed against the wealthy and powerful, and tends to be hostile to foreigners.

These were precisely the characteristics of the crowd in Quito. By rioting, it made forceful, extralegal representation of its opposition to tax reform; by attacking official buildings, government officers, and wealthy Spaniards, it directed its antagonism against targets which symbolized the abuse of power and the inequity of the social order; finally, by focusing on peninsular Spaniards, the rioters combined animosity toward the wealthy with that xenophobia so characteristic of urban crowds. However, as we have seen, the rebels were also eager to avoid any suggestion of disloyalty to the crown and, indeed, sought to legitimize their rebellion by protestations of loyalty to the king and demands for royal pardons. Moreover, although by asserting their right to express their views to the king over the heads of his ministers, and by their resistance to new taxation, Quito's plebeians voiced their political ideas in direct action, their behavior after the St. John's night riot shows that they did not trespass beyond the boundaries of a traditional political culture, founded on deference toward the existing social and political hierarchy. The appointment of barrio captains, chosen by the Audiencia from among the creole elite, reflects this plebeian deference toward the traditional social order and customary methods of government. In accepting creole notables as their captains, the plebeians showed their acceptance of the normal methods of municipal government, whereby men were selected according to their rank and wealth. Nor was popular preference for local men in government and rejection of rule by outsiders in any real sense a radical departure from the axioms of the existing political culture. Conflicts between creole and peninsular factions had long been a major theme in the politics of the city, and popular involvement in such factional politics does not imply any protonationalist rejection of colonial rule. It was, perhaps, more akin to the "municipal patriotism" which Hobsbawm found to be common among the city mobs in Europe.

Another major factor which helped to limit the development of the rebellion was the conciliatory stance taken by those members of the Audiencia who remained after the June riot, and the growing willingness of leading creoles to cooperate in the restoration of normal government in the months that followed. After the defeat inflicted on the authorities and their peninsular allies on the "noche de San Juan," the Audiencia had little choice but to conciliate, since it could not call on any military force to impose its will on the rebels. But, by formally conceding an end to fiscal reform, offering general pardons to the rioters and rebels, and expelling the European Spaniards whom the Quiteños had identified as their enemies, the Audiencia succeeded—as it had intended—in lowering tension and reestablishing the legitimacy and authority of government. This was, nevertheless, a slow process, and the cooperation of leading creoles was vital to its success. The reports of the creole captains show why this cooperation was forthcoming. Now that they no longer needed popular violence to oppose the reforms, and as popular "lawlessness" grew, they became alarmed by such behavior and anxious to reconstruct the old order.

Faced with a wave of crime against property, with disrespect for their own persons and property, and with popular questioning of their decisions as magistrates, the creole leaders sought to check the rebellion before it threatened their own privileged position. They did this by organizing militia companies in the main districts of the city, and by taking advantage of divisions within the populace. Thus, in seeking to repress those challenges which still arose from the ranks of the plebeians, the captains allied themselves with those elements that they considered "more rational, more obedient, and more committed to the obligations of vassallage," and persuaded them that, if necessary, they should expel "the ungovernable and the vagabonds."[125] Furthermore, to pacify the populace, the creoles did not rely simply on persuasion by argument and appeals to deference. When Nicolás Calixto de Alarcón asked for permission to retire from his task as a barrio captain, he argued that he had not

only exhausted himself in the effort of restoring government, but
had spent much of his wealth on presents and bribes needed to win
popular support.[126]

These efforts by the creole elites, working with the Audiencia,
gradually bore fruit. In mid-September, the viceroy officially ratified the general pardon announced by the Audiencia in early July,
and this seems to have marked a turning point in the rebellion. For,
apart from some minor tumults, popular restiveness began to sub-
side. By the beginning of October, the president reported that the
city was stable and showed signs of submission to authority. Nonetheless, his optimism was still tempered by misgivings, for much
remained to be done. Hundreds of illegal stills were operating in
the city, turning out aguardiente at low prices, while an official
agreement suspended the collection of revenues from the farmers
of the aguardiente monopoly in Quito and its jurisdiction, for fear
that any effort to operate the monopoly would lead to renewed disturbances. Rubio de Arévalo also testified to the continuing weakness of royal government, stating that it was unable to influence
appointments to minor municipal posts, which had consequently
fallen into the hands of "criminals." Nor was he entirely confident
of the future. Like the fiscal Cistué, who continued to send alarmist reports to the viceroy from his exile, Rubio de Arévalo lamented
the erosion of deference and the decay of social discipline. The
mob, he said, had triumphed, it had chosen its tribunes, and it would
rise again whenever it was challenged.[127]

In fact, any renewal of confrontation was avoided. From December, when Rubio de Arévalo retired and was replaced as interim president by Oidor Santa Cruz, the Audiencia gradually
restored its authority. This was partly because the rebels had
achieved their objectives: the new excise had been suspended, a
pardon had been ratified, and, so long as they were not provoked
by any show of force or retribution, they had nothing left to fight
for. Another factor in the restoration of the Audiencia was the diplomacy of its new president, Santa Cruz, who sought to co-opt
and cooperate with the barrios. Thus, when disturbances were threatened at the end of December, he called the delegates of the barrios
to his house and negotiated with them; when there was a conflict in
the election of alcaldes in January 1766, he resolved the problem
by electing two extra alcaldes; and, when the corregidor refused to
cooperate with Francisco de Borja, Santa Cruz not only ordered
him to do so, but also showed his confidence in the creole Borja by
placing him in command of the presidential guard, thereby con-

verting an erstwhile opponent of government into its principal de-
fender.[128] Furthermore, to stiffen creole commitment to the pacifi-
cation of Quito, Santa Cruz prevented the departure of leading
citizens, on pain of confiscation of their property, and encouraged
the return of those who had left, arguing that their presence contributed to containing "the pride of the mob."[129]

With cooperation within the patriciate, as well as between the
creole elite and members of the government, the city slowly returned to normalcy. It seems that, after the June riot had infused the
antitax movement with dangerous popular animosities towards
Europeans and colonial government, the urban patriciate chose to
side with the Audiencia in order to bring the people back under
control. Gradually, under the careful supervision of select members of the creole elite and the Audiencia, the popular parishes were
brought to heel, a process no doubt helped by lax collection of sales
taxes and the removal of controls on the manufacture and sale of
aguardiente.

By the early months of 1766, the lingering symptoms of disaffection and fear of rebellion faded. In early March, an Indian rebellion in nearby Latacunga was rapidly suppressed without
repercussion in Quito.[130] At the end of March, news that a military
expedition was being sent to the city, something which had previously been a closely guarded secret, was received in Quito.[131] According to the exiled fiscal Cistué, this news brought a sharp change
in attitudes, spreading apprehension and encouraging the "nobles"
to shift blame for the rebellion onto the leaders of the barrios.[132] In
early May, Francisco de Borja reported to the viceroy that the city
was quietly awaiting the arrival of troops, and he raised no objec-
tion to the sending of the military expedition.[133] Other reports indicate, however, that there was still a groundswell of opposition among
the lower classes. At the end of May, a Spaniard in Quito pointed to
the dangers of another uprising, induced by popular rumors that
the arrival of troops would lead to mass executions and the imposition of heavy tributes on the mestizos.[134] However, the creole patriciate, working with the Audiencia, retained its grip on the city. On
September 1, 1766, the troops entered the city, to be warmly received by its inhabitants.[135] Command of the city was now transferred to the military commander, Pedro Zelaya, who, though he
emphasized reconciliation rather than retribution, took the precau-
tion of forming a battalion of Europeans to prevent any further plebeian insults to authority.[136] After a respectable interval, the
Audiencia was purged of all surviving ministers associated with

the debacle of 1765, pending an investigation into the events of that year.[137] And, on February 14, 1767, the aguardiente monopoly, source of so much discord, was restored without opposition from any quarter.[138] Quito, now occupied by a garrison, had been brought firmly back under Bourbon control.

Conclusions

In his brilliant analysis of rebellion in a sixteenth-century French town, Ladurie has proposed two paradigms for classifying urban revolts; though they pertain to a quite different historical context, they provide a starting point for some closing comments on the Quito insurrection of 1765. The first—the "Ibn Khaldun paradigm"—approaches urban violence as a function of rivalries between families or clans, and their clienteles. The second—the "Karl Marx paradigm"—sees it as a class struggle, rooted in the conflicts of social groups with contradictory economic interests.[139] While the Quito case cannot be accommodated within either of these models, analysis in their terms offers a useful perspective.

The "Ibn Khaldun paradigm" is useful because it draws attention to a common feature of urban political life in colonial Spanish America, and to its role in generating local political conflict: namely, the rivalries and enmities of leading families, often expressed in conflicts over municipal and bureaucratic office, in judicial disputes over property, and in other conflicts over local resources. Of course, in America such conflicts had an additional edge, for they tended to divide along the social lines which divided American and European Spaniards. Although the history of Quito remains to be written, the evidence available suggests that it was at least as prone to such divisions as was any comparable city, and that rivalries between creole and peninsular factions were intense. But, in the Quito case, the "Ibn Khaldun paradigm" must be adapted to its context in order to be useful. In Quito, the conflict within the elite cannot be reduced to that of rival families or clans: it was much more complicated, drawing on disputes between clergy and government, between officials within government, between cabildo and corregidor, and between European and American Spaniards. Nor was this simply a conflict between creoles and peninsulars as rivals within the dominant social group. The conflict also had an important political dimension, as the creole patriciate and its allies were evidently moved by a determination to resist the encroachments of a reformist and centralizing monarchy.

The rebellion in Quito was, then, in part the expression of several overlapping disputes within the urban elite and government. Indeed, for the viceroys of New Granada and Peru, this was all it was. Viceroy Messía de la Cerda finally concluded that it had stemmed from the "seditious spirit of the principal citizens of that city," who had promoted hatred of taxes and Europeans, aided by the partiality of ministers in the Audiencia and by conflict between the secular clergy and the government. Thus, with Viceroy Amat of Peru, he concurred in attributing responsibility to the creole patriciate, whom they both saw as the "hidden hand" impelling and guiding an ignorant and disorganized populace for its own purposes.[140] This official view of the rebellion is, however, only partly correct, and historiographical interpretations based on it need to be revised. For, while it is clear that the creoles colluded in the rebellion—if only by failing to defend the royal government against attack—the patriciate was simply one element in a loose coalition of social and corporate groups drawn into a temporary alliance. If factional quarrels within the dominant groups played a part in preparing the ground for rebellion, the rebellion also demonstrated the grievances of plebeian groups who were capable of organized collective action in defense of their own interests.

In this sense, the Marxian model of urban insurrection as a class struggle of artisans and city workers against merchants and nobles also has relevance to Quito's rebellion. The latter was clearly not an undiluted class struggle, dominated by the clash of social groups with opposing economic interests. But there can be little doubt that the political mobilization of the plebeians owed much of its force to the strains imposed by recent economic dislocations. It was not economic decline in itself that generated rebellion: if contemporary reports are to be believed, this had been slowly crippling the city for many years. Much more important was the experience of a recent sharp downturn, described by the merchants' delegate as a "profound depression," which had undermined exports, reduced trade in the city to the exchange of basic necessities, and caught merchants and traders in a chain of credit where none could hope for payment.[141] This economic squeeze brought class and ethnic tensions to the surface. The expulsion of peninsulars after the June riot was prompted by the desire to punish the Europeans for their behavior on St. John's night, but it also reflected a division along class lines, in which plebeian artisans and tradesmen vented their anger on merchants. Europeans dominated Quito's trade. Thus, as the importers of the very textiles harmful to the city's economy—

and possibly also because they stood at the head of the chains of credit which bound merchants to shopkeepers and shopkeepers to consumers—they could be identified as profiting from the city's economic decline. There is, then, the possibility that the Quito rebellion was tinged by conflict between artisans and merchants, though not in the conventional European sense of a struggle between groups involved in the production and distribution of the same product. The attack on merchants would have been, rather, a sign that the rebels attributed responsibility for their economic ills to the Spanish government because of its changes in commercial policy, and to Spanish merchants because they not only were identified with this policy, but also appeared to be profiting from it. Thus, the revolt was not propelled by mere poverty, but given shape and direction by the identification of specific agents for Quito's social ills.

In its later stages, the rebellion showed more direct symptoms of a struggle between rich and poor, as a wave of delinquency brought property under attack. But such activity remained on its fringes, and the rebellion cannot be regarded as a struggle between the upper and lower classes of urban society. Inevitably, in a society in which differences of ethnic status were at least as important as divisions defined by wealth and occupation, if not more so, conflicts of class gave way to conflicts rooted in differences of race. In this sense—and like most other rebellions in late colonial Spanish America—the Quito insurrection was the rebellion of a community rather than a class. In Quito, that community was an agglomeration of urban whites, mestizos, and Indians, who could unite briefly behind the common goal of resisting changes in taxation but could not find any lasting cohesion nor develop links which went beyond the urban community into its rural hinterland. With the European Spaniards to serve as scapegoats, with fears that the Indian peasants might enter and overwhelm the city, and with the moderating leadership of a creole patriciate anxious to retain its own privileges, there was little scope for popular resentments to build into an organized attack on the social order. Despite rumors of slave and Indian emancipation, plebeian discontents were channeled into retribution rather than revolution. Ultimately, the Quito rebellion remained a protest against a policy, not against the power from which policy emanated.

The rebellion did not put forward any written program nor any systematic account of the ideas which might have been held by participants. This should not, however, disguise the ideological currents present in the rebellion, nor shroud their importance. On the one hand, the arguments of the creole elites and their allies, both in the *cabildo abierto* and in supporting correspondence with the authorities, all allude to a belief in a kind of constitutionalism in the conduct of state business. It would be a mistake to dismiss the arguments concerning the need to recognize local needs, customs, and conventions as mere rhetoric, cynically employed to disguise selfish sectoral interests. Of course, the creole opponents of reform were concerned with protecting and defending their economic interests. But they did not need to disguise this, for they saw it as a right, facilitated and sanctioned by the traditional procedures of government, with their lengthy consultations, delayed deliberations, and tendency to respect the status quo. Thus, while the rebellion did not produce a manifesto, the letters and petitions of the leading opponents of reform reveal a patrician, primarily creole discourse concerning the distribution and exercise of power within the colonial state.

Another ideological dimension of the rebellion is found among the plebeians. This is much more difficult to identify and define, because it was not articulated in any written form, nor, without prosecution of the rebels, can we even attempt to trace it among the testimonies of defendants and witnesses at trials. Nevertheless, as E. P. Thompson has suggested in another historical context, glimpses of an unsophisticated and unsystematic "ideology" can be gained by studying the behavior of rioting crowds.[142] Thompson found that the actions of the eighteenth-century English mob were underpinned by a sense of legitimacy—the belief that they were defending some rights or traditional customs—and that this was reflected in disciplined and directed action, governed by certain norms and geared towards certain goals.

The riots which provided the main expressions of plebeian participation in the Quito rebellion display such a notion of legitimacy. In the May riot, there were some references to the drunkenness and insolence of the mob, but, beneath its disorderly surface, the riot displayed elements of structure and discipline. That there was some drunkenness is hardly surprising: the rioters' target housed a distillery and liquor store. But there was no indiscriminate violence or plunder. Damage was inflicted on the excise building, but in a manner which displays a purposeful attitude. Its contents were destroyed, not simply stolen, and the systematic demolition of the excise building suggests a deliberate symbolic gesture rather than a disordered attack. Throughout the period of the riot, the crowd remained in

the area of the excise office, and, although the Audiencia took precautions to defend the Plaza Mayor, the riot showed no signs of
turning into a general assault on government. Nor was there any
deliberate assault on the persons of officials: Díaz de Herrera and
his subordinates were able to escape and take religious sanctuary,
and none of the officials involved in trying to restrain the rioters
reported any direct attack against them. Clearly, the rioters had what
they regarded as legitimate goals, signalled by their choice of targets and the restraint exercised in unleashing their anger on these
targets. Furthermore, having directly vented its anger against the
symbols of fiscal oppression, the crowd then emphasized its claim
to legitimacy by seeking formal recognition for its rejection of the
reform, using clerical intermediaries to negotiate with the authorities. Once its demands were met, the crowd disbanded peacefully.

The June riot was more violent, but displayed similar elements
of structure. Rallied by the bells of the barrios' parish churches,
the rioters turned against the corregidor's patrol because it represented a form and style of government which, in the wake of the
May riot, had lost its legitimacy. Indeed, the crowd was drawn into
an attack on government because it was itself attacked; though there
was loss of life and property, the riot never became simply a destructive rampage by an infuriated and mindless mob. Moreover,
though there were signs of growing indiscipline among the urban
lower classes after the riots, especially in the weeks after the "noche
de San Juan," not even the most prejudiced observers suggested
that the city had been submerged by a tide of uncontrollable
violence.

There were many facets of civil disorder and popular protest in
late colonial Spanish America, among all ethnic groups and at different social levels. Rebelliousness was most evident, of course, at
the lower ends of the social scale, among people of color, most of
whom were poor. This included the rebellions of black slaves who
took collective actions to improve their conditions or to secure their
freedom; it also encompassed the many outbursts of agrarian communities against those they perceived to be predators, whether tax
collectors, abusive officials, or competing communities. Riots of
urban mobs, again usually against tax collectors or other officials,
fall within the same broad spectrum. More rarely, rebellion was
actively promoted by relatively wealthy creoles as in the case of
the Caracas rebellion of 1749–52, in which creole landowners protested against their economic subordination to a Spanish monopoly.
Occasionally, these protests might cluster together within a short

time span, to form a recognizable conjuncture of rebellion. Or, again on rare occasions, the disparate strands of rebellion might merge in time and space to produce great regional rebellions which blended the discontents of disparate groups, even different cultures, into prolonged upheavals which, as with the rebellions of Tupac Amaru in Peru or Hidalgo in Mexico, might become veritable civil wars.

Quito's "rebellion of the barrios" did not become a great regional social and political movement, of the kind that was to occur in neighboring Peru and New Granada during the early 1780s. It has, indeed, been overshadowed by those great rebellions, especially by that of the southern Andes, where several overlapping revolts, mainly among the native peasantry, unleashed a conflict of unparalleled duration and violence. It was, nevertheless, a significant episode in the history of rebellion in colonial Spanish America. First, it was part of a cluster of rebellions that affected the southern regions of the Viceroyalty of New Granada during the early 1760s and signalled the first widespread, if scattered, resistance to Bourbon fiscal reform among both urban and rural communities.[143] Thus, it stands as an important moment in a major regional conjuncture of resistance to that new phase of Bourbon reformism, associated with the government of Charles III, that started in the 1760s. By the same token, it also constitutes a striking episode in that wider, pancontinental movement of rebellion which developed during the final half-century of the colonial regime—a movement better known for its great regional exemplars in Peru and New Granada.

The Quito rebellion is also important because of its character as an urban movement. It was indeed the first in a series of urban uprisings directed against colonial government during the last 50 years of Bourbon rule. Such uprisings—of the kind found among townspeople in the Socorro region of New Granada and in towns in different parts of Peru and Upper Peru in the early 1780s—constituted important elements in the conjunctures of rebellion that occurred in this period, and contributed to the development of the larger, regional movements which challenged the crown's new policies. Urban popular protests were, moreover, to play an important role in politics again in 1810, when urban mobs were frequently to engage in the political struggles that gave rise to the first movements for colonial autonomy.

This tradition of urban revolt—which has tended to be submerged in analyses of larger rebellions or political movements—deserves more attention from historians. For Spanish American towns, with their concentrations of population and more intense social stratification, were—like their contemporary North American counterparts—often more susceptible to economic change, and had a more active political life, than the small, scattered settlements of the countryside.[144] Often, perhaps invariably, this political life was confined to small oligarchies, with the inevitable tendency for politics to decline into mere factionalism. But, as the Quito rebellion shows, there were moments when this narrow and exclusive political system could open up through conflict, revealing divisions within the community and providing some scope for wider political participation and for changing political attitudes. Although these urban movements were less violently disruptive in their impact and less radical in their implications than the great peasant movements, such as those found among the Quechua- and Aymara-speaking natives of the central and southern Andes, they are nevertheless important. Born in towns and cities, they were at the heart of colonial culture, where the tensions generated by economic change, political centralization, and ethnic and social rivalries were concentrated, and where, during the great crisis of imperial rule in the early nineteenth century, the final struggle between colonies and metropolis was to be played out.

Notes

1. See Segundo Moreno Yáñez, *Sublevaciones indígenas en la Audiencia de Quito, desde comienzos del siglo XVIII hasta finales de la colonia* (Bonn, 1976).
2. The earliest history of the rebellion appeared in 1789, in Juan de Velasco, *Historia del Reino de Quito*, 2 vols. (Quito, 1971 ed.), I, 136–149; another account is given in the classic nineteenth-century history of Federico González Suárez, *Historia general de la república del Ecuador*, 9 vols. in 3 (Quito, 1979 ed.), III, 1,126–1,139. A more recent account is found in Carlos de la Torre Reyes, *La revolución de Quito del 10 de agosto de 1809* (Quito, 1961), 147–154.
3. Joseph Pérez, *Los movimientos precursores de la emancipación en Hispanoamérica* (Madrid, 1977), 46–63.
4. The main source for the rebellion used in this article is the collection of correspondence relating to the events of 1764–66 compiled by the secretary of the viceroy of New Granada, and now located in the Archivo General de Indias, Seville (hereafter AGI), Quito 398 and 399. The numbers of the documents cited here from the AGI Quito legajos conform to the numbers given in the original index, in Quito 398; the folio numbers conform to the modern foliation. This documentation has been supplemented by some material drawn from the Colombian national archives in Bogotá. Regrettably, I have not been able to use Ecuadorian archives directly. However, the two legs. of documentation relating to the rebellion found in the Archivo de Indias do offer an unrivaled source. Indeed, their compilation of correspondence and other documents constitutes a kind of "official history" of the rebellion, which, because it contains so many firsthand accounts of events, provides a source unlikely to be surpassed even in the ar-

chives of Quito itself. The Quito archives would, however, undoubtedly be indispensable for a thorough analysis of the social and economic history of the city during this period.

5. Eduardo Posada and P. M. Ibáñez, *Relaciones de mando: Memorias presentadas por los gobernantes del Nuevo Reino de Granada* (Bogotá, 1910), 80–81.

6. Ibid., 99.

7. AGI Quito 398 (No. 1), fols. 32–35. The viceroy's order was not officially approved by the crown until more than a year after it was issued. See Julián de Arriaga to Viceroy Messía de la Cerda, Aranjuez, June 5, 1765, Archivo Histórico Nacional de Colombia (hereafter AHNC), Impuestos Varios (Cartas), tomo 17, fol. 21.

8. Viceroy Messía de la Cerda, Oct. 10, 1765, AGI Quito 398 (no. 149).

9. Joseph de Cistué to Viceroy Messía de la Cerda, Apr. 1, 1766, AHNC Historia, tomo 3, fols. 33–34.

10. Cabildo of Quito to viceroy, Sept. 7, 1752, AHNC, Impuestos Varios (Cartas), tomo 23, fols. 754–756.

11. Joseph Gómez Lasso de la Vega to viceroy, Mar. 5, 1764, ibid., tomo 22, fols. 761–764.

12. Pedro Guerrero y Otañón to viceroy, Mar. 8, 1764, ibid., fol. 769.

13. Francisco de Borja to crown, Jan. 24, 1767, AGI Quito 399 (no. 423).

14. For general comment on the city's politics from the 1730s until the 1760s, see González Suárez, *Historia general*, V, chaps. 3 and 4.

15. Luis de la Cuesta to viceroy, Oct. 29, 1764, AGI Quito 398 (no. 6), fols. 61–62.

16. Borja sought to delay the establishment of a royal aguardiente distillery on the ground that it interfered with the public water supply. He also persuaded the Audiencia that the corregidor of Quito should not participate in the cabildo's deliberations on the new policy, as he was personally prejudiced. Díaz de Herrera to viceroy, Dec. 8, 1764, AGI Quito 398 (no. 148), fol. 601.

17. For some data on Borja's social connections and their positions in the local economy, see Javier Ortiz de la Tabla, "Panorama económico y social del corregimiento de Quito (1768–1775)," *Revista de Indias*, 36:145–146 (1976), 92–95.

18. AHNC, Impuestos Varios (Cartas), tomo 22, fols. 372–375. In a "Memoria de los individuos, en hacendados, quienes se han prorrateado de su libre voluntad por las quadras de caña dulce que tienen en sus haciendas de trapiches en donde se fabrican aguardientes de caña que se expende en esta ciudad y sus cinco leguas" drawn up in Aug. 1752, Juan de Chiriboga appears as the second largest contributor, after the Jesuits, with 150 cuadras devoted to the production of sugarcane.

19. "Testimonio del ocurso hecho por las Religiones y Commun del Vecindario de la Ciudad de Quito," fol. 601, AGI Quito 398, no. 148.

20. Ibid., fols. 605–606.

21. Ibid., fol. 604.

22. Information on the Audiencia members is from Mark A. Burkholder and D. S. Chandler, *From Impotence to Authority: The Spanish Crown and the American Audiencias* (Columbia, MO, 1977), 219–221.

23. González Suárez, *Historia general*, II, 1,054–1,057.

24. Viceroy to Arriaga, July 5, 1765, AGI Quito 398 (no. 59), fol. 358.

25. Llano to viceroy, Nov. 20, 1764, ibid. (nos. 8 and 9). Llano's fears of an uprising were not necessarily exaggerated: he had only recently returned from

Riobamba, where his efforts to count the Indian population had sparked a local rebellion. See Moreno Yáñez, *Sublevaciones indígenas*, 42–107.

26. Díaz de Herrera to viceroy, Jan. 18, 1765, AGI Quito 398 (no. 21).

27. Díaz de Herrera to viceroy, Feb. 2, 1765, ibid. (no. 24).

28. Díaz de Herrera to viceroy, Dec. 8, 1765, ibid. (no. 12).

29. Ibid. (no. 35), fols. 205–215; Díaz de Herrera also reported that it had been agreed that the hacendados and vecinos of the province of Quito should raise six to eight thousand pesos by pro rata contributions, in order to meet the costs of sending Borja to Spain to present their case at court. Díaz de Herrera to viceroy, Dec. 13, 1764, ibid. (no. 16).

30. According to Díaz de Herrera, the monasteries regularly contravened the *estanco* regulations but could not easily be controlled because aguardiente was distilled in the cloisters, where guards could not enter and from which it was often taken out by women. Díaz de Herrera to viceroy, Dec. 8, 1764, ibid. (no. 10).

31. Llano to viceroy, Nov. 20, 1764, ibid. (no. 8), fol. 67.

32. Joseph Gómez Lasso de la Vega to viceroy, Mar. 5, 1764, AHNC, Impuestos Varios (Cartas), tomo 22, fol. 760.

33. Díaz de Herrera to viceroy, Dec. 8, 1764, AGI Quito 398 (no. 12). These threats were serious enough for Díaz to ask for a guard to protect him and for the Audiencia to set up an investigation. See Díaz de Herrera to viceroy, Dec. 8, 1764, ibid. (no. 11) and Audiencia to viceroy, Dec. 13, 1764, ibid. (no. 17).

34. Borja, "Informe por el vecindario," Nov. 28, 1764, ibid., fols. 215–225.

35. Informe de los vecinos de Tacunga, ibid., fols. 230–233. Of the two signatures on this document, one was that of the Marqués de Maenza who, it should be noted, had been involved in the recent successful bid for the aguardiente monopoly, as a guarantor for Melchor de Rivadeneyra. See AHNC, Impuestos Varios (Cartas), tomo 22, fol. 769.

36. Informe de los hacendados; informe de los trapicheros, ibid., fols. 238–244.

37. Informe del comercio, ibid., fols. 233–238.

38. Informes de la Compañía de Jesús, Fray Jacinto de la Cruz, and rector del Colegio Imperial de San Buenaventura, ibid., fols. 244–247.

39. In 1752, the Jesuits had headed the list of landholders contributing on the basis of their acreage under sugar production, with the convents of San Agustín and la Merced also being among the leading contributors. See AHNC, Impuestos Varios (Cartas), tomo 22, fols. 372–375. In the same year, the cabildo said of the haciendas of Quito that they were "so burdened with mortgages that their owners are in reality no more than mayordomos for the mortgagors," ibid., tomo 23, fol. 754. For further comment on clerical involvement in the agrarian and urban economy of Quito, see Jorge Juan and Antonio de Ulloa, in *Discourse and Political Reflections on the Kingdoms of Peru*, John TePaske, ed. (Norman, 1978), 306–307.

40. After a major demographic crisis in the 1690s, the Quito textile industry had entered a phase of decline from which it never fully emerged. See John Leddy Phelan, *The Kingdom of Quito in the Seventeenth Century: Bureaucratic Politics in the Spanish Empire* (Madison, 1967), 66–71.

41. Robson B. Tyrer, "The Demographic and Economic History of the Audiencia of Quito: Indian Population and the Textile Industry, 1600–1800" (Ph.D. diss., University of California, Berkeley, 1976), 184–341. For a classic contemporary statement concerning the problems facing Quito around midcentury, see "Razón que cerca del Estado y Gobernación Política y Militar de las Provincias, Villas y

Lugares que contiene la Jurisdicción de la Real Audiencia de Quito da . . . el Marqués de Selva Alegre" (1754), in *Arbitraje de límites entre Perú y el Ecuador. Documentos anexos al alegato del Perú* (Madrid, 1905), I, 138–169.

The view that Quito suffered economic decline during the eighteenth century has recently been questioned. Carlos Marchán asserts that there was no such general decline in the Audiencia of Quito, and that the image of general decline was propagated by the *obraje* owners of the north-central sierra in order to defend themselves from the competition of textile imports. It is indeed unlikely that the whole Audiencia of Quito suffered uniform economic decline, and it is true that the *obraje* owners were among those hardest hit by changes in external trade. But the fact remains that, when discussing the city of Quito and its hinterland, contemporary sources constantly reiterate the theme of depression, and invariably link it to the loss of specie caused by the contraction of Quito's textile trade with Peru. Without new evidence to the contrary, the "depression thesis" for the economy of highland Quito stands. For Marchán's arguments, see Leoncio López-Ocón Cabrera, "El protagonismo del clero en la insurgencia quiteña (1790–1812)," *Revista de Indias*, 46:17 (1986), 109–112.

42. See Antonio García-Baquero González, *Cádiz y el Atlántico (1717–1778) (El comercio colonial espanol bajo el monopolio gaditano)*, 2 vols. (Seville, 1976), II, 173.

43. For a general account of the *cabildo abierto*, see John Preston Moore, *The Cabildo in Peru under the Hapsburgs* (Durham, 1954), 125–135.

44. "El cabildo secular . . .," AGI Quito 398 (no. 35), fols. 248–249.

45. On Spanish medieval practice, see José Antonio Maravall, *Las comunidades de Castilla: Una primera revolución moderna*, 2d ed. (Madrid, 1979), 117–118.

46. "El cabildo secular . . .," AGI Quito 398 (no. 35), fol. 220.

47. "Informe del señor procurador," ibid., fols. 227–228.

48. Luis de Santa Cruz to viceroy, Feb. 1, 1765, ibid. (no. 22).

49. Phelan, *The People and the King: The Comunero Revolution in Colombia, 1781* (Madison, 1978), 35.

50. Ibid., 79–88.

51. Viceroy Messía de la Cerda to Arriaga, Feb. 1, 1765, AGI Quito 398 (no. 23).

52. "El cabildo secular . . .," ibid. (no. 35), fols. 265–267.

53. Díaz de Herrera to viceroy, Dec. 8 and 9, 1764, ibid. (nos. 10, 11, 12, 13, 14) documents these antireformist activities.

54. Díaz de Herrera to viceroy, Jan. 18, 1765, ibid. (nos. 20 and 24).

55. Llano to viceroy, Mar. 4, 1765, ibid. (no. 26); Díaz de Herrera to viceroy, Mar. 22, 1765, ibid. (no. 27).

56. Llano to viceroy, May 3, 1765, ibid. (no. 29).

57. Díaz de Herrera to viceroy, May 12, 1765, ibid. (no. 33).

58. For an account of events leading up to the riot, see the anonymous "Relación sumaria de las dos sublevaciones de la Pleve de Quito," *Boletín de la Academia Nacional de Historia*, 15: 42–45 (Quito, 1937), 103 and Domingo de Araujo to viceroy, July 13, 1765, AGI Quito 398 (no. 65).

59. Information on the social composition of these barrios is from A. M. Minchom, "Urban Popular Society in Colonial Quito, c. 1700–1800" (Ph.D. diss., University of Liverpool, 1984), 220–221, 236.

60. The following reconstruction of the May 22 riot is based on several first-hand accounts, all sent to the viceroy within days of the riot. First, from the Audiencia tribunal: AGI Quito 398 (no. 39), fols. 281–288; second, from Oidor Hurtado de Mendoza, ibid. (no. 38), fols. 276–280; third, from the corregidor of

Quito, ibid. (no. 40), fols. 289–294; fourth, from the prelates of the religious communities, ibid. (no. 36), fols. 269–271; and fifth, from the bishop of Quito, ibid. (no. 37), fols. 272–275.

61. Biblioteca Nacional de Colombia, Bogotá (hereafter BNC), Sala de Libros Raros y Curiosos, Fondo Quijano Otero mss. 179, no. 5; Hurtado de Mendoza to viceroy, May 24, 1765, AGI Quito 398 (no. 38).

62. AGI Quito 398 (no. 67), fols. 426–431.

63. Ibid., fol. 429.

64. Domingo de Araujo to viceroy, July 13, 1765, ibid. (no. 65).

65. Audiencia to viceroy, May 24, 1765, ibid. (no. 34), fols. 281–288.

66. Bishop of Quito to viceroy, May 24, 1765, ibid. (no. 37).

67. Audiencia to viceroy, May 24, 1765, ibid. (no. 34).

68. Bishop of Quito to viceroy, May 24, 1765, ibid. (no. 37). This is the only account of this meeting.

69. Audiencia to viceroy, May 24, 1765, ibid. (no. 34).

70. Manuel Sánchez Osorio y Pareja to viceroy, May 26, 1765, ibid. (no. 35).

71. Hurtado recorded sending the results of this secret investigation to the viceroy in Aug. 1765, and said that it included the testimonies of 81 witnesses, from "all classes and hierarchies," Hurtado de Mendoza to viceroy, Sept. 30, 1765, AHNC, Milicias y Marina, tomo 123, fols. 138–139. Unfortunately, this document is not included among the papers directly related to the rebellion, and though there are other references to it, it has not been found. The references suggest that it was sent on to the viceroy in Bogotá and subsequently to the Consejo de Indias, but, despite a search in the correspondence of the Audiencia of Quito, the viceroy of New Granada, and the Consejo de Indias, found in the archives of Bogotá, Seville, and Madrid, these papers have not been traced.

72. Velasco, *Historia del Reino de Quito*, I, 144.

73. Domingo de Araujo, who was later appointed as counsel for the barrios of San Roque, San Blas, and San Sebastián, referred to "mestizos and criollo plebeians," whom he distinguished from the Indians who dismantled the excise building. AGI Quito 398 (no. 65), fol. 412.

74. For a description of the social groups of Quito, see Juan and Ulloa, *A Voyage to South America*, John Adams, trans. (New York, 1964), 135–146.

75. AGI Quito 398 (no. 42), fols. 297–305.

76. Bishop of Quito to viceroy, May 22, 1765, AGI Quito 398 (no. 34).

77. Viceroy Messía de la Cerda to Arriaga, Apr. 9, 1767, AGI Quito 399 (no. 419).

78. Juan and Ulloa, *Discourse and Political Reflections*, 283–286.

79. Ibid., 294–298.

80. Minchom, "Urban Popular Society," 340–346.

81. On this festival, see Minchom, "Urban Popular Society," 145–149.

82. "Relación sumaria," 104.

83. Díaz de Herrera sought sanctuary in a Franciscan convent, where he remained until June 21, when he finally left the city under cover of darkness, with an armed escort provided by the Marqués de Villa Orellana, and returned to Bogotá. Díaz de Herrera to viceroy, Popayán, July 22, 1765, AHNC, Milicias y Marina, tomo 123, fols. 88–93.

84. BNC, Libros Raros y Curiosos, Fondo Quijano Otero mss. 179, no. 5.

85. Hurtado de Mendoza to viceroy, July 4, 1765, AGI Quito 398, fol. 341.

86. "Relación sumaria," 104.

87. BNC, Libros Raros y Curiosos, Fondo Quijano Otero mss. 179, no. 5.

88. AHNC, Milicias y Marina, tomo 125, fols. 93–95; AGI Quito 398 (no. 67), fol. 43.

89. Unless otherwise indicated, this account of events leading up to the June 24 riot is based on the report made by the Audiencia president. Rubio de Arévalo to viceroy, July 11, 1765, AGI Quito 398 (no. 62), fols. 391–400.

90. This was reported by Fernando de Echandía, a peninsular Spaniard who was personally involved in the events. "Relación del nuevo tumulto popular acaecido en la Ciudad de Quito," AHNC, Milicias y Marina, tomo 123, fols. 93–95.

91. This reconstruction of the riot and events which followed is based on several sources: the report of the Audiencia (AGI Quito 398 [no. 52], fols. 324–335); that of Domingo de Araujo (ibid. [no. 65], fols. 409–417); and the anonymous "Relación sumaria" (pp. 105–109). Where other sources provide additional detail, they are cited separately.

92. A graphic personal account of the riot and the attack on Izquierdo's house, including the ordeal of his wife, was given by Izquierdo himself. It is reprinted in "Noticia de los movimientos de Quito en el año de 1765," *Museo Histórico*, 3:9 (Quito, 1951), 37–54.

93. Eyewitness accounts of the fighting were given by soldiers who testified to the leading role of Alcalde Mariano Monteserín, in the defense of the palace. These are reprinted in "Sublevación de Quito por la Aduana y los Estancos," *Museo Histórico*, 2:7 (Quito, 1950), 25–37 and 3:8 (1951), 16–31. Domingo de Araujo reported that between three and five hundred persons among the "gente miserable" were killed without the death of a single European. The two whites killed were both creoles. AGI Quito 398 (no. 65), fol. 417.

94. AGI Quito 398 (no. 52), fol. 327.

95. Domingo de Araujo argued that the riot would not have occurred if it had not been for the behavior of the "European faction." He explained that the Europeans, who despised American Spaniards in Quito and even more the plebeian mestizos and Indians, persuaded the corregidor to punish the rioters, using the street patrol as a pretext for violent retribution against the barrios for their pride and ardor. Ibid. (no. 65), fol. 412.

96. St. John's Day was a "día de precepto," a holiday when attendance at mass was obligatory. See "Notas históricas. Fiestas que se celebran en Quito a fines del siglo XVIII," *Boletín de la Academia Nacional de Historia*, 7:19 (1923), 262–266. As no contemporary description of the festival is available for the city of Quito itself, it is not clear what specific ritual activities it might have involved. However, in the provincial town of Otavalo, it was a major festival in which barrios competed, masks and disguises were used, and Indians engaged in dances and mock battles. See Pedro de Carvalho Neto, *Antología del folklore ecuatoriano, 1653–1963* (Quito, 1964), 168–174.

97. AHNC, Milicias y Marina, tomo 123, fols. 93–95; AGI Quito 398 (no. 62), fol. 396.

98. "Relación sumaria," 110.

99. AGI Quito 398 (no. 55), fols. 340–345.

100. AGI Quito 398 (no. 52), fol. 331.

101. Domingo de Araujo to viceroy, July 13, 1765, AGI Quito 398 (no. 65). Araujo was the only observer to detail the response of the barrios to the threat of an Indian invasion; he also stated that Indians attacked various entrances of the city. There is, however, no other evidence of such armed conflict between the Indian peasants and urban mestizos.

102. "Relación del nuevo tumulto . . . ," AHNC, Milicias y Marina, tomo 123, fols. 93–95. Echandía was among the peninsulars expelled from Quito, and he sent his account of events in the city while in Pasto on July 11, en route to Popayán. It was sent to Pedro Agustín de Valencia in Popayán, who forwarded it to the viceroy.

103. "Relación sumaria," 111. A list of 81 peninsulars was drawn up, of whom 25 were liable for expulsion.

104. Romualdo Navarro to Arriaga, July 24, 1765, AGI Quito 398 (no. 67), fol. 434.

105. Ibid. (no. 53), fols. 336–337; ibid. (no. 54), fol. 339.

106. Cistué to viceroy, Sept. 9, 1765, ibid. (no. 105), fol. 507.

107. Ibid. (no. 62), fol. 399.

108. Ibid. (no. 52), fol. 333.

109. Ibid. (no. 53), fols. 336–338.

110. Ibid. (no. 56), fols. 346–347; ibid. (no. 57), fols. 348–349.

111. Valencia to viceroy, Popayán, July 17, 1765, AHNC, Milicias y Marina, tomo 123, fol. 85.

112. AGI Quito 398 (no. 58), fol. 350.

113. Audiencia to viceroy, July 13, 1765, ibid. (no. 64). In this letter the Audiencia stated that these captains were "from the highest nobility" and that their purpose was to serve "as interlocutors and emissaries" with the "vulgo," so that the latter might communicate its ideas. Those appointed were the Conde de Selva Florida (for the barrio de San Roque). Don Nicolás Calixto de Alarcón (for San Sebastián), Don Mariano Pérez de Ubillas (for San Blas), Don Joseph Lasso de la Vega (for Santa Bárbara), Don Manuel González and Don Francisco de Borja (for San Marcos). Two priests (Don Ramón Yepes and Don Ramón Monteserín González) were also involved in negotiation with the barrios. The two *alcaldes ordinarios*, together with some of the regidores of the cabildo, also played a part in government, but Corregidor Sánchez Osorio remained in hiding.

114. Sánchez Pareja and Juan Antonio Abel de Blas to viceroy, Aug. 3, 1765, ibid. (no. 92), fols. 480–481.

115. Audiencia to viceroy, Aug. 25, 1765, ibid. (no. 99), fols. 495–496.

116. Diputados de los barrios to viceroy, Sept. 19, 1765, ibid. (no. 106), fols. 519–522.

117. Cistué to viceroy, Sept. 8, 1765, ibid. (no. 105), fol. 509. In this letter, Cistué referred to mestizo leaders; his list of leaders includes several Indian names.

118. Ibid., fol. 511.

119. Phelipe Baquero, Sept. 19, 1765, ibid. (no. 110).

120. AHNC, Impuestos Varios (Cartas), tomo 22, fols. 94, 99, 723–725.

121. Ibid., fol. 100.

122. Ibid., fols. 513–514.

123. E. J. Hobsbawm, *Primitive Rebels. Studies in Archaic Forms of Social Movement in the 19th and 20th Centuries* (Manchester, England, 1959), 108–205.

124. Ibid., 110.

125. Bishop of Quito to viceroy, Sept. 19, 1765, AGI Quito 398 (no. 108), fol. 521.

126. Calixto de Alarcón to viceroy, Sept. 19, 1765, ibid. (no. 109), fols. 530–531.

127. Manuel Rubio de Arévalo to viceroy, Oct. 2, 1765, AHNC, Milicias y Marina, tomo 123, fols. 155–156.

128. Santa Cruz to viceroy, Dec. 29, 1765, AGI Quito 398 (no. 212), fols. 893–894; Viceroy Messía de la Cerda to Corregidor Sánchez Osorio, Feb. 13, 1766, AGI Quito 399 (no. 247), fol. 73; Santa Cruz to viceroy, May 17, 1766, ibid. (no. 339), fols. 215–216.

129. Viceroy Messía de la Cerda to Santa Cruz, Mar. 5, 1766, ibid. (no. 279), fols. 214–216.

130. Santa Cruz to Viceroy Messía de la Cerda, May 17, 1766, AHNC, Juicios Criminales, tomo. 129, fols. 848–853.

131. Viceroy Messía de la Cerda to governor of Guayaquil, May 22, 1766, AGI Quito 399 (no. 283), fol. 263.

132. Cistué to Viceroy Messía de la Cerda, Apr. 29, 1766, AHNC, Milicias y Marina, tomo 123, fol. 114.

133. Borja to viceroy, May 2, 1766, AGI Quito 399 (no. 323), fol. 194.

134. Cistué to Viceroy Messía de la Cerda, May 29, 1766, AHNC, Milicias y Marina, tomo 126, fols. 258–260.

135. Baquero, Sept. 2, 1766, AGI Quito 399 (no. 397), fols. 363–366.

136. Audiencia to Arriaga, Oct. 12, 1766, ibid. (no. 404). A company of voluntary cavalry, made up of European residents in Quito, was established in Nov. 1766; ibid. (no. 416).

137. Real orden, Jan. 1767, AGI Quito 269. By this order, all the ministers of the Audiencia, with the exception of Santa Cruz, were suspended while an investigation of the rebellion took place, and three new oidores were appointed.

138. Zelaya to Arriaga, Apr. 3, 1767, AGI Quito 399 (no. 418), fol. 481.

139. Emmanuel Le Roy Ladurie, *Carnival in Romans. A People's Uprising at Romans, 1579–1580* (Harmondsworth, England, 1981), 269.

140. Viceroy Messía de la Cerda to Arriaga, Apr. 9, 1767, AGI Quito 399 (no. 419), fol. 483; Viceroy Amat to Gregorio Hurtado, July 16, 1765, AHNC, Historia, tomo 3, fol. 24.

141. Informe del comercio, AGI Quito 398 (no. 35), fols. 237–238.

142. E. P. Thompson, "The Moral Economy of the English Crowd in the Eighteenth Century," *Past and Present*, 50 (Feb. 1971).

143. On this conjuncture of rebellion, see Anthony McFarlane, "Civil Disorders and Popular Protests in Late Colonial New Granada," *Hispanic American Historical Review*, 64:1 (Feb. 1984), 22–27.

144. These comments draw on the excellent and suggestive discussion of the urban polity in North America found in Gary B. Nash, *The Urban Crucible. Social Change, Political Consciousness and the Origins of the American Revolution* (Cambridge, MA, 1979), 27–53.

2

Popular Politics in Mexico City: The Parián Riot, 1828

Silvia Marina Arrom

Silvia Marina Arrom is a historian whose research explores social groups and issues—women, the poor, and personal and class relations—that have been invisible in traditional accounts of Mexican history. Her publications include La mujer mexicana ante el divorcio eclesiástico, 1800–1856 *(1976),* The Women of Mexico City, 1790–1857 *(1985), and articles on the family, elite policies toward the urban poor, and their responses to these initiatives. Professor Arrom is the Jane's Professor of Latin American Studies at Brandeis University.*

The following essay is part of a larger project on class relations in Mexico City that focuses on the capital's Poor House from 1774 to 1871. Like that work, this study challenges the social control "school," epitomized by Michel Foucault, that views the poor as helpless victims against an increasingly powerful state. Yet, Arrom does not merely celebrate the agency of the city's popular classes, for she shows that in some respects this action backfired. Occurring only seven years after Mexican independence, the riot described here was pivotal in souring the elites' perceptions of the urban poor and in dampening their enthusiasm for democracy.

On Thursday, December 4, 1828, as the Acordada revolt prevailed against the government of Guadalupe Victoria, a crowd five thousand strong attacked and pillaged the cluster of luxurious shops in the Parián building, located in Mexico City's central square. Governor José María Tornel y Mendivil, in charge of restoring order to the shaken city, recalled how

> numerous groups of insolent plebes forced the doors of the Parián, . . . [and] then began sacking the building, or Bazaar, which for more than a century was the emporium of commerce, . . . [and] contained cash and goods worth the enormous sum of two-and-

From *Hispanic American Historical Review* 68, no. 2 (May 1988): 245–68. © 1988 by Duke University Press. Reprinted by permission.

a-half million pesos. . . . Throughout that disgraceful day and all
of the night, they stole without intermission and committed
abominable crimes, including murders in cold blood to dispute
both valuable articles and trinkets that passed from the hands of
one thief to another. The devastation of the Parián was like that
of a voracious fire: all the doors were unhinged and broken; some
roofs burned, and not one display case was spared, nor a single
shop.[1]

The writer Guillermo Prieto, then a child whose father and uncle
owned shops in the building, described in his memoirs how the
Parián, "that temple of good taste," suffered a "savage invasion,"
an "avalanche of furies" who "broke down doors, flung jewelry
and lace over the ground, shattered strongboxes full of treasure,
wounded each other, and smothered themselves carrying off their
loot."[2]

Although the rioting had dissipated within 24 hours, this uprising of the lower classes shook propertied Mexicans to the core.
Those who lived through the violent episode never forgot that "stain
on the pages of our history,"[3] which discredited Mexico in the eyes
of the world and reminded the elites of their fragile control over
the urban poor. Yet the Parián riot has received little attention from
twentieth-century historians, even though it was one of the few riots in the Mexican capital—indeed, the first in 136 years and the
only large-scale riot of the nineteenth century. While rural communities were the scene of numerous popular protests in the eighteenth
and nineteenth centuries, and while provincial cities experienced
violent outbreaks during the Bourbon reforms and independence
wars, Mexico City—the stronghold first of colonial domination and
then of republican rule—remained relatively quiet.

Historians have much to learn from this incident. Like any
moment of crisis, it highlights the way in which the system normally worked. The causes and development of the crisis show where
the established order was vulnerable as well as where it was strong,
for the riot failed to evolve into a meaningful mass movement. As
studies of Europe and, more recently, Latin America indicate, the
analysis of popular disturbances can illuminate the values and beliefs of the lower classes, who rarely appear in historical records.
The elites' response, in turn, reveals their views of the poor and
their understanding of how social control is maintained. Finally, a
comparison with other popular rebellions suggests some distinctive features of the Mexican capital, and how it had changed since
the great riots of 1624 and 1692.

In the 1950s, Eric Hobsbawm and George Rudé, the eminent historians of urban riots in Europe, developed a powerful model for the study of crowds.[4] Their portrayal of eighteenth- and nineteenth-century rioters as heroic protesters, motivated by shared goals and an incipient sense of class struggle, changed the way historians see the nature of collective violence. This view contrasted sharply with previous elite condemnations of rioters as an irrational rabble, more criminals than champions of the people. Hobsbawm and Rudé's approach provides many insights that help rescue the Parián rioters from the negative portrayal in contemporary Mexican accounts, for a close reading of the evidence reveals rational patterns in the crowd's behavior. This essay finds, however, that if the rioters were not simply crazed criminals, neither were they as respectable, orderly, and purposeful as the crowds depicted by Hobsbawm and Rudé. Indeed, an emphasis on class solidarity, though not totally misplaced, obscures much of the significance of the incident. The riot, occurring against a background of economic discontent and electoral tension, reveals a new kind of populist politics where elite politicians mobilized the masses. Because the riot followed the lines of partisan politics, it was not directed against a particular class. Yet elite revulsion to the tumult caused politicians to shun popular support in the future, and helped usher in a century of increased social conservatism. Putting the Parián riot in this context supports the recent scholarly reappraisal of early republican Mexico. Far from being a laughable "opéra bouffe," sometimes dismissed as a period of "marking time" until the Porfiriato,[5] the early republic was in fact the crucible where many characteristics of the later nineteenth century were forged.

The Riot

The Parián riot is not easily studied, for the documentation is sparse and often contradictory. Although the standard histories of the period present their descriptions of the tumult as "fact," there are few facts contemporary authors agreed on.[6] Their version of the events depended largely on their stance toward the Acordada revolt, which culminated in the riot as the populace celebrated the rebels' victory. The coup followed months of economic crisis and bitter factionalism. As the government approached bankruptcy and the general economy declined, discontent focused on the hotly contested presidential election of September 1828. The government party, the *escoceses* organized in a Scottish rite lodge [of

Freemasons], ostensibly won the election and prepared to place their candidate, Minister of Defense Manuel Gómez Pedraza, in the presidency. The *yorkino* opposition, organized in a York rite lodge, claimed fraud and pronounced in order to install their own candidate, Vicente Guerrero, in office. The *yorkinos* won, with Guerrero named president in January. Their victory was short-lived, however, since Guerrero was ousted from office and executed 12 tense months later.

Contemporary accounts of the riot are found in highly polemical works by supporters or opponents of the coup. These include, on the *escocés* side, the works of journalist Carlos María de Bustamante, professor of painting Francisco Ibar, and statesman Lucas Alamán, blaming the rebel leaders for the popular disorder; on the *yorkino* side, coup leaders Lorenzo de Zavala and Anastasio Zerecero, attempting to absolve themselves of guilt for the shameful incident, and Tornel, appointed interim governor of the Federal District on the day of the riot, defending himself from accusations of incompetence and corruption.[7] Despite the reams of paper devoted to the Acordada revolt, only a few pages deal directly with the riot, although every historian and memoirist of the period mentioned the tumult in passages charged with emotion. Thus, Zavala observed that, "filled with consternation at the sight of the terrible scenes caused by civil war," he "sincerely would prefer to have suffered the effects of tyranny . . . in the flesh than to have been witness and party to this catastrophe." Bustamante repeatedly referred to the horrible specter of the "ignominious" masses, a "memory that despite the passage of time still distresses my spirit." Prieto, in even more purple prose, insisted that "neither delirium, nor fire, nor earthquake, could have rivaled that invasion [of the Parián], cause of eternal shame and opprobrium to its authors." And Deputy José María Bocanegra, decades later writing what he claimed was the only objective history of the period, labeled the event so "lamentable and disastrous" that "my memory saddens when remembering it, and my pen refuses to record it."[8] So the riot was an embarrassment writers did not elaborate on beyond a paragraph or two.

Indeed, they probably could not provide a fuller description because they lacked concrete information about the episode. Even the few supposedly firsthand accounts—all by elite observers—are severely flawed by questions about how much their authors actually saw. Ibar described the looters as they left the central square, but he was not present where they rioted. Tornel saw the crowd as it surged into the National Palace, where he was with the president, but he did not witness the events in the Parián either, or at least he chose to tell us little more than the paragraph quoted above. Prieto's description is clearly secondhand, based on the impressions of one of his father's friends who went to the Parián in a vain attempt to save his merchandise. And that account, which Prieto first heard when he was ten years old, was undoubtedly embellished and distorted by the time it appeared decades later in his memoirs. Similarly, though Bustamante described the tumult in his diary, his may not be a true eyewitness description either since he was apparently in bed with a fever that day. Bustamante provided vivid detail only for events after December 15, perhaps the first day he ventured out of his quarters. Indeed, Bustamante himself credits "some people who were there, including several deputies," for part of his information.[9]

It is easy to understand why few nonparticipants witnessed the rioting. Because the Parián had closed sometime after the Acordada revolt began on November 30, the owners of its shops were absent at the time of the pillaging. By December 4, most wealthy residents of the capital had fled the city or locked themselves in their houses. Business throughout the city was at a virtual standstill, and no newspapers were published that week. The government's forces had surrendered the night before, though the president did not capitulate until that evening. The congress and the city council, which normally met close to the Parián building, had adjourned earlier that day and had left the center of the city. The leaders of the Acordada revolt were busy holding down their positions and negotiating with President Guadalupe Victoria. And in the absence of any effective civil authority, the guards posted at the entrances of the Parián had left, and the municipal police had ceased functioning.

We do not even have police records or court cases that might provide descriptions of the event by the participants themselves, the sort of documents Rudé used to determine the composition and ideology of the European crowds he studied. Zavala, who masterminded the Acordada revolt, claimed that on hearing the news of the mob outburst he sent a highly disciplined artillery troop to stop the looting. His men were unsuccessful, he explained, because "the torrent of more than five thousand men from the barrios and from the army itself was impossible to contain."[10] As far as I can tell, the troop left without making any arrests, and the crowd was dispersed that evening only by the firing of a cannon. In fact, surviving criminal records do not record arrests for theft or disorderly conduct connected with the riots—or, for that matter, arrests for possession and sale of stolen property—either on December 4 or the next few days.

The minutes of the city council touch on the incident, but they shed more light on its aftermath than on the riot itself. The council met twice on December 4, without mentioning the tumult. In an emergency session at 9 A.M., the members voted to draft a proclamation upholding the legitimate government of Guadalupe Victoria and denouncing the "anarchic" Acordada insurgents; at noon they returned and approved the final statement, still apparently unaware of any popular disturbance. At their next meeting on December 6, and in subsequent sessions, the council members discussed methods of restoring public order, recovering stolen goods, compensating shopowners, and—most important for them—ingratiating themselves with the new government many of them had originally opposed; they did not, however, directly discuss the riot.[11]

Consequently, there is much that we do not know about the incident. We cannot be certain who the rioters were, only that they were members of the lower orders, and apparently soldiers as well. In a city of 160,000, a crowd of 5,000 was but a small percentage of the poor, though, and we do not know whether the rioters were mostly unemployed vagrants, solid artisans, occupants of nearby streets, or—as Zavala said—residents of outlying (and largely Indian) barrios. These distinctions, so important for Rudé in documenting the respectability of the crowd, were in any case lost on most elite Mexican observers, who betrayed their prejudices by referring to the mob not only as *el pueblo* and *la plebe* but also by such derogatory terms as *léperos* and *la chusma*. Indeed, Ibar recalled several months later how he had seen looters on their way home, their faces displaying "the rabidity of the most savage and inhuman cannibals."[12]

There is a consensus that soldiers participated in the looting; even Zavala's description suggests that some of the men he sent to check the disorder joined the fray. There is disagreement, however, as to whether *yorkino* officers were involved. Ibar claimed that he had seen not only soldiers and "*léperos* in the streets burdened with their loot," but also "anarchist" officers "with sabers in hand conducting to their homes the fruit of their perfidy and ambition." Bustamante similarly charged that "the principal robbers were the captains" of the *yorkino* army.[13] Still, their statements are not entirely reliable, because they were trying to discredit the *yorkinos*, just as Alamán later did by accusing the rebel officers (as well as soldiers) of participating in the crimes of the day.

The subject of the most heated controversy is whether the *yorkino* leaders authorized the pillage. On this question contemporaries again divided along partisan lines. Alamán accused both Zavala and the rebel General Lobato, who led the victorious troops into the Zócalo that day, of "offering the sack of the Parián" to the people of the capital in order to attract followers to their cause. Ibar blamed only Lobato. H. G. Ward, the former British chargé d'affaires, claimed (on information sent to him in England) that Vicente Guerrero, the defeated *yorkino* presidential candidate, publicly licensed the sack from the windows of the Acordada by promising the assembled crowd, "¡Hijos, para ustedes es el Parián!" Tornel and Bustamante, instead of fingering any individual, blamed the *yorkinos* in general for marking the Parián, in Tornel's phrase, "as booty in the immoral war that gripped the unhappy city." Bustamante also held the entire movement accountable for undermining the rule of law and order, thereby giving rise to the frenzy of the mob.[14]

Although Zavala and Zerecero accepted indirect responsibility for having led a movement that unleashed the masses, they vigorously denied any direct responsibility for the riot. They insisted that it was unforeseen and beyond their control, despite the concerted efforts of *yorkino* officers to quell the disorder. Indeed, Zavala not only defended himself, but also Guerrero, by saying that the general had only been at the Acordada a few hours before leaving the capital, and Lobato, by saying that "at the time no one mentioned anything about Lobato's authorizing the sack."[15] Taking a position between these two, several contemporaries absolved the *yorkinos* of guilt in instigating the riots, but accused them of failing to take energetic measures to bring the mob under control.[16] Since all these positions are plausible, new eyewitness accounts will have to be discovered if the controversy is ever to be resolved.

Other contradictions in surviving accounts, such as about the time the rioting began and how long it lasted, can be resolved more easily. Most eyewitnesses time the riot from the early afternoon of December 4, after the de facto surrender of the National Palace. Bustamante and Senator Luis Gonzaga Cuevas merely wrote that it began in the afternoon; Joel Poinsett, the U.S. minister in Mexico City, placed it shortly after noon; and military officer Juan Suárez Navarro specified that it began after two o'clock, while the president met with Zavala in rebel headquarters at the Acordada prison.[17]

Zavala alone claimed that the riot began at ten in the morning. The other accounts seem more plausible, however. At ten in the morning, Zavala was in the Acordada, more than ten blocks away from the central square. The Chamber of Deputies, meeting in the National Palace until two minutes to twelve, and the city council, meeting at noon in the municipal building across the street from the Parián, were unaware of any tumult, even though it would have been within earshot of their chambers. It is, furthermore, improbable that the city council members would have walked through an angry crowd to keep their noon appointment, as 11 of them did. By 3 P.M., however, the situation had changed. Bustamante reported that, though Congress had dissolved that morning, some senators and deputies still in the National Palace had to leave through the stables in disguise to avoid the dangerous mob.[18]

Zavala's account of the evening appears more reliable, since he actually walked through the Zócalo that night to meet with President Guadalupe Victoria. In a passage since copied by most writers on the tumult, Zavala described how

> the [national] palace was without any guards but those Zavala [*sic*] had ordered; the city was frightfully silent. The pillaging . . . had ceased by nightfall; a sepulchral silence reigned over the vast capital of Mexico; in the palace there was no one but Victoria, abandoned even by his servants. Many shops were open, their merchandise on the streets, in the plazas; their doors fractured. Not a voice could be heard; only the sound of the hours, announcing the passage of time, interrupted the profound dream that enveloped all mortals. What a night! What a terrible night!

In another of his writings, Zavala reiterated his view of the evening quiet: "It is very rare that a sack can be contained on the afternoon of the first day, being worthy of note that no robbery at all occurred during the night, and though the next morning some looting did occur, the excesses did not last longer than two hours."[19]

Although Bustamante and Tornel claimed that the riot continued all night, it appears to have ended that evening, as Zavala indicated. Indeed, Tornel contradicted his own statement by praising Lieutenant Colonel Alejandro Zamora for services rendered on the evening of December 4, when he took a squad and cannon to the Zócalo and "made the looters of the Parián retire, thereby saving several exterior shops that had not yet been sacked." Tornel also supported Zavala's claim that by the next morning the fury of the mob had been spent, for Tornel claimed that on December 5—though

he found part of the Parián still burning and a crowd milling about—
it took him and his men but half an hour to snuff out the flames,
disperse the crowd, and set up pickets to guard the desolate building.[20] Thus, the incident was basically over the first day. Its duration was somewhere between 2 to 3 hours (according to Poinsett)
and less than 12 (according to the merchants of the Parián).[21]

This was, as the liberal theoretician José María Luis Mora emphasized eight years later in his *México y sus revoluciones*, a relatively short time as riots went. Indeed, Mora, attempting to correct
European misconceptions about Mexico, argued that the Parián riot
demonstrated the good nature of the Mexican people.

> The riot of the Acordada, the most atrocious which Mexico has
> known, is in no way comparable to the insurrections and popular
> movements that have existed in France and England even in their
> present stage of civilization, for neither were buildings destroyed
> nor was there loss of life (with the sole exception of two mur-
> ders, and an unsuccessful murder attempt); the looting was re-
> stricted to a few, fixed points, and it was easily contained once
> we put our minds to it. Compare this with the Lord Gordon riots
> in London, or the French Revolution in its early period

where hundreds died, large sections of the cities were destroyed,
and the rioting lasted for days before it could be quelled. Europe,
he concluded, was more "ferocious and barbaric" than Mexico.[22]
Mora had conveniently forgotten the Mexico City riots of 1692,
when the National (then Viceregal) Palace as well as the original
Parián were burned to the ground. Beside that earlier tumult, the
1828 riot also paled.

Still, the Parián riot was not quite as tame as Mora claimed.
The two murders he referred to may have been the only casualties
among upper-class Mexicans—and, significantly, carried out by the
hands of their peers, not the lower orders—but numerous rioters
died, according to Tornel's description of "corpses strewn here and
there" in the streets.[23] Thus, we cannot say, as Rudé does of European crowds, that they consistently attacked property rather than
people. Further, though it is true that the looting was mostly restricted to the Parián, it was not their only target. The National
Palace and a few portals surrounding the Zócalo (especially the
shops in the Portal de Mercaderes) appear to have suffered some
damage. Both Bustamante and Alamán said that warehouses in the
palace were sacked, and Bustamante added that the chambers of
Congress were broken into. Tornel self-servingly credited himself

and two colonels with fighting off the surging mob before it pillaged the entire palace.[24]

Although Bustamante stated that a few private houses close to the Zócalo were also sacked, there is no evidence to support Ward's claim that "the Léperos . . . spread themselves, like a torrent over the town, where they committed every species of excess," breaking into and plundering the houses of many wealthy individuals. Zerecero insisted that the timely intervention of General Lobato prevented the pillage from spreading beyond the Zócalo. And Ibar, who emphasized the violence, only blamed the looters for destruction in the central square; he attributed other losses to the previous three days of street fighting and crossfire between government and rebel forces that damaged buildings throughout the city and created, by his estimate, two thousand victims. Ward's description thus illustrates how events became exaggerated as they were retold, especially among potential investors in far-away London.[25]

Most accounts suggest that though the rioting was restricted to a relatively small time and space, anarchy reigned for days afterward. There were those who took advantage of the disorder to settle old scores. The statesman Manuel Payno, then a student in Mexico City, later wrote that "during that time, robbery, murders, and the most outrageous scandals were the order of the day."[26] Unlike the three days of street fighting that preceded the tumult, the riot scared the well-to-do off the streets; for more than a week afterward the capital belonged to the lower orders and the victorious soldiers. Ibar recounted that "the *hombre de bien* did not dare step out of his house because of the provocations and insults of those triumphant tigers." And Bustamante, who set out for the post office on December 15, soon returned home because of "the multitude of *canaille*" that populated the streets, showering him with insults, and the dismaying scenes of plundered jewels, crystal, and cloth sold on the streets with impunity—soldiers allegedly carrying off the best of the loot.[27] The disorder was such that food became scarce because, as Bustamante explained, the city's suppliers stayed away when they learned of the commotion. The price of bread shot sky high and had to be fixed by a decree of December 7, which also ordered the bakers back to work. And, though Tornel claimed that the situation was under control by December 8, when he allowed the city's markets and bars to reopen,[28] the city council minutes demonstrate that it was several weeks before complete order was restored. Indeed, for more than a month, according to Payno, "stolen goods were sold publicly in the *plazuela* of Santo Domingo"—where some of the original owners managed to recover a few of their belongings, especially, according to Bustamante, the book dealers whose wares were not appreciated by those who stole them.[29]

Moreover, the riot had a lasting impact on the merchants of the Parián. Some lost everything and were, in their own words, "reduced to mendicity in less than twelve hours."[30] Other merchants recovered what they could and opened shops in new locations away from the central square—or moved to Europe when the decree expelling Spaniards was promulgated early the next year. The few who stayed in the Parián had to wait five months for the building to reopen. Even then, it was only partially repaired, remaining a half-empty eyesore and constant reminder of that "black day" until it was torn down in 1843. For 23 years, the shopowners unsuccessfully petitioned the government for compensation; only in 1851 was an indemnization finally approved. And the city also suffered a loss, for with its demolition the ayuntamiento lost the rents the Parián shopowners had paid.[31]

Popular Objectives

It is difficult to determine with certainty what ideas motivated the rioters. Unlike the elites, the rioters left no written records, had no spokesmen, and made no demands on any authorities. Given the unreliability of existing accounts, we cannot even be sure of the slogans they may have voiced as they milled about the central square. It is nonetheless possible to draw several tentative conclusions about popular objectives.

First, it appears that the rioters broadly supported the Acordada revolt, since chroniclers on both sides agree that the *yorkino* rebels enjoyed wide popular allegiance, while the *escoceses* did not. By all accounts, thousands of lower-class supporters joined the insurgency. Soon after the coup began on November 30, enthusiastic crowds began forming outside the Acordada and other rebel strongholds; in the next few days the rabble—or the citizenry, depending on the writer's viewpoint—were decisive in assuring the *yorkino* victory. As Tornel described it, "the semidisciplined corps of rebels fought surrounded by an immense sea of riffraff, armed with whatever they managed to pick up in a moment of ire, . . . and giving the impression of a swarm of terrifying furies from hell." Zavala, more sympathetic to his party's supporters, described how "the people of Mexico en masse decided for those who were in the Acordada: the most humble and poverty-stricken citizens ran to their aid, carrying munitions, pulling the artillery, moving the wounded, and helping in whatever way they could a cause they believed to be theirs." Indeed, if we are to believe Zavala's numbers, 30,000 to 40,000 people, perhaps one-fourth of the capital's residents, fought with the rebels.[32] In contrast, not a single observer mentioned any popular support for the government; and Ibar noted that most government soldiers deserted to the rebel side, leaving the government defenseless.[33]

Why did the masses consider the *yorkino* party their own? There is no controversy about the rebel goals; they called for the annulment of the allegedly fraudulent presidential election and the installation of their candidate, Vicente Guerrero, in office; at the same time, they denounced the infringement of political liberties under Guadalupe Victoria, demanded the immediate resignation of the minister of defense and *escocés* presidential candidate Gómez Pedraza, and—taking up the issue that divided the two parties most bitterly—called for the expulsion of Spaniards from Mexican territory. It is unlikely that the curtailment of elite politicians' freedoms aroused strong feeling among the populace, but the *yorkino* candidate and two of his policies did.

The candidacy of Guerrero, the uneducated mestizo hero of the independence wars, was immensely popular. Because of his past heroism, he embodied the untarnished cause of national independence. The lower classes could identify with him because of his social background, his dark complexion, and the derision he elicited from high society. On a personal level, he represented the possibility for upward mobility; on a political level, he also represented egalitarian aspirations, for his supporters and opponents alike believed that he wanted to establish, in Zavala's words, "absolute equality, despite the present state of society, and democratic liberty, despite the differences in civilization" among Mexico's citizens.[34] Although the texts of Guerrero's public speeches have not survived, he apparently appealed to the "leveling instinct" that Rudé identified as a value consistently held by the crowds he studied. And, as Zerecero and Zavala recounted, Guerrero cultivated a highly populist style in his public pronouncements.[35] His leadership of the party made plausible the *yorkinos'* claim that they were the "popular" party opposing the "aristocratic" and "hierarchical" *escoceses*.[36]

Guerrero struck a popular chord on another issue as well, for at a time when Mexican artisans were buffeted by competition from cheap European imports, he favored high tariffs to protect the domestic textile industry on which so many in the lower and lower-middle classes depended. Their situation had been growing increasingly desperate since independence, as Mexico experimented with freer trade. In the months preceding the coup, artisans (as well as industrialists and cotton producers) petitioned the government to exclude the damaging textile imports. And, as Robert Potash has noted, artisan discontent played a significant—though largely unexplored—role in the *yorkino* victory. Indeed, one of Guerrero's first acts in office was to raise tariffs on imported textiles, a measure that might be construed as a reward to his followers.[37]

Guerrero's call for the expulsion of Spaniards (again translated into law soon after he became president) also gained his party a mass following, for most observers believed that anti-Spanish measures "complied with the demands of the multitude."[38] Barely seven years after independence was won, the few thousand Spaniards residing in Mexico not only symbolized colonial rule, but also became scapegoats for the new nation's ills. Because many of them still retained great wealth and influence, they were the target of popular resentment. They were, in addition, the large-scale import merchants most visible to protectionists. Finally, as rumors spread of Spanish plans to reconquer the former colony, they were suspected of being an enemy within. The expulsion measure was heatedly debated in elite circles, and—at a time when popular opinion counted because there were few restrictions on male suffrage—the *yorkinos'* anti-Spanish rhetoric helped them win local elections. A weak version of the expulsion bill passed in December of 1827, but it failed to bring public calm because most Spaniards obtained exemptions. The tension, heightened by the discovery of an alleged Spanish invasion plot and by mass demonstrations against Spaniards in small towns surrounding the capital, reached fever pitch during the electoral campaign of August 1828, for the *escoceses* were known as the pro-Spanish party. Their victory was therefore considered (in *yorkino* circles at least) a victory for Spain.[39]

Of course, we cannot be sure that these views were held by the rioters who sacked the Parián; we cannot even be certain that the crowds of *yorkino* supporters were the same as those who pillaged. Some individuals lacking political motivation surely took advantage of the temporary absence of public authority to steal at will. Yet observers on both sides believed that most rioters were *yorkino* followers reveling in their party's triumph. Ibar claimed that as the mob surged into the Zócalo, ringing the bells of the cathedral and charging the National Palace, it cried "¡Viva Guerrero!" and "to the Parián!" Payno said that the looters cried "vivas to liberty" as they threw themselves on the building. And Zavala, though intent on defending his party, admitted that discipline deteriorated among the mass of his volunteer followers, as "the sovereign people" celebrated the *yorkino* victory "in their terrible and accustomed manner."[40]

Historian Manuel Rivera Cambas claimed a half century later that, as the *léperos* rushed to the Parián, they raised the old cry of "¡Mueran los españoles!"[41] Although I have not been able to substantiate his version in earlier accounts, it certainly fits the contemporary view that the rioters were propelled by hatred of Spaniards. The mob chose as its main target a building not only conveniently located and full of riches, but also one that had long symbolized Spanish domination, for most Spanish import merchants had their shops there. Indeed, during the Mexico City riots of 1692, furious crowds had similarly attacked the Parián while shouting anti-Spanish slogans.[42] The building was further marked as a Spanish stronghold when, in 1808, Spanish merchants plotted from within its walls against a viceroy sympathetic to Mexicans.[43] In the weeks preceding the tumult, the *yorkino* newspaper, *Correo de la Federación Mexicana*, had targeted the "*parianistas*" as staunch supporters of the pro-Spanish *escocés* party.[44]

Bustamante and Ibar, who vehemently opposed the expulsion of the Spaniards, tried to persuade their readers that the Mexican people were not really hostile to Spaniards, because they indiscriminately pillaged the property of Mexicans who had recently come to own shops in the Parián.[45] It is unreasonable, however, to expect the average resident of the capital to have known this, especially since the shopkeepers of the Parián, according to Prieto, scrupulously maintained Spanish traditions. Although it is certainly possible that for some rioters the Spaniards merely provided a pretext for stealing from the wealthy, even the *escocés* Alamán acknowledged that the Parián was the center of Spanish commerce.[46] It thus remained the symbol of both the centuries of Spanish exploitation and the continuing Spanish presence despite the achievement of independence. And—though contemporaries failed to mention this connection—the imported goods sold in the Parián represented unwelcome European competition for Mexican artisans as well.[47]

Moreover, there are other indications of virulent anti-Spanish sentiment. In provincial cities, mass demonstrations erupted against Spaniards throughout 1828. In Mexico City itself, immediately after the riot, Tornel genuinely feared for the lives of Spaniards when the populace, exhibiting a classic conspiracy mentality, apparently

blamed them for the shortages of food. He accordingly took precautions to ensure their safety, even escorting a group of Spanish
citizens out of the capital under armed guard.[48] The hostility against
Spaniards did not, apparently, extend to foreigners in general. Only
Ibar raised this possibility. But his claim that during the riot the
"rabble" attacked the British Consulate in Mexico City and trampled
its flag is called into question by the omission of this incident from
British consular records. His contention that a few English and
German shops were sacked is contradicted by assurances from Ward,
as well as from the British chargé d'affaires, Robert Pakenham,
that "not a single British merchant was plundered." Poinsett likewise reported no attacks on U.S. citizens or property.[49] It therefore
appears that the Spaniards were singled out as a symbol of colo-
nialism, wealth, foreign imports, and the *escocés* party simultaneously. The tense climate caused by the threat of a Spanish
invasion, the economic decline of the artisans, and the hotly contested election made the combination electric.

This evidence suggests that the rioters were not as irrational,
senseless, and disorderly as many elite observers believed. Although
it is dangerous to assume that everyone in the crowd shared common ideas and motives, it appears likely that many shared what
sociologist Neil Smelser terms the "generalized beliefs" that direct
collective behavior.[50] In this case, such beliefs included, as I have
argued, enthusiasm for Guerrero and his party, a desire for the protection of domestic industry, and hostility toward Spaniards. Indeed, the latter fits Smelser's conclusion that most riots vent popular
rage against a particular individual, group, or institution held responsible for an undesirable state of affairs. Moreover, since the
rioters for the most part limited themselves to looting the Parián,
their behavior—though seemingly chaotic—had an internal structure. Not only did their main target correspond to their politics, but
the looters may have believed they had some kind of permission
for attacking the Parián. For even if we reject the charges that
yorkino leaders instigated the looting, the rhetoric that targeted
Spaniards and *"parianistas"* gave a patina of legitimacy to the violence. Certainly the looting was partly sanctioned by the type of
ideas voiced by a member of the city council a month after the riot:
in a discussion on whether to compensate the Spanish shopkeepers
of the Parián, the first *síndico* held that their property was the ill-
gotten fruit of conquest and, by implication, fair game.[51] Thus, as
Hamlet might have said, the crowd had a certain method to its
madness.

The riot further suggests that the xenophobia so prevalent during the Mexican Revolution of the twentieth century had deep roots, at least in urban areas. Since antiforeignism, even in its more restricted anticolonial form, is an incipient form of nationalism, this conclusion challenges the views of Mexican leaders of the midnineteenth century who bemoaned the lack of national loyalty among their people. Indifference to the fate of the nation may have characterized Indian villagers, especially during the Mexican-American War, but indifference did not characterize the lower classes in the capital, who in 1828 as well as 1848 exhibited as much nationalism as their social superiors.

Still, it is easy, in following Rudé and Hobsbawn, to overemphasize the rioting crowd as the embodiment of national identity and as champions of the people. Both logic and the paucity of data caution against forcing five thousand people into a homogeneous mold, especially when the available evidence shows untidiness at every turn. We know, for example, that though the Spanish stronghold of the Parián was their main target, it was not the only building they looted, and more widespread damage might have occurred had it not been for the timely intervention of authorities. Furthermore, though the Parián riot demonstrates that class conflict was always beneath the surface in such a highly stratified society, it was given focus by nationalism and partisan politics. The opportunity to pillage, a kind of leveling by taking from the rich, certainly played a part. It is difficult, however, to argue that a crowd that killed its peers but not its social superiors, and that allied itself with one elite faction, was primarily motivated by an unconscious sense of class solidarity.

The Political Context

In discussing the causes of riots, Hobsbawm emphasizes the economic context, where the dislocations of expanding capitalism undermined the social order. Certainly, the impoverishment of the artisans through foreign competition helped prepare the ground for the Parián riot, as did the hardships created by the increasingly penurious government which was unable to pay many of its employees by 1828. Yet in the next three decades the Mexican capital suffered a downwardly spiraling economy without producing another major popular disturbance. Thus, economic distress is a necessary, but not sufficient, explanatory factor. What distinguishes the 1828 incident is the political context. It is important to remember that this riot, like many outbreaks of lawlessness in Latin America studied in Richard Slatta's *Bandidos*,[52] coincided with partisan struggles among the elites that weakened the central authority. One further factor was necessary: as with provincial riots during the independence wars, the populace had been mobilized by one elite faction. Although elite leaders soon lost control, it is doubtful that the urban poor would have risen up without their initial encouragement. Especially in the huge capital, where nearly half the poor were migrants from widely disparate areas, they lacked the communal structure and leadership that facilitated organization in Indian villages. And they had not yet developed strong associational organizations that would foster collective independent action.

The Parián riot must therefore be viewed as the by-product of a new kind of democratic politics ushered in by the independence wars. Since 1810, members of the Mexican elites appealed to the people, first to support them in the struggle against Spain, and then to support their candidates at the ballot box. The result, as Alamán noted, was not infrequently violence and looting, the Parián riot and Hidalgo revolt being the most extreme examples.[53] The politics of the early republic thus differed from colonial politics in the extent of mobilization of the urban poor. Many contemporaries charged the *yorkinos* with being demagogues, pandering to the masses in order to build a following. Bustamante and Ward accused them of organizing the demonstrations that shattered the peace throughout 1828. Suárez Navarro, exonerating the Mexican masses, accused the *yorkinos* of "seducing the simple people" and taking advantage of their innocence.[54] Whether or not the rioters actually understood or agreed with *yorkino* politics, it is apparent that they came from the crowd mobilized by the *yorkino* cause, and the *yorkino* rhetoric helped to define the context in which the rioters acted.

Because of its relationship to partisan politics, the tumult of the Parián fits Eric Hobsbawm's and Charles Tilly's classification of a "modern" rather than "traditional" riot of the "Church and King" variety (which Tilly later termed a "proactive" rather than "reactive" collective action). Although the distinction is probably overdrawn, it is useful for highlighting the unusual features of the riot. According to Hobsbawm's and Tilly's formulation, crowds in the earlier type of riot, prevalent in Europe until the eighteenth century, invoked the name of "Church and King" as they tried to defend traditional rights and customs, either by resisting new demands imposed by outsiders (as in the tax revolt) or by fighting to enforce popular standards of justice (as in the food riot). In contrast, modern crowds wanted to change rather than preserve an old way of life; instead of invoking traditional norms and symbols, they proclaimed the goals of political clubs or parties, secret societies, and workers' organizations; and their riots often grew out of political demonstrations and strikes. As Richard Bendix has pointed out, the new forms of popular protest reflected the growth of democracy in Europe. But they also reflected deep-seated changes in the organization of daily life. For while traditional rioters usually represented a close-knit community, modern rioters usually represented supporters of a particular creed or program. Thus, in Tilly's words, "collective violence, like so many other features of social life, changed from a communal basis [of organization] to an associational one."[55]

The Parián riot indicates that, to the extent that Mexico City had made the transition from "traditional" to "modern" forms of collective violence, it had more in common with European cities of the time than with the rural areas of Latin America. Recent studies of Latin American village riots in the nineteenth century, as well as the colonial period, indicate that they were of the "Church and King" variety, as were the great riots that shook Mexico City in the seventeenth century. Unlike the Parián rioters, rural protesters throughout Latin America reacted against a specific injustice imposed on them from the outside, made well-defined demands (such as the return of a parcel of land or the removal of an abusive official), and usually had visible leaders.[56] The Mexico City rioters of 1624 and 1692, though not representing a cohesive community, also wanted to preserve certain customary arrangements, the tumult of 1692 being a fairly classic food riot (albeit with anticolonial overtones), and that of 1624 protesting a viceroy who trampled community norms.[57] It might be argued that the Parián riot similarly embodied a desire to return to the norms of colonial commerce overturned by free trade; but its anticolonial character, along with the fact that Spain never intentionally protected the Mexican textile industry, makes this argument difficult to sustain. The rioters' affiliation with electoral politics highlights the degree to which Mexican politics had changed over a century and a half. The contrast with village riots that appealed to authorities to right specific wrongs also suggests the degree to which the nineteenth-century capital (along with a few provincial cities) remained distinctive in a largely rural country.[58]

Yet the new populist politics did not last, in part because of elite revulsion to the riot. The immediate reaction of the capital's propertied classes was to call for a stronger police force to maintain public order. This was not the first time they had done so—the city had reorganized its police force in the late eighteenth century, and only the preceding spring, as the effects of the economic crisis became evident, the city council had set up a vagrants' tribunal to round up potential troublemakers. But the tribunal barely functioned in the months before the riot, and the police force was likewise ineffective.[59] In fact, in the days after the tumult, it became obvious that the police contributed more to the city's problems than to their solution, for the city council received so many complaints about corrupt policemen carrying out new robberies in the guise of recovering stolen loot that it had to revoke a decree ordering the police to search the city for plundered goods.[60] Thus, as Tornel explained, public order before the riot had been maintained not so much by force as by the "docility" of the lower orders.[61] And their betters had exhibited a remarkable complacency, fearing threats from the rural areas far more than they feared an uprising of the urban poor. By labeling the Parián riot the worst catastrophe ever to befall the capital, Mora and Ibar suggest that the well-to-do had quite forgotten the outbursts of the seventeenth century.[62] In the aftermath of the uprising, however, the *gente decente* regarded congregations of poor people with horror, the city government reorganized and strengthened the police force, and the vagrants' tribunal began pursuing the capital's paupers in earnest.[63]

It is interesting to note that the church played a smaller part in restoring order in 1828 than it had in 1692, when processions of friars and a Nahuatl-speaking priest had calmed the rioting crowd.[64] To be sure, after the Parián riot, the governor of the Federal District convinced the church to excommunicate those who possessed looted goods,[65] but it was soldiers and cannon—not churchmen—that dispersed the rioters at the Zócalo. Despite the proximity of the Parián to the cathedral and numerous convents, not a single religious attempted to halt the disturbance, probably viewed as the *yorkinos'* doing. Their reluctance not only suggests the growing estrangement of the *yorkinos* from the church, but also its lower profile in an increasingly secular world. My impression from reading the minutes of the city council is that the decline in the role of the church was not entirely due to partisan politics, for *escocés* as well as *yorkino* members preferred reliance on an expanded armed force to reliance on a strong church.

Just as the riot led the elites to conclude that the city needed
more armed force to control the poor, it also helped persuade them
that it needed less democracy, now stained by association with riot,
plunder, and the threat of class war. Tornel believed the Parián riot
"effectively dissipated all illusions" about democracy. Contemporary writers proved him right by deploring "popular doctrines that
undermine subordination and obedience" and denouncing "the ills
of unlimited popularism and exaggerated democracy."[66] Indeed,
Prieto, who admitted that his first political notions were forged by
the tumult, stated that "the democratic program was summarized
by the plebs in the phrase, '¡Vivan Guerrero y Lobato / y viva lo
que arrebato!' "[67] Even Zavala and Zerecero were repelled by the
uprising of the poor. Thus, Zerecero later regretted his part in the
Acordada revolt, confessing "before God and man" that he had
"done wrong" because the revolt ended in the sack of the Parián.
Zavala likewise denounced that "horrible revolution," disastrous
because of the popular disorders that accompanied it.[68] And though
it is hardly surprising that in its aftermath Bustamante and Ibar
openly proclaimed their disdain for the masses, these sentiments
were also expressed by Zavala about the lower-class followers he
had originally courted.[69] The riot therefore reinforced class prejudice, as *yorkinos* and *escoceses* alike feared that mobilization of
the masses might lead to anarchy and class war.[70]

The unhappy experience with popular participation contributed
to the social conservatism that would characterize both liberal and
conservative parties throughout the nineteenth century. The riot,
though just one episode in one city, was a pivotal event in dampening the democratic idealism of early independent Mexico. Because
it elicited such generalized repugnance among the establishment,
the triumph of the Acordada revolt was, as many commentators
noted, the downfall of the popular party. Those who a year later
deposed Guerrero and imposed a dictatorial regime were able to
portray themselves as "fighting the war of civilization against barbarism, of property against thieves, of order against anarchy."[71] The
new government soon began to revise the surprisingly democratic
electoral laws that granted suffrage to men regardless of literacy
and wealth.[72] And the Constitution of 1836 introduced literacy and
income requirements for suffrage. Thus, within 12 years, Mexico's
leaders had lost the optimism that informed the first constitution in
1824.[73] By revealing the dangers of mass mobilization, the summer
and fall of 1828 may have witnessed the last populist campaign
until the elections of 1909 unleashed the Mexican Revolution.

The contrasts between the two upheavals are instructive, since every riot carries with it the potential for a prolonged breakdown in social control. Both the twentieth-century revolution and the Parián riot came on the heels of economic crises, widespread dissatisfaction, and a division among elites. Controversial elections followed by repression of the opposition caused the government to lose some of its legitimacy. And the disaffected faction of the elites appealed to the people for support in its bid for power. Yet in 1828, the popular uprising quickly subsided. Elite factions, not yet alienated from the system, immediately closed ranks without providing sustained leadership for the masses. Since the urban lower classes did not have strong associational organizations of their own, even the vicious intraelite conflicts that followed during the Reforma did not lead to major popular disturbances. Without a crossclass alliance, mass protest did not develop into a challenge to the established order. But Mexican leaders had forgotten that lesson by 1910. As in the century after the great riots of the seventeenth century, they had become complacent and ignored the reservoir of dissent among the lower orders that could easily ignite when it became linked with the grievances of other social groups.

Notes

1. Tornel contradicted himself on two points a few pages later. First, he described how the mob was dispersed on the evening of the riot, rather than continuing to loot all night; and second, he commented that several shops were spared by chance. José María Tornel y Mendivil, *Breve reseña histórica de los acontecimientos más notables de la nación mexicana, desde el año de 1821 hasta' nuestros días* (Mexico City, 1852), 393–394, 403. Unless otherwise noted, the translations are mine.

2. Guillermo Prieto, *Memorias de mis tiempos: 1828 a 1840* (Mexico City, 1906), 35.

3. Carlos María de Bustamante, *Continuación del cuadro histórico de la revolución mexicana*, 3 vols. (Mexico City, 1954), III, 199.

4. George F. Rudé, *Paris and London in the Eighteenth Century: Studies in Popular Protest* (London, 1952) and *The Crowd in History: A Study of Popular Disturbances in France and England, 1730–1848* (New York, 1964); Eric J. Hobsbawm, *Primitive Rebels: Studies in Archaic Forms of Social Movement in the 19th and 20th Centuries* (Manchester, 1959), esp. chap. 7, "The City Mob." See also the influential article by E. P. Thompson, "The Moral Economy of the English Crowd in the Eighteenth Century," *Past and Present*, 50 (Feb. 1971), 76–136.

5. Lesley Byrd Simpson, *Many Mexicos* (Berkeley, 1966), 199; Charles C. Cumberland, *Mexico: The Struggle for Modernity* (New York, 1968), title of chap. 7.

6. Well-known histories touching on the riot, such as those by Francisco de Paula de Arrangoiz y Berzábal (*Méjico desde 1808 hasta 1867...*, 4 vols. [Madrid,

1871 72]) and Niceto de Zamacois (*Historia de Méjico desde sus tiempos más remotos hasta nuestros días* . . . [Mexico City, 1879]), follow the *escocés* accounts. In contrast, Hubert Howe Bancroft (*History of Mexico*, vol. V, which is Vol. XIII in *The Works of Hubert Howe Bancroft*, 39 vols. [San Francisco, 1882–90]); Manuel Rivera Cambas (*México pintoresco, artístico y monumental* [Mexico City, 1880]); Justo Sierra (*The Political Evolution of the Mexican People* [1902], Charles Ramsdell, trans. [Austin, 1969]); and most twentieth-century historians generally follow the *yorkino* version.

7. Lorenzo de Zavala, *Manifiesto del gobernador del estado de México* (Tlalpan, 1829), *Juicio imparcial sobre los acontecimientos de México en 1828 y 1829* (New York, 1830), *Ensayo histórico de las revoluciones de México, desde 1808 hasta 1830* (Mexico City, 1845), II, and *Albores de la república* (Mexico City, 1949); Anastasio Zerecero, *Memorias para la historia de las revoluciones en México* . . . (Mexico City, 1869); Francisco Ibar, pamphlets published from Jan. to Aug. 1829 collected in *Muerte política de la república mexicana* (Mexico City, 1829); Lucas Alamán, *Historia de Méjico* . . . (Mexico City, 1852), V; Tornel, *Breve reseña*. Bustamante published a series of articles on the Acordada revolt in his newspaper, especially "Tristes recuerdos de la Acordada por un militar antiguo," *Voz de la Patria*, July 1, 1829, pp. 1–7; "Estracto del diario de las ocurrencias acaecidas en esta capital de México el 1 de diciembre hasta el 4 del mismo," *Voz de la Patria*, July 8, 1829, pp. 2–8, and "Continúa la historia del desgobierno de Victoria. . . ," published in seven installments in *Voz de la Patria*, July 10–Aug. 21, 1830. His *Continuación del cuadro* collects much of the material in these articles. Both sources were in turn largely excerpted from his diary (see n. 9).

8. Zavala, *Manifiesto*, 17; Bustamante, *Continuación*, III, 200, 204; Prieto, *Memorias*, 35; José María Bocanegra, *Memorias para la historia de México independiente, 1822–1846*, 2 vols. (Mexico City, 1892–97), I, 492.

9. Bustamante's first entry in December was on the 13th ("Diario de lo especialmente ocurrido en México," XVIII, Nettie Lee Benson Collection, University of Texas Library, microfilm reel no. 6). See also *Continuación*, III, 204, 207.

10. Zavala, *Manifiesto*, 17.

11. See Archivo Histórico de la Ciudad de México (hereafter cited as AHCM), Actas de Cabildo, Dec. 4, 1828ff. (vol. 148-A); Actas Secretas, Dec. 9, 1828ff. (vols. 290-A, 291-A); Hacienda-Propios Parián, Jan. 6, 1829 (vol. 149-A, no. 159).

12. Ibar, *Muerte*, "Introducción," 5. Follows the translation by Frederick J. Shaw, Jr., in "Poverty and Politics in Mexico City, 1824–1854" (Ph.D. diss., University of Florida, 1975), 332.

13. Ibar, *Muerte*, "Introducción," 5; Bustamante, "Continúa la historia," *Voz de la Patria*, July 17, 1830, p. 3.

14. Alamán, *Historia*, V, 842; Ibar, *Muerte*, "Introducción," 4–5; H. G. Ward, *Mexico*, 2d ed., 2 vols. (London, 1829), II, 610; Tornel, *Breve reseña*, 393; Bustamante, *Continuación*, III, 201, 205, "Infeliz México," *Voz de la Patria*, July 1, 1829, p. 3; and "Continúa," *Voz de la Patria*, July 17, 1830, p. 3. Also Luis Gonzaga Cuevas, *Porvenir de México, o juicio sobre su estado político en 1821 y 1851* (Mexico City, 1851), 491. The British chargé d'affaires in Mexico City, Robert Pakenham, also asserted that "the pillage of the houses of the Old Spaniards had been promised" to the soldiers; despatch of Dec. 10, 1828, Great Britain, Public Record Office, Foreign Office, 50/45. f. 325 (General Correspondence, Mexico City).

15. Zavala, *Juicio*, 28–29 and *Manifiesto*, 17; Zerecero, *Memorias*, 109.

16. Manuel Payno, *Compendio de la historia de México para el uso de los establecimientos de instrucción pública de la República Mexicana* (Mexico City, 1876), 154; Bocanegra, *Memorias*, I, 496; Juan Suárez Navarro, *Historia de México y el General Antonio López de Santa Anna* . . . , 2 vols. (Mexico City, 1850–51), I, 130.

17. Bustamante, *Continuación*, III, 204–205; Gonzaga Cuevas, *Porvenir*, 491–492; Joel Poinsett, despatch of Dec. 10, 1828, in National Archives, Department of State, Record Group 59, Diplomatic Despatches, Mexico, vol. IV, no. 157; Suárez Navarro, *Historia*, I, 129. Note that Gonzaga Cuevas claimed that Tornel, rather than President Guadalupe Victoria, met with Zavala.

18. Note that two days later so few city council members dared brave the city streets, still gripped by confusion and disorder, that only six members attended the meeting of Dec. 6. AHCM, Actas de Cabildo, Dec. 4 and Dec. 6, 1828, vol. 148-A. On the congressional meetings of Dec. 4, see Bocanegra, *Memorias*, I, 499; Bustamante, *Continuación*, III, 203–204; and Ward, *Mexico*, II, 481, 484.

19. Zavala, *Ensayo*, I, 102 and *Juicio*, 29.

20. Tornel, *Breve reseña*, 394, 403. See also Gonzaga Cuevas, *Porvenir*, 491–492; Suárez Navarro, *Historia*, I, 129.

21. Poinsett, despatch of Dec. 10, 1828; Ramón Gamboa and Manuel Lozano, *Representación del comercio solicitando una indemnización* . . . (Mexico City, 1829), 16, inserted in AIICM, Hacienda-Propios Parián, vol. 2238, no. 159. Although the *North American Review* claimed that the rioting lasted two full days ("Politics of Mexico," no. 31 [1830], 146), this claim seems to be based on a misreading of Ward, who said that "such disorders" (apparently referring to the resale of stolen goods rather than rioting) lasted until General Guerrero returned to check them "after the lapse of two days" (*Mexico*, II, 482). Ward's information was in any case based on secondhand reports and was often faulty.

22. José María Luis Mora, *México y sus revoluciones*, 3 vols. (1836; reprint ed., Mexico City, 1950), I, 80–81; see also p. 469.

23. Tornel, *Breve reseña*, 394. On the highly publicized elite casualties, see Gonzaga Cuevas, *Porvenir*, 492; Rivera Cambas, *México*, I, 231–233; and Bustamante, *Continuación*, III, 208.

24. Bustamante, *Continuación*, III, 205, 221; Alamán, *Historia*, V, 845; Tornel, *Breve reseña*, 394.

25. Bustamante, *Continuación*, III, 221; Ward, *Mexico*, II, 481; Zerecero, *Memorias*, 110; Ibar, *Muerte*, pamphlet 1 (originally published Jan. 30, 1829), 6.

26. Payno, *Compendio*, 154.

27. Ibar, *Muerte*, "Introducción," 5; Bustamante, *Continuación*, III, 207–208 and "Continúa la historia," 2.

28. Bando of Dec. 7, 1828 in Basilio J. Arrillaga, ed., *Recopilación de leyes* . . . , 17 vols. in 16 (Mexico City, 1834–50), II, 278–279; Bustamante, *Continuación*, III, 210; Tornel, *Breve reseña*, 403–404.

29. Payno, *Compendio*, 154; Bustamante, *Continuación*, III, 211.

30. Gamboa and Lozano, *Representación del comercio*, 16.

31. It is unclear whether the indemnization was ever paid. See Bustamante, *Continuación*, III, 211, 247–248; Rivera Cambas, *México*, I, 115–119. The rents received by the city government belie the view that the Parián remained unprofitable after 1828, for the rents paid by its shopkeepers actually increased after new classes of native merchants (*manteros* and *zapateras*) replaced those who left: *Documentos oficiales relativos a la construcción y demolición del Parián* . . . (Mexico City, 1843).

32. Tornel, *Breve reseña*, 392; Zavala, *Juicio*, 29.

33. Ibar, *Muerte*, pamphlet 1, p. 6.

34. Zavala, *Ensayo*, II, 101. In addition, Zavala claimed (ibid., 114) that Guerrero wanted to level the social classes.

35. Zerecero, *Memorias*, 278; Zavala, *Juicio*, 32. On Guerrero's popularity, see also Tornel, *Breve reseña*, 408; Prieto, *Memorias*, 38–41; and Zavala, *Ensayo*, II, 48–49.

36. See Zavala, *Ensayo*, II, 92, 103, and 111.

37. Robert A. Potash, *Mexican Government and Industrial Development in the Early Republic: The Banco de Avío* (Amherst, 1983), 12–33; Luis Chávez Orozco, *El comercio exterior y el artesanado mexicano, 1825–1830* (Mexico City, 1965).

38. Tornel, *Breve reseña*, 167. See also "Politics of Mexico," 127–128, 132–133.

39. Romeo R. Flores Caballero, *Counterrevolution: The Role of the Spaniards in the Independence of Mexico, 1804–38*, Jaime E. Rodríguez, trans. (Lincoln, 1974), esp. 82–121.

40. Ibar, *Muerte*, pamphlet 1, p. 7; Payno, *Compendio*, 154; Zavala, *Juicio*, 29 and *Albores*, 276.

41. Rivera Cambas, *México*, I, 118. Shortly thereafter, Bancroft repeated this version in his *History of Mexico*, V, 43.

42. See Chester L. Guthrie, "Riots in Seventeenth-Century Mexico City: A Study of Social and Economic Conditions," in *Greater America: Essays in Honor of Herbert Eugene Bolton*, Adele Ogden and Engel Sluiter, eds. (Berkeley, 1945), 248; Rosa Feijóo, "El tumulto de 1692," *Historia Mexicana*, 14:4 (Apr.–June 1965), 661, 676.

43. Tornel, *Breve reseña*, 393.

44. Michael P. Costeloe, *La primera república federal de México (1824–1835): Un estudio de los partidos políticos en el México independiente*, Manuel Fernández Gasalla, trans. (Mexico City, 1975), 215.

45. Bustamante, "Diario," Dec. 13, 1828; Ibar, *Muerte*, "Introducción," 5; also Ward, *Mexico*, II, 481. Payno (*Compendio*, 154) also pointed out that the mob plundered Mexican and Spanish shops alike.

46. Alamán, *Historia*, V, 842. See also Tornel, *Breve reseña*, 393 and Prieto, *Memorias*, 34–35.

47. Although we do not know how many rioters were artisans, the confirmed presence of soldiers in the crowd fits the anti-Spanish theory, since—as David Sowell pointed out to me—many could have been veterans of the war against Spain. Research on soldiers' backgrounds is sorely needed for this period, along the lines suggested by Anthony P. Maingot, "Social Structure, Social Status, and Civil-Military Conflict in Urban Colombia, 1810–1858," in *Nineteenth-Century Cities: Essays in the New Urban History*, Stephen Thernstrom and Richard Sennett, eds. (New Haven, 1969), 297–355. Maingot's thesis that the importance of lower-class soldiers reflected the democratization of the political process after independence might also apply here, where the army recruited largely from the lower orders abandoned the *escocés* government for the more popular *yorkinos*.

48. Tornel, *Breve reseña*, 403–405. On anti-Spanish riots elsewhere, see Zavala, *Ensayo*, II, 103–104; Bustamante, "Continúa," *Voz de la Patria*, Aug. 4, 1830, p. 1; Ward, *Mexico*, II, 490–491; and Flores Caballero, *Counterrevolution*, 95, 102.

49. Ibar, *Muerte*, pamphlet 1, p. 2; Pakenham, despatch of Dec. 10, 1828ff., 324–327; Ward, *Mexico*, II, 490; Poinsett, despatches of Dec. 10–11, nos. 157–158. Quote in text is from Ward; Pakenham reported that outside of the Parián,

"the damage . . . , all things considered, has been much less than might have been expected. I have the satisfaction to acquaint your Lordship that not one of the Houses of the British Merchants has been pillaged." Their loss was indirect, since the ruined Spanish retail dealers would not be able to pay for the goods sold them on credit by the British wholesalers.

50. Neil J. Smelser, *Theory of Collective Behavior* (New York, 1962), esp. 8–9. On the logic and discipline of crowds, see also the works cited in n. 4 and Nevitt Sanford, Craig Comstock et al., *Sanctions for Evil* (San Francisco, 1971), esp. ix, 3, 21, 25.

51. AHCM, Actas Secretas de Cabildo, Jan. 5, 1829, vol. 291-A.

52. Richard W. Slatta, ed., *Bandidos: The Varieties of Latin American Banditry* (Westport, 1987). In *The Rebellious Century, 1830–1930*, Charles, Louise, and Richard Tilly found that in Europe the crests of collective violence similarly coincided with national struggles for power rather than economic distress (Cambridge, MA, 1975, esp. 247–248, 252).

53. Alamán, *Historia*, V, 842. See also Christon I. Archer, *The Army in Bourbon Mexico, 1760–1810* (Albuquerque, 1977), 73–74.

54. Bustamante, *Continuación*, III, 173–174, 228; Ward, *Mexico*, II, 614; Suárez Navarro, *Historia*, I, vii. See also Gonzaga Cuevas, *Porvenir*, 484; and Mariano Otero, *Ensayo sobre el verdadero estado de la cuestión social y política que se agita en la República Mexicana* (Guadalajara, 1852), 70.

55. Charles Tilly, "Collective Violence in European Perspective," in *The History of Violence in America: Historical and Comparative Perspectives*, Hugh D. Graham and Ted R. Gurr, eds. (New York, 1969), 4–45; with Louise and Richard Tilly, *The Rebellious Century*; Hobsbawm, *Primitive Rebels*, esp. 116–122; Richard Bendix, "The Lower Classes and the 'Democratic Revolution,' " *Industrial Relations*, 1:1 (Oct. 1961), 91–116.

56. See especially William B. Taylor, *Drinking, Homicide, and Rebellion in Colonial Mexican Villages* (Stanford, 1979), chap. 4; Jean Meyer, *Problemas campesinos y revueltas agrarias (1821–1910)* (Mexico City, 1973); Luis González Obregón, *Rebeliones indígenas y precursores de la independencia mexicana en los siglos XVI, XVII, y XVIII*, 2d rev. ed. (Mexico City, 1952); Segundo Moreno Yáñez, *Sublevaciones indígenas en la audiencia de Quito: Desde comienzos del siglo XVIII hasta finales de la colonia* (Bonn, 1976); and Anthony McFarlane, "Civil Disorders and Popular Protests in Late Colonial New Granada," *Hispanic American Historical Review*, 64:1 (Feb. 1984), 17–54.

57. See Guthrie, "Riots"; Feijóo, "El tumulto de 1624," *Historia Mexicana*, 14:1 (July–Sept. 1964), 42–70; and Feijóo, "Tumulto de 1692."

58. The dearth of research on nineteenth-century urban riots in Latin America makes it difficult to compare Mexico City to other Latin American cities. Sandra Lauderdale Graham's pathbreaking piece on an 1880 riot in Brazil suggests, however, that Mexico's early experiment with populist politics was unusual [Note: Graham's article is reprinted in this volume as Chapter 4.] Her article also underlines the importance of the elite response in determining the effect of a riot. In Rio de Janeiro, establishment groups did not, as in Mexico, join forces to suppress popular participation because it served them in discrediting the monarchy.

59. On the reorganization of the police in the eighteenth century, see Gabriel J. Haslip, "Crime and the Administration of Justice in Colonial Mexico City, 1692–1810" (Ph.D. diss., Columbia University, 1980), esp. 94–101. On the vagrants' tribunal, see decree of Mar. 7, 1828 in AHCM, Vagos, vol. 4151, no. 2; Shaw, "Poverty," 278–292. On their ineffectiveness, see Tornel, *Breve reseña*, 403;

AHCM, Actas Secretas de Cabildo, Feb. 13 and 14, 1829, vol. 291-A; and Shaw, "Poverty," 295–302.

60. AHCM, Actas de Cabildo, Dec. 9–16, 1829, vol. 148-A. Ibar also claimed that policemen were exacting stiff bribes from merchants who had been spared by claiming to have protected them from the looters (*Muerte*, "Introducción," 6).

61. Tornel, *Breve reseña*, 403–404.

62. Mora, *México*, I, 80; Ibar, *Muerte*, "Introducción," 6.

63. Tornel, *Breve reseña*, 406, 409; Ibar, *Muerte*, "Introducción," 6; Bustamante, *Continuación*, III, 211, 228; AHCM, Actas Secretas de Cabildo, Dec. 16, 1828, vol. 290-A, and Feb. 14, 1829, vol. 291-A; AHCM, Vagos, vols. 4151–4152; laws of Dec. 14 and 20, 1828 and Feb. 20, 1829 in Arrillaga, *Recopilación*, III, 22–35, 176–182.

64. Guthrie,"Riots," 248–249.

65. Tornel, *Breve reseña*, 417; Ibar, *Muerte*, "Introducción," 6.

66. Tornel, *Breve reseña*, 394; Gonzaga Cuevas, *Porvenir*, 261; *El Sol*, Jan. 11, 1830 quoted in Costeloe, *Primera república*, 275.

67. Prieto, *Memorias*, 37.

68. Zerecero, *Memorias*, 109; Zavala, *Ensayo*, I, 110 and *Albores*, 266, 275, 278.

69. Bustamante, *Continuación*, III, 204; Ibar, *Muerte*, "Introducción"; Zavala, *Ensayo*, II, 92, 109–110 and *Albores*, 276, 278.

70. See Tornel, *Breve reseña*, 393–394; Mora, *México*, I, 81; and Bustamante, *Continuación*, III, 205.

71. Editorial in *Registro Oficial*, quoted in Costeloe, *Primera república*, 274. See also José María Luis Mora, *Obras sueltas* . . . (1837; reprint ed. Mexico City, 1963), 11.

72. The national constitution of 1824, in fact, gave the states the right to regulate elections and define who was eligible to vote. See tit. III, 2:9 in Felipe Tena Ramírez, *Leyes fundamentales de México, 1808–1973*, 5th rev. ed. (Mexico City, 1973), 207–208. Most state constitutions imposed few restrictions on male suffrage, however. For example, the constitution of the State of Jalisco disqualified only those men who lacked a "useful occupation" (*Constitución Federal de los Estados Unidos Mexicanos y Constitución Política del Estado Libre de Jalisco* [Guadalajara, 1973], 65–66). The regulations applying in Mexico City itself excluded domestic servants but specifically granted the vote to day laborers (*jornaleros*) (*Legislación electoral mexicana, 1812–1973* [Mexico City, 1973], 34, 44).

73. Bases Constitucionales of 1836 in Tena Ramírez, *Leyes*, 207–208. See also Shaw, "Poverty," 319–325.

3

"Death to the Cemetery": Funerary Reform and Rebellion in Salvador, Brazil, 1836

João José Reis

João José Reis is a professor of history at the University of Bahia, Brazil. He has published extensively on slave resistance and popular culture in nineteenth-century Brazil; his books include Slave Rebellion in Brazil: The Muslim Uprising of 1835 in Bahia *(1986; English ed., 1993),* Negociação e conflito: Resistência negra no Brasil escravista *(with Eduardo Silva, 1989), and* História do Quilombo no Brasil *(with Flávio Gomes, 1996).*

This study of a riot against funerary reform is based on his book on death in Brazilian culture, A morte é uma festa: Ritos fúnebres e revolta popular no Brasil no século XIX *(1991), which won Brazil's National Book Award, the Premio Jabuti, for the best work of nonfiction in 1992. Professor Reis shows that this riot cannot be explained adequately without understanding its cultural context, but he warns against oversimplifying the view of popular culture, since the motivations for participating were different for members of different social groups. The* Cemiterada *illustrates what Eric Van Young describes as "the resilience of popular culture, and the recalcitrance of large segments of civil society in the face of statist projects."**

On 25 October 1836 a remarkable revolt took place in Salvador, capital of the then province of Bahia, in north-eastern Brazil: an uprising against a cemetery. It occurred one day before a law

From *History Workshop Journal* 34 (Autumn 1992): 33–46. Reprinted by permission of Oxford University Press and the author. [Revisions added by author.]
*Eric Van Young, "Conclusion: The State as Vampire—Hegemonic Projects, Public Ritual, and Popular Culture in Mexico, 1600–1990," in *Rituals of Rule, Rituals of Resistance: Public Celebrations and Popular Culture in Mexico*, ed. William H. Beezley, Cheryl English Martin, and William E. French (Wilmington, DE, 1994), 344.

proscribing burials inside local churches was to take effect. The same law granted a private company the monopoly of interments for thirty years.

The revolt started with a rally organized by Catholic lay brotherhoods in front of the provincial government palace. The brotherhoods were associations dedicated to the festive devotion to specific saints, and membership in them followed class, national and ethnic lines; they functioned as mutual-aid societies which, among other things, provided funerals for their members. In the morning of 25 October, the bells of brotherhood churches all over town sounded continuously inviting members and others to protest against the new law. Brothers and sisters went to the palace square wearing the attire of religious galas, and carrying crosses, flags and other insignia identifying each association. The number of people was calculated by the police at between two and four thousand. It was no doubt the biggest street demonstration Salvador had ever seen, despite the fact that those were not peaceful days.

Faced with such a crowd outside his door, the president of the province agreed to discuss the matter with representatives of the brotherhoods, but a good number of other demonstrators also forced their way into the palace. Under pressure, the president promised that within two weeks he would call for an extraordinary meeting of the Provincial Legislature to review the law, a move that appeared to calm feelings down. In the meantime burials could continue as before.

Peace, however, lasted but a few minutes. A group approached the town office of the cemetery company just two steps from the palace shouting 'Long live the brotherhoods, death to the Freemasons'. Stones were thrown against a placard on which bright letters announced: 'The Cemetery Company'—the placard was destroyed and windowpanes were broken. An eyewitness later said that the stones had been brought (under their habits) by a group of lay sisters. At one point someone shouted: 'Death to the Cemetery', and the crowd marched to the Campo Santo cemetery located some three kilometers away, outside the urban perimeter.

There destruction was almost complete. The surrounding walls were knocked down, a heavy iron gate was removed, the chapel's roof dismantled, still unused sepulchres and tombstones were destroyed. Mortuary carts decorated with mortuary cloth were burned; and one was carried ritually to the town centre and broken into pieces near the palace, in defiance of the government.

The procession was closely followed by the police, who decided not to intervene. Later the police chief explained that it would have been improper to use violence against men carrying crosses, and still more against women, and, moreover, that it was impossible to control a crowd of that size.

The demonstration continued into the night, when Bahians lit their windows with candles and torches, a traditional sign of public rejoicing; church bells sounded again for hours. The demonstrators chose to ritualize their rebellion just as they were accustomed to ritualize death.[1]

This movement—which received the name of Cemiterada—is an obvious example of the conflict between tradition and reform so common in the formation of capitalism and nation-states. More specifically, it may be linked to long-term change of attitudes towards death and the dead in parts of the Catholic world from around the middle of the eighteenth century to the first decades of the nineteenth. This process has been discussed by French historians such as Philippe Ariès, Michel Vovelle, Pierre Chaunu, Jacqueline Thibaut-Payen and others. They have shown that during the eighteenth century the baroque 'way of death' was in decline.[2]

Baroque funerals were characterized by spectacular ceremonies that mobilized numerous priests, the poor, friends and family of the deceased, all carrying many—sometimes hundreds—of candles; these funerals usually had as their final destination graves inside churches or parish cemeteries inside towns. The world of the dead and the world of the living were integrated in the same urban space. By the end of the eighteenth century, these funerals had been replaced in Europe by simpler ceremonies, and for medical reasons burial grounds had been transferred outside towns and villages.

Little opposition seems to have been raised against the transferral of cemeteries in France, for example, except for delaying tactics and a few minor violent incidents in small towns, mentioned by Thibaut-Payen and John McManners. In general burial reforms—which were made together with other urban reforms—followed the decline of religious devotion. In other predominantly Catholic countries of Europe the trend seems to have been the same.[3]

There was, however, at least one exception in Europe. In Portugal, Brazil's mother-country, more specifically in the northern province of Minho, rural folk fiercely opposed the enforcement of the 1846 sanitary laws of the Liberal government which prohibited burials inside churches. The conflict—known as the Maria da Fonte rebellion—began with a confrontation between country women and soldiers over illegal burial practices and soon spread, merging with the conservative *miguelista* movement.[4]

Unless further research suggests otherwise we may suppose that it was in the Portuguese world that there occurred the most radical reaction to the closing of churches to the dead. Of course, the Bahian uprising of 1836 did not have a direct link with the Portuguese uprising ten years later, but it should be recalled that most immigrants from Portugal to Bahia came from the Minho region. And they certainly brought deeply rooted traditions concerning death and the care of the dead, traditions that owed much to old European pagan cults and magical beliefs.

One of these was the belief in wandering souls. In Portugal, individuals who died tragic deaths, who did not receive proper funerals, or who were not buried in consecrated soil became 'wandering souls' among the living, against whom they could play all kinds of tricks, ask difficult favours, sometimes avenge old wrongs. But generally these damned spirits asked only for a proper mass, decent burials, payment of debts and so on. These measures would help them overcome their liminal state and join for good the world of the dead, either to enjoy death in heaven or, more realistically I guess, to await rehabilitation in purgatory.[5]

Parallel traditions reached Bahia from Africa. In 1836 the majority of Salvador's 66,000 inhabitants were either slaves or descendants of slaves brought to work in Bahian sugar plantations and in the port-city of Salvador. Africans in Bahia came from west and southern-central Africa, and were primarily of the Aja-Fon-Ewe, Yoruba, Hausa, Umbundo and Ovimbundo peoples from present-day Nigeria, Benin and Angola. All of these groups possessed complex escatologies and funerary rituals. All of them regarded ancestor spirits as important forces monitoring their daily lives and securing them good deaths and a smooth integration in the world of the dead. They also believed in wailing souls who would be created in similar circumstances to those believed in by the Portuguese, particularly concerning lack of proper burial.[6]

Of course, once in Brazil, as slaves of Brazilian white and mestizo masters, Africans were often forced to abide by Catholic rules; but they did not abandon old ways of life and death. Whites and blacks, slaves or freedmen, had their own brotherhoods. But in their confraternities Africans and creole blacks reinvented Catholicism according to their own traditions. They celebrated patron saints with masquerades, drumming, songs sung in African languages and the election of allegoric kings and queens.[7] Baroque Portuguese Catholicism, with its effusion of rituals, symbols and colours, and with its processional street culture, was not completely foreign to Africans. And given the flexibility of African religiosity, there was always room for new rituals, symbols and gods. In addition, despite the protest of purists the Church accepted—or closed its eyes to—African funerary ceremonies. French traveller Jean Baptiste Debret painted scenes of funeral corteges of blacks in which Catholic priests intervened only after the corpses had crossed the doors of church buildings.[8] However, there is no doubt that even among slaves Catholic rules were predominant in Bahia's funerary culture, especially in its public dimensions.

According to the norms of this culture, the first strategy for salvation was careful organization of one's own death. Many did this orally, often in the last moments of life, preferably in the presence of a priest. But many Bahians, including ex-slaves, also arranged their deaths by dictating testaments where, besides disposing of their property, they organized their funerals and the departure of their souls. They named saints as defence lawyers in the 'divine tribunal', and indicated the number and type of masses they thought necessary to curtail their stay in purgatory; they chose the funerary shroud, on occasion the model of the coffin, the number of priests and musicians for the procession and burial, and the specific place of burial.

Many of the secular features of wills nevertheless had religious implications. In a merchant city like Salvador, death represented an important mechanism for settling outstanding business affairs. As in Portugal, the dead could not find rest, or would not escape the purgatorial flames, until their debts to the living had been paid. Debts to heavenly creditors and to human creditors, quoted in currency, were often listed side by side (one could die owing money to a tavern owner and owing masses to a saint, masses that also cost money). It was also an act of faith to be fair with those left behind. Old 'sins of the flesh' were corrected at this moment, when fathers recognized children born of illicit relationships. Many men married long-term companions, sometimes black women, making them legal heirs. Others would deny paternity, like a certain Luiz Pedro de Carvalho, who in 1835 accused the mothers of two girls known as his children of being prostitutes. Rocha wrote: 'If they were my daughters, I would not conceal it, especially now that I am close to settling my account with the Creator'.[9]

For Bahians a fundamental funerary belief linked the treatment of the corpse with the fate of the soul, a common conception found in a variety of cultures.[10] When death arrived, a number of domestic rituals were immediately performed with or around the corpse to keep evil spirits at bay and to guarantee the peaceful departure of the deceased. Death was announced by wailing women, often specialists in the task—as is common in the Mediterranean. Sometimes women were hired to wash the corpse with special infusions or perfumes, and then to dress it. More commonly this was done by family members or neighbours who had been there at the end and perhaps had helped the deceased to die a good death.

The funerary wardrobe of Bahians was a complex one. Few corpses were dressed in secular clothes. In 1836, adult corpses were most commonly attired in white, black or Franciscan shrouds (*mortalhas*). White robes made of ordinary cotton cloth were popular among the Africans, white being the funerary colour of many ethnic groups such as the Yoruba and the Fon-Ewe, and among Muslims. For the Yoruba, for instance, whiteness was linked to Orisha Obatatala, the creator of living beings. But whiteness had important meanings in the symbolism of Christian death as well.[11] As Victor Turner has written, in the Christian tradition it 'helps to reveal the order of grace'. Bahians were even more direct: in 1832 one of them asked to be buried 'dressed in a white cloth imitating Our Lord Jesus Christ', a reference to the Holy Shroud.[12]

The use of black *mortalhas* increased from the beginning of the nineteenth century, primarily among married women. When combined with a crucifix around the neck, these constituted the habit of Saint Rita, protector of sufferers. The wearing of habits of saints was very common, especially that of Saint Francis, used in Portugal since the Middle Ages.[13] Saint Francis had a prominent place in Catholic eschatology. An eighteenth-century painting in the magnificent Franciscan church in Bahia shows the saint using the cord from his habit to rescue souls from purgatory.

Judging by a sample of over a thousand entries in parish records in 1835–36, white shrouds were worn by forty-four percent of Bahian dead, black shrouds by sixteen percent and the Franciscan habit by nine percent. The remaining thirty-one percent were buried with other types of clothes, including the habits of other saints. Boys, for example, wore the military uniform of Saint Michael the Archangel—which included helmet, armour and sword—an appropriate costume for those who according to popular belief were, if baptized, to be recruited to the angelical army immediately after death. Boys also dressed as Saint John the Baptist, while girls dressed as Our Lady of Conception, both patrons of fertility in Brazil. In both cases parents seemed to be taking propitiatory measures to guarantee the survival of future children in a demographic environment characterized by high rates of infant mortality.[14]

The use of these habits represented an appeal to the saints thus represented for protection. It expressed the importance of the corpse in the passage to the afterlife and of the belief in resurrection on the day of Apocalypse. It was also often a representation of the desire of grace, of being closer to God, and evoked membership in the Divine Court, or it worked as an element in a ritual of fertility. Funerary garb could communicate other meanings. According to the French consul in Bahia, African slaves who rebelled in the early 1830s fought in the streets of Salvador wearing their best African robes in the belief that, if they were to die, they would return in spirit to their homeland.[15]

Once properly dressed, the dead were ready for the wake which usually happened in the house parlour, sometimes profusely decorated for the occasion with large black curtains embroidered in silver or gold. Until the moment of burial the deceased was never to be left alone, for a solitary corpse was easy prey for evil forces. During the wake, wailing women prayed aloud, often singing funerary songs. Family members, friends and neighbours kept their eyes vigilantly open with the help of food and drink.

Funeral corteges left the house at sunset, for the night shadows protected the living from the shadows of death. Funerals could be spectacular, imitating Corpus Christi processions or the Procession of Our Lady of Good Death, when music, fireworks and food and drink abounded.

Bahians were deeply attracted by funerals which, according to more than one foreign traveller, they adopted as a favourite pastime.[16] The ability to recruit a large crowd was a sign of the family's social prestige, a symbol of earthly power, and at the same time a protection for the soul of the deceased, who would profit from the prayers of many mourners. Rich families sent out hundreds of invitations. Passers-by were welcome to join the procession, receiving candles to help open the way for the dead, candles which rarely melted completely and were later sold by mourners or used to light their homes. The poor—and they were many in Bahia in 1836— were professional funeral goers, for which they received, besides candles, money or food. They were organized in groups around the city led by *capatazes* (foremen) responsible for the redistribution of alms. Their prayers were considered particularly effective. The poor served the rich not only in life but also in death.[17]

In 1817 a rich Portuguese merchant hired 500 beggars, an orchestra and twenty priests to take him to the grave. The presence of priests was very important, for they were experts in saving souls, and Bahians tried to mobilize as many as they could afford. At the peak of the baroque age—in the late seventeenth century—there were persons who asked for as many as one hundred priests, though the maximum number had fallen to half that on the eve of the Cemiterada.

This wealthy Portuguese merchant also reminded the executors of his last wishes to announce his death to the four brotherhoods to which he was affiliated. With these, the five hundred poor, and friends and neighbours, a crowd of probably more than a thousand people brightened his funeral.[18]

But he was a rich man. The poor usually joined brotherhoods precisely so that they could better solemnize their deaths. The brotherhoods were good at mobilizing members, properly dressed, carrying candles, crosses, flags and their collective biers. Black brotherhoods elected officers whose task was to go around the city announcing the passing-away of brothers. The by-laws of the black brotherhood of Saint Benedict established that any member who failed to attend funerals would not be accompanied by the brotherhood at his own death—a terrible threat.[19]

For my purpose the main focus of Bahian funerals is the place of burial. Death without proper burial was greatly feared. Death by drowning in the high seas was particularly dreaded and in the Brazilian countryside prayers are to this day annually made for 'the souls of the sea waves', a custom certainly learned from the coast at a time when it was not 'sweet to die in the sea', as a popular singer much later expressed it. In 1823 a merchant who made frequent trips to Lisbon wrote in his will: 'I hope, by the divine mercy, that I will die ashore'. Three years later he died crossing the Atlantic and certainly became a sea ghost.[20]

It was important to die on *terra firma* and to have a grave in a consecrated place. For Bahians this place was the church. Just as the funeral cortege imitated the processions of Christ's funeral, the graves were associated with the Lord's house. The physical proximity between the corpse and divine images of saints and angels represented spiritual proximity between the soul and celestial beings. The church building was an entrance to Paradise. It was at the same time a perfect and desirable place to await the resurrection on Judgement Day, a conception widely accepted in the Catholic world from the Middle Ages. In 1764, the black brothers of Santa Ifigênia protested against the disrespectful way blacks were being interred by the local charity, expressing concern for 'the immortality of their souls and the future resurrection of their bodies'.[21]

To have a grave inside a temple was also a way of keeping in touch with the world of the living, so that the latter did not forget the dead in their prayers. This is how the 1707 Bahian synod explained the advantages of ecclesiastical burial, adding that the daily view of death would prevent the faithful from sinning.[22] The dead came to occupy the same temples they had attended in life, where they would still witness and influence community affairs. Church buildings at that time served as classrooms, electoral precincts, auditoria for trials and political debates. The living trod on graves while attending these activities.

In the decade before the revolt against the Campo Santo, the majority of will-makers (60 percent) asked to be buried either in their brotherhoods' temples or their parish churches, which suggests that the spirit of community was projected beyond life itself. The individual wanted a grave located in familiar territory, near those with whom he or she had shared their life. Attitudes toward death thus revealed concepts of spatial organization and community which were common to the neighbourhood and parish. Jeronima Maria dos Santos wrote in 1836: 'I declare that I want to be buried in the Parish of Passos, which is my parish'. In 1828, Jacinta Tereza de São José asked to be buried in the parish in which she lived, and in the same church she had received baptism.[23] Signs of life and death converged spatially, marking the end of the individual's time on earth with promises of a new beginning.

Although a church represented *the* burial place par excellence, there was a geography of death which reflected the social hierarchies and other forms of social segmentation. Few whites, for instance, had graves in black churches. One exception was a powerful planter and owner of over two hundred slaves who, in 1824, hoped to avoid the underworld by being buried in the church of Our Lady of the Rosary that belonged to the black brotherhood of the same name. He received a private tomb near the main altar, in return for a donation of two thousand *contos*, approximately one thousand three hundred dollars. Without any specific request from him, the black brothers inscribed on his tombstone: 'Here lies the mortal remains of our brother and benefactor Mariscal José Ignacio Acciavoli, who passed away on 9 February, 1826'.[24] The slave master was commemorated as a brother of slaves.

Family or individual tombs—granted in perpetuity, with the right to inscribe the name, occupation, titles of the dead, the family coat of arms and devout messages—were occupied by the most powerful figures of Bahian society. The temple's common graves were themselves divided according to their position in relation to the altars and other significant places in the architecture of the church. The order of importance varied from graves in the churchyard to those near the main altar. Rita dos Anjos in 1829 asked her husband, a sugar plantation owner, to bury her near the font of the Franciscan church.[25] She certainly hoped that her soul would profit from holy water falling on her grave.

During the eighteenth century brotherhoods, and later parish churches, built burial niches along underground walls for their brothers and well-to-do parishioners. This innovation, besides introducing new forms of class segregation, separated the dead from the images of the saints, and also isolated the dead from the living. It was a decisive step towards a more individualistic death, for it separated the dead not only from one another but from the earth, which in Brazil was believed to have an equivalence with the cadaver, as French traveller Ferdinand Denis noted in 1818.[26]

Not everyone in Bahia was buried in Catholic churches. British citizens, for example, had their own cemetery. Most slaves, although some were allocated graves in churches, were taken to a cemetery on the outskirts of Salvador. In the first half of the eighteenth century the city council deposited there slave corpses abandoned by masters on the road, beaches and streets, or the bodies of those who died during quarantine in slave ships. The removal of these corpses was conducted without any religious ceremony, nor did things improve significantly after control of the cemetery passed to the Holy House of Mercy, the most prominent philanthropic institution in Salvador, formed by powerful slavemasters, planters and merchants. Slaves joined black brotherhoods to escape this shameful fate. The brotherhood substituted in both life and death for family ties severed by slavery. In Africa, the Yoruba, the Fon-Ewe, the Nupe—groups well represented within the Bahian slave population—interred their dead inside family compounds; in Bahia they chose burial among religious brothers, their new, fictive family.

The church, then, was generally considered to be the proper place of burial. But from the beginning of the nineteenth century Brazilian medical opinion began to shift, projecting a more 'enlightened', 'rational' solution. After independence from Portugal in 1822, European—especially French—hygienist ideas captured the minds of the cultivated, liberal elite. Doctors in particular believed themselves to be in the vanguard of enlightenment in the tropics, and they fought, as they repeatedly wrote, to 'elevate Brazil to the heights of European nations'. Funerary reforms represented one aspect of this bid to bring civilization to the country. Many had learned their lessons in France, being graduates of Montpellier or Paris. In 1831 Manoel Maurício Rebouças, a mulatto Bahian doctor, defended a thesis at the Ecole de Médecine de Paris criticizing burials within urban areas, particularly churches.[27] When he returned to Bahia the following year he became professor at the newly inaugurated School of Medicine.

In his thesis, Rebouças repeated arguments, stories, and explanations he had read in the French medical literature or heard in the classroom. The decomposition of corpses produced miasmas that affected the health of the living who should, he proclaimed, transfer the dead to cemeteries located outside the urban perimeter, on top of hills, surrounded by high trees, away from water sources and winds blowing towards the city. The new cemeteries were to have twice as many graves as the size of the population, and a period of two years should separate burials in the same grave—two years being the ideal time for safe decomposition in the tropics. Graves were to be seven feet deep and kept an appropriate distance from each other so as to 'deflect the miasmatic rays', he wrote. Besides being the most hygienic resting place for the dead, 'extramural' cemeteries were—in this rational utopia—to become showrooms of civic attitudes, where citizens would find monuments of exemplary countrymen who had served with distinction the nation and humankind. In the model cemetery, civic virtue would thus replace religion. That was a bourgeois funerary programme for a society based on slavery.

Rebouças himself, trained in Paris, had almost nothing to say specifically about Brazilian miasmas. But in Brazil the medical profession published numerous articles and reports with horror stories about the activities of deadly effluvia. Lino Coutinho, first director of Bahia's Medical School, poet and minister of the Brazilian Empire, told a meeting of the Medical Society of Rio de Janeiro that his sister had died from attending mass early in the morning, this being the most dangerous hour to visit a church on account of the concentration of cadaverous effusions during the night behind closed doors. Women, moreover, were considered to be the most common victims of miasmas, not only because they attended mass more assiduously, but because of their supposedly more delicate physical and psychological structure.[28]

In Salvador and other urban centers the medical campaign won the opinion of the legislators, a few of them doctors themselves. As part of the liberal reforms promised by Emperor Pedro I, in 1828 a national law that reorganized municipal government also ordered town councils to take measures to remove all burials from urban areas. The following year Salvador's council issued sanitary laws, one of which prohibited burials within the city after the next two years. Meanwhile parishes and brotherhoods were to build cemeteries outside Salvador.

Except for a cemetery to serve the local American community, on expiration date no cemetery had yet been built. The municipal authorities began fining heavily those who persisted in using churches for burials. Fortunately for the brotherhoods—and for the deceased—both the Bahian archbishop, D. Romualdo Seixas, and the provincial government intervened against the municipal council.[29]

In early 1835 the recently inaugurated provincial legislature received a proposal from a private company formed by two businessmen and a judge. (The judge's speciality was the settlement of inheritance disputes, a position that gave him inside knowledge of funeral costs and so also of the commercial potential of a funerary venture.) In the proposal, these men echoed medical arguments against traditional interment and explained that theirs would be, more than a commercial venture, a patriotic contribution to the country, for the planned cemetery would 'bring civilization to Bahia'. But since they needed some sort of return, they asked for the monopoly of graves and funerary transportation for the next thirty years, which was accepted by the Provincial Assembly, by the government and by the archbishop who, as it happened, was also the president of the Assembly. Law number 17 of 25 June 1835 formalized the contract.[30]

Despite the archbishop's support, many priests, monks and particularly the lay brotherhoods fought vigorously against the Cemetery Company. Initially, they petitioned the provincial government and the legislature. In these petitions, paradoxically, the brothers invoked constitutional rights, as citizens of a recently born nation, drawing upon the modern language of liberalism in order to defend the pre-modern customs of traditional burials.

They argued that the monopoly was unconstitutional because it harmed property rights and thwarted long-held religious privileges. The prohibition, they believed, would result in declining membership of the brotherhoods, since people joined primarily in order to have decent burials inside their temples. The end of burials in the convent of Saint Francis, complained the friars, would eliminate their main source of income and jeopardize plans to recruit new members. The brotherhood of Saint Domingo foresaw the decline of religion, the closing of churches, the abandonment of devotion, the insurrection of the faithful and even the destruction of the state. More than one petition warned of the possibility of a popular uprising. The movement against the cemetery presented as its goal the regeneration of an order contracted between the state and the citizen, a movement made in the name of religion, the constitution and property rights. In the logic of the brotherhoods the existing funerary order was part of the political order of monarchic Brazil: one could not survive without the other. The petitioners expected their arguments to have special resonance in a period of republican and federalist unrest.[31]

The Church itself was not spared in these petitions. The law exempted from the prohibition members of certain religious orders which were subject to strict rules of seclusion, a measure which established a discrimination within the Catholic community. Even worse, the law was silent about the British and American cemeteries, which meant that it was only Catholics, formally most fully entitled to protection by Church and state, who would be denied freedom of burial.

But the archbishop had a plan. For Romualdo, the new law was to be a step in the process of romanization of the Brazilian Church, functioning to undermine the national-popular Catholicism embedded in the culture of the brotherhoods. Like the doctors, higher Church officials were of the opinion that true religion dispensed with burials within church buildings and that those who insisted on the old practice were following no more than superstition. The Church fought, above all, to separate divine worship from the cult of the dead—a ritual mixture that evoked pagan ancestor cults of both European and African origins—while for the brotherhoods, on the contrary, the living, the dead and the divine formed an inseparable ritual family. Romualdo knew that this separation would undermine the influence of brotherhoods and increase the power of the ecclesiastical hierarchy.[32]

At the same time, Bahian brotherhoods were not in their best days. Research on wills, inventories and parish records shows that membership had been falling since the beginning of the nineteenth century. The popularity of patron saints, as reflected in demands for protection after death, was also in decline. Even the popularity of brotherhood temples as places of burial, though still high at the time of the rebellion, was also declining. These shifts closely followed a slow secularization manifest in Bahian wills. Thus the Cemiterada happened at a time of declining devotion, as though to forestall a definitive fall. As the main channel of traditional devotion, the brotherhoods became the vanguard of this reaction.

Church and state resisted the brothers' pressure long enough to allow the inauguration of the cemetery on 23 October, a very hot Sunday. But two days later the rebels won a complete victory with the attack on Campo Santo. Later the Provincial Assembly cancelled the prohibition law, and church burials continued for another twenty years. Although a judicial inquiry was made, no one was ever indicted, no one was even arrested, and no leader found. However, there was in fact a leader, the Viscount of Pirajá, son of an important local family, conservative member of the provincial legislature, a man of strong monarchist positions, and a follower of traditional baroque Catholicism, who belonged to at least two prestigious brotherhoods and who valued the full ostentation of the traditional funeral and the family tomb. During the rebellion, demonstrators shouted 'Death to José Araújo [one of the owners of the Campo Santo] and long live Santinho [or "Little Saint"]', as the viscount was popularly known.[33] His name headed a petition against the cemetery that circulated in Salvador for ten days and received 280 signatures, a notable achievement in a highly illiterate society. Members of other important families, primarily merchants and public servants, but also artisans and common people, signed this document, which again threatened a break with the social and political order if prohibition of church burials were maintained.[34]

Other sources indicate the range of participants in the uprising itself. One witness saw barefooted black men and women, their lack of shoes usually signifying their slave status. The majority of the testimonies, however, pointed out that individuals of 'different classes and sexes' formed the crowd.[35] This was probably the first time Bahian free women, normally secluded, had participated in a street demonstration. They restated what seems to be a cross-cultural rule in traditional societies: that women are important agents of popular religion and in particular they have a pre-eminent role in things related to death.

The movement, then, was multi-racial, multi-class and composed of both men and women. But within this range of support there were widely varying positions. Although viscount and slave both had a stake in the maintenance of traditional funerary practices, their motivations differed. The viscount was defending seigneurial interests: his family tomb in the convent of Saint Francis was a symbol of long-held aristocratic privilege and of the hope that it would continue in the afterlife. The slave defended tradition from the other end of the social spectrum. For him (or perhaps her), a grave in a brotherhood chapel signalled respect and standing previously denied, and the hope of a better future. Thus the slave sought a dignity in death which had never been available in life and which the cemetery could not provide. At the same time, all those who participated in the Cemiterada followed that basic impulse, to which Freud refers, of "denying it [death] the significance of annihilation."[36] The rebels kept this conviction deeply buried in their souls.

Notes

1. For the complete story of the movement, see João J. Reis, *A morte é uma festa: Ritos fúnebres e revolta popular no Brasil no século XIX*, São Paulo, 1991.

2. Philippe Ariès, *The Hour of Our Death*, trans. by Helen Weaver, Harmondsworth, 1981; and *Images de l'homme devant la mort*, Paris, 1983; Michel Vovelle, *Piété baroque et déchristianisation en Provence au XVIIIe siècle*, Paris, 1978; Pierre Chaunu, *La Mort à Paris: 16e, 17e, 18e siècles*, Paris, 1978; Jacqueline Thibaut-Payen, *Les morts, l'Eglise et l'Etat: Recherches d'histoire administrative sur la sépulture et les cimetières dans le ressort du parlement de Paris aux XVIIe et XVIIIe siècles*, Paris, 1977; François Lebrun, *Les hommes et la mort en Anjou aux 17e et 18e siècles*, Paris, 1971. In England the transition came with the Reformation: Clare Gittings, *Death, Burial and the Individual in Early Modern England*, London, 1984.

3. Thibaut-Payen, *Les morts*, pp. 417ff; John McManners, *Death and the Enlightenment: Changing Attitudes to Death among Christians and Unbelievers in Eighteenth-century France*, Oxford, 1981, p. 313; see also Lebrun, *Les hommes et la mort*, p. 486.

4. João Pina-Cabral and Rui Feijó, 'Conflicting Attitudes to Death in Modern Portugal', in Feijó et al. (eds.), *Death in Portugal*, Oxford, 1983, pp. 17–43; Maria de Fátima Mello Ferreira, 'Formas de mobilização popular no liberalismo' and Rui Feijó, 'Mobilização rural e urbana na "Maria da Fonte" ', in M. H. Pereira et al. (eds.), *O liberalismo na Peninsula Ibérica*, Lisbon, 1982, II, pp. 161–168, 183–193.

5. See Feijó et al., *Death in Portugal*, passim. On Brazil see for example the works of Luís da Câmara Cascudo, *Anúbis e outros ensaios*, Rio de Janeiro, 1983;

Dicionário do folclore Brasileiro, Brasília, 1972; and *Antologia do folclore brasileiro*, São Paulo, 1956, among others. See also José de Souza Martins (ed.), *A morte e os mortos na sociedade brasileira*, São Paulo, 1983, and the bibliography cited therein.

6. On African death culture see Louis-Vincent Thomas, *La mort africaine: Idéologie funéraire en Afrique noire*, Paris, 1982; Peter Morton-Williams, 'Yoruba Responses to the Fear of Death', *Africa*, 30: 1, 1960, pp. 34–40; S. F. Nadel, *Nupe Religion*, New York, 1970, pp. 121–130; M. L. Rodrigues Areia, *L'Angola traditionnel*, Coimbra, 1974, pp. 152–168. On Afro-Brazilian death: Roger Bastide, *Estudos afro/brasileiros*, São Paulo, 1973, ch. 6; Juana and Deoscoredes dos Santos, 'O culto dos ancestrais na Bahia', in C. Moura (ed.), *Oloorisa*, São Paulo, 1981, pp. 153–188; Jean Ziegler, *Os vivos e a morte*, Rio de Janeiro, 1977, among others.

7. On black brotherhoods see A. J. R. Russell-Wood, 'Black and Mulatto Brotherhoods in Colonial Brazil', *Hispanic American Historical Review*, 54: 4, 1974, pp. 567–602; Patricia Mulvey, 'The Black Lay Brotherhoods of Colonial Brazil', Ph.D., CUNY, 1976.

8. Jean Baptiste Debret, *Viagem pitoresca e histórica ao Brasil*, São Paulo, 1940 [orig. 1835], II, plate 16. See also Adalgisa A. Campos, 'Notas sobre os rituais de morte na sociedade escravista', *Revista do Departamento de História da UFMG*, 1988, pp. 109–122.

9. Arquivo Público do Estado da Bahia (Bahia State Public Archives, hereafter APEBa), *Livro de registro de testamentos*, vol. 23, fl. 80. These and other aspects of old Brazilian ways of death are discussed at length in Reis, *A morte é uma festa*, passim; see also Katia M. Q. Mattoso, *Testamentos de escravos libertos na Bahia no século XIX*, Salvador, 1979; and Maria Inês C. de Oliveira, *O liberto*, São Paulo, 1988.

10. R. Huntington and P. Metcalf, *Celebrations of Death*, Cambridge, 1979, Part II.

11. White as African funerary color: Thomas, *La mort africaine*, p. 215; Melville Herskovits, *Dahomey: An Ancient West African Kingdom*, Evanston, 1967, I, p. 353; Ziegler, *Os vivos e a morte*, pp. 28–29.

12. Victor Turner, *Revelation and Divination in Ndembu Ritual*, Ithaca, 1975, p. 197; APEBa, *Inventário e testamento*, vol. 731, doc. 1.

13. A. H. de Oliveira Marques, *A sociedade medieval portuguesa*, Lisbon, 1974, p. 211.

14. Based on parish records of the Arquivo da Cúria de Salvador (Curia Archives of Salvador).

15. Armand Marcescheau to the French Minister of Foreign Affairs, Salvador, 22 February 1831, Archives du Ministère des Relations Extérieures (Paris), *Correspondance Politique, Brésil*, vol. 12, fl. 206–207.

16. See for example, Thomas Lindley, *Narrative of a Voyage to Brazil*, London, 1808, p. 275 (Lindley, an Englishman arrested in Bahia for smuggling, was himself an assiduous funeral-goer); Maximiliano des Wied-Neuwied, *Viagem ao Brasil*, São Paulo, 1940 (orig. 1820–21), II, p. 450.

17. Based on data from *post mortem* inventories from the APEBa.

18. APEBa, *Livro de registro de testamentos*, vol. 6, fl. 25v–26.

19. 'Compromisso da Irmandade de São Benedicto Erecta no Convento de São Francisco . . . [1770]', ch. 11, Arquivo Nacional da Torre do Tombo (Lisbon), *Ordem de Christo*, vol. 293.

20. APEBa, *Inventários*, no. 04/1721/2193/03, fls. 2, 8, 8v.

21. Cited by Mulvey, 'The Black Lay Brotherhoods', p. 197.

22. D. Sebastião Monteyro da Vide, *Constituiçoens Primeyras do Arcebispado da Bahia, etc.*, Coimbra, 1720, LIII: 843.

23. APEBa, *Livro de registro de testamentos*, vol. 24, fl. 65; vol. 17, fl. 162v.

24. This inscription, which has disappeared, was registered in the 1940s by Fellipe Scarlata, 'Inscrições lapidares da cidade do Salvador', 1949, fl. 405, mss. Arquivo Municipal de Salvador (Municipal Archives of Salvador, hereafter AMS).

25. APEBa, *Inventários*, no. 04/1723/2193/03, fl. 13.

26. Ferdinand Denis, *Brasil*, Salvador, 1955 [orig. 1837], I, p. 266.

27. Manoel M. Rebouças, *Dissertation sur les inhumations en général (leurs résultats fâcheux lorsqu'on les pratique dans les églises et dans l'enceinte des villes, et les moyens d'y remédier par des cimetières extra-muros)*, Paris, 1831 (a Portuguese translation was published in Bahia in 1832).

28. José Martins da Cruz Jobim, 'Reflexões sobre a inhumação dos corpos', *Semanário de Saúde Pública*, 11 (12 March 1831): 60: J. C. da Costa e Oliveira, 'Inconvenientes de se fazerem os enterros dentro das Igrejas', *Archivo Médico Brasileiro*, II: 2(Oct. 1845): 31.

29. AMS, *Livro de posturas, 1829–1859*, vol. 566, fls. 15–20; AMS, *Oficios ao governo*, vol. 111.8, fls. 233–234; Romualdo to the Minister of Justice, Rio de Janeiro, 28 August 1834, APEBa, *Câmaras*, maço 1433; Municipal Council's minutes of session, 31 October 1834, AMS, *Atas da Câmara*, 1833–34, vol. 9.41, fl. 146.

30. The petition and the law are registered in *Resoluções e Leis do Governo*, Salvador, 1837, unpaginated.

31. APEBa, *Legislativa, Abaixo-assinados, 1835–36*, maço 979 and 980. On social and political unrest in Bahia in the 1820s and 1830s see João J. Reis, *Slave Rebellion in Brazil: The Muslim Uprising of 1835 in Bahia*, Baltimore, 1993.

32. On the romanization of the Brazilian Church see João F. Hauck et al., *História da Igreja no Brasil*, Petrópolis, 1985, ch. 3; and on Romualdo's role, Candido Costa e Silva and Rolando Azzi, *Dois estudos sobre Romualdo*, Salvador, 1982, 17–38.

33. APEBa, *Cemiterada*, maço 2858, fl. 22 on the police inquiry.

34. APEBa, *Legislativa, Representações, 1834–1925*, uncatalogued.

35. APEBa, *Cemiterada*, maço 2858, throughout.

36. Sigmund Freud, "Reflections upon War and Death," in Philip Rieff, ed., *S. Freud: Character and Culture*, New York, 1963, p. 127.

4

The Vintem Riot and Political Culture: Rio de Janeiro, 1880

Sandra Lauderdale Graham

Sandra Lauderdale Graham holds degrees in both sociology and history and teaches as senior lecturer in history at the University of Texas at Austin. Her work focuses on the social history of nineteenth-century Brazil. In addition to articles on slavery, women, and legal change, she has published a book on urban domestic life, House and Street: The Domestic World of Servants and Masters in Nineteenth-Century Rio de Janeiro *(1988). She is currently working on two research projects, one on slavery and the other on family conflict and death.*

In this essay Professor Graham analyzes the first of two major riots to shake the then capital of Brazil in less than twenty-five years (the second is analyzed in Chapter 6). She compares conflicting accounts of the Vintem Riot by participants and authorities and shows how different groups used the riot for their own ends. Finally, she concludes that the riot was one of those decisive moments that traumatized a city and transformed the political culture of its residents.

Rioting marked the first days of January in the summer of 1880 in Rio de Janeiro. They were confusing, uncertain days in which public meetings to protest a one-*vintem* city tramways tax escalated into street violence. Although armed struggle between protesters and the authorities persisted only a few hours, the imprint of the Vintem Riot cut deeply and lastingly into the political life of both the city and the empire by redefining the actors, audience, and stage-setting of political culture.[1] The decade initiated by rioting and influenced by the political style it presaged would continue as one of conflict. By the closing years of the 1880s, the broad contours of Brazilian society would be altered; Parliament would

From *Hispanic American Historical Review* 60, no. 3 (August 1980): 431–49.
© 1980 by Duke University Press. Reprinted by permission.

finally abolish slavery and a republican government would replace the constitutional monarchy of the empire. At the time, however, contemporaries could not know the long-ranging outcomes that their actions would shape. Events of the riot had for them more immediate significance.

During the several decades of Brazil's Second Empire since 1850, politics had been the domain of a socially cohesive, if geographically dispersed, and essentially secure elite. Politics existed as the exclusive concern of gentlemen acting in what they would have unhesitatingly claimed to be everyone's best interest. Within Parliament they might differ bitterly, yet they differed with the comfortable sense that the business of politics would be conducted and contained according to rules they all accepted. It was a politics based finally on patronage and deference, where political favors were carefully weighed against electoral advantage. To that fine balancing act, the public might appear as spectator or commentator but not as active, initiating participant. A shared vision of those rules formed the political culture dominant before 1880.[2]

Events in Rio in January of 1880 rent that view. The Riot of the Vintem marked a decisive shift in the ways political action could be publicly and directly stated and understood and by whom. That is, it marked a shift in political culture. City residents, respectable but without formal political connections or political positions, for the first time in over forty years engaged in demonstrations of popular protest.[3] Poor workers from the city's slums, also for the first time, joined demonstrations. Cabinet ministers, city councilmen, members of Parliament, and journalists publicly assumed new political postures consciously altered as a result of the riot. Clearly and emphatically they stated the several larger meanings they attributed to the riot, identifying links between the riot and other issues. All participants—whether those already recognized as political spokesmen or those who remained nameless—behaved in dramatically novel ways. They took politics to the city's streets and squares, they distributed pamphlets, they paraded past newspaper offices soliciting support, they confronted police, army, and emperor, they defied the law. Their socially visible methods engaged the entire Rio community in political issues that ultimately challenged basic social structures. In these ways, Rio residents projected the first traces of a new political style, a style that would be elaborated during the decade of the 1880s. The Vintem Riot proved to be for contemporaries an "instructive explosion" and, because instructive for them, it is instructive for us.[4]

The riot occurred against a background of urban changes that had already transformed the city politically, economically, and demographically. Particularly since becoming Portugal's royal court in 1808 and then capital of an independent empire from 1822, Rio served as Brazil's political center. Meanwhile the country's economic force had also shifted south to Rio. Through its port passed Brazil's great wealth in coffee bound for European and North American markets. At its docks foreign merchants unloaded the endlessly varied goods supplied to wealthy Brazilians from the capitals of Europe. Even after the end of the African slave trade in about 1850, slaves from northern provinces continued to enter the more prosperous south and center regions through Rio de Janeiro.[5]

Changes in political and economic importance propelled shifts that altered the city's social composition. In the fifty-year period up to 1870, Rio's population had doubled. But in only twenty years, from 1870 to 1890, Rio again more than doubled to a total population of over 500,000. In large measure, the city's swollen population can be attributed to the influx of European migrants who numbered nearly 80,000 between 1870 and 1890.[6] Midway in that span of spectacular growth the 1880 riot occurred.

Rio's upper- and middle-class citizenry did not reckon that all change had yielded increased power, wealth, or progress. Certainly by 1880 city life had produced its own unique problems. Rio residents voiced alarm over the multiplying slums that festered in the low-lying center of the city. Poor Brazilians together with Italian and Portuguese immigrants, freed blacks, and slaves who worked for wages despite their bondage crowded into those damp, dark, and filthy rooms. Slum dwellers in these "beehives," as they were commonly and derogatorily named, posed a visible threat to public health and by extension to public order, at least for more privileged Rio residents. The issue became for them a matter of how to control the laboring classes.[7] Against mounting preoccupation with public order, the riot of the Vintem exploded.

Passed by Parliament the previous October in order to bolster government revenue at a time of national financial crisis, the tram tax was one of several taxes leveled specifically at urban dwellers. In its final form, however, the tax applied only to the city of Rio and not to other cities of the empire. Nor did it fall to the tram companies, as originally proposed, but instead beginning January 1 it was to be collected directly from passengers on all city tram lines.[8] Rio residents believed they had reason, then, for discontent, and as December passed their discontent mounted.

Four days before the tax would become effective, dissatisfaction developed into popular protest when a crowd 5,000-strong gathered, probably in response to a newspaper announcement, in the spacious and treeless Campo de São Cristovão near the imperial palace. Roused by a speech from the colorful and provocative José Lopes da Silva Trovão, a militant Republican journalist and self-declared gadfly, the crowd set off to deliver to Emperor Pedro II a petition requesting that he revoke the "unjust and vexatious" tram tax.[9] That such a demonstration took place at all and that it succeeded in drawing a huge crowd were events unparalleled in the city's recent history.

Faced with a most unusual situation for which there could be no well-tried response, authorities reacted with alarm. The festive air of the procession quickly evaporated as marchers found their way to the imperial residence, blocked by a threatening array of police that included District Police Chief Felix José da Costa e Silva, backed by a line of police cavalry and 100 secret agents armed with truncheons. The crowd obeyed Costa's gesture to halt and then turned back across the square, away from the palace toward the city. The meeting finished quietly, as Trovão had promised, but not before he accused police of unlawfully "forcing themselves between the people and the emperor."[10]

Besides a startling encounter with the police, the protesters' attempt to petition the emperor had failed—as Trovão intended it should. No head of state could open his private residence to 5,000 demonstrators, but by not acting personally and firmly at the start, arranging early to meet with a delegation from the march, and relying instead on armed police, Pedro II was drawn into the Vintem controversy, cast in a most ineffectual role. Too late that day he sent Trovão a message that he would receive a delegation.[11] Trovão refused the invitation. "The people," he declared, "would never return having once had the palace doors closed to them by secret police who . . . appeared more as the toughs they really were than the maintainers of law and order they pretended to be."[12] The distance between protesters and the authorities had been widened and the emperor's authority weakened.

The unusual events of the next days moved with tense, uncertain speed. Trovão and others organized, by means of leaflets scattered throughout the city, a second meeting scheduled for January 1, the first day of the tax.[13] No longer did they appeal for its revocation; instead they now urged passengers to resist payment, thus openly challenging the law. That change in purpose, symbolized by their electing to meet at a central, downtown square, pushed the controversy a step further. The second meeting went not to an intransigent emperor but to the people.

Despite an air of growing expectation, the early hours of January 1 passed calmly. Trams of the four city lines ran on schedule without serious protest from passengers who generally paid the tax.[14] The mid-day rally, with participants numbering about 4,000, once again ended in a protest march. From the square they proceeded through Rio's most fashionable and densely commercial center toward the Largo do São Francisco from which all downtown trams departed.[15] A block from their destination, however, at the corners of the streets Uruguayana and Ouvidor, the march divided into several groups: two remained there while others continued to the Largo do São Francisco or dispersed to other parts of the city.[16] Whether they acted spontaneously or followed a previously agreed-upon plan remains unknown.

In either case, at that moment peaceable protest triggered into violence. Rioters tore up tram tracks, stabbed mules, and overturned cars belonging to several different lines. They fired pistols and beat up tram conductors. With the arrival of each new tram, the tumult mounted. The overturned cars, reinforced with paving stones and lengths of track, served as barricades at the intersections of Uruguayana with the streets Ouvidor and Sete de Setembro. From late afternoon on, tram companies suspended all services.[17]

Police, unsuccessful in their attempt to stop the rioters, combined with over 600 army infantry and cavalry to confront them in Uruguayana Street. Commander Antonio Enéas Gustavo Galvão's orders were to take the barricades, break their resistance, and thereby disperse the rioters. To that end, Galvão ordered the cavalry to charge the crowd. Soldiers advanced on the barricades, swords drawn. Some fired shots. At the same time in the Largo do São Francisco cavalry charged into a crowd of protesters who tried to obstruct trams.[18] Rain, as much as the army, eventually cleared the streets, and by eleven o'clock that night the city was again quiet. Only small groups of curious onlookers wandered the streets. But while doctors treated the fifteen or twenty wounded, on Uruguayana three men lay dead. The Vintem Riot had had its martyrs; lighted candles flickered at the places where they lay.[19]

Over the next several days, only lesser, isolated disturbances took place although troops remained on alert. By January 5, police could report that "nothing occurred to disturb the public calm." Trams ran regularly; only an occasional passenger refused to pay the tax.[20] Officially the Vintem Riot had ended. Rio de Janeiro had returned to order.

The straightforward reporting of external events kaleidoscopes into very different renderings, however, when seen from the distinct accounts provided by participants. According to Commander Galvão's report, he ordered troops to advance only after rioters had fired shots. Observers who had watched the melee from nearby office windows claimed that cavalry had charged without provocation and that mounted police had even pursued people into shops where they had hastily sought refuge.[21] Not only did participants differ over the sequence of events, but at crucial points they differed profoundly over the meaning of what had taken place. José Carlos de Carvalho, the one rioter to leave a lengthy, detailed version of what occurred, characterized the violence of the protesters as wholly defensive. He explained how that understanding came to him during those confused, hot hours: "Once in the streets, we knew [we had] to organize means of protecting the people against attack by the authorities. . . . We overturned trams . . . with the aim of avoiding charges from the cavalry."[22] For the police that "necessary defense" was wanton destruction directed against the tram companies, and their own response, in turn, defensive. No additional information would have convinced Carvalho, after the riot, that the combined forces of police and army ever intended to permit a peaceful end to the protest. Similarly no statement about the protesters would have altered the police chief's view that "intervention by the public authorities became inevitable."[23]

It was also true, however, that before the rioting began neither protesters nor authorities could have held such crystallized views of one another. The Vintem Riot did not begin as a confrontation between sides able to predict or identify in a meaningful way one another's moves. Rather, violence spiraled out of what was an uncertain situation, where no precedents or agreed-upon rules guided action. Each side tested the reaction of the other until suddenly the balance tipped toward bloody conflict. Their separate understandings of what the rioting signified, fixed by their actions in those few bewildering hours, remained in contradiction. This contradiction was itself a new result of the riot: each side now knew where the other stood.

The Vintem Riot instructively summoned the beginnings of a new political style. Not only did bitterly divergent interpretations harden around the rioting itself, but sizeable numbers of city residents had come forward to engage in new forms of participation.

Demonstrators had succeeded in dragging politics from the chambers of Parliament into the city squares, while rioters made real the tough fact that street violence could be an element in the political equation. For the authorities, their presence justified an alert police force and even armed repression.

Simultaneously city residents served as audience to the play of political action. Dom Pedro had revealed himself to be an unresponsive ruler, lacking in vision, energy, and decisiveness. All sides condemned the emperor's refusal to deal responsively but firmly with the early protests against the tax in such a manner as to have avoided the rioting. The audience of city residents had witnessed the frailty of old-style politics that had, when challenged, immediately resorted to the extreme of military repression. Before the first public meeting on December 28, authorities had insisted that the tax was law and must therefore be enforced. If necessary, conductors could rely on promised police assistance in collecting the tax. There was even the suggestion that public meetings be banned.[24] Thus authorities had assumed that by loud threats they could contain an uncertain and increasingly tense situation. The rioting of January 1 proved them wrong. Even the emperor acknowledged that "during almost forty years it has not been necessary to employ force such as this against the people."[25] What mattered more than the failure of customary controls, however, was that an entire city had witnessed that failure.

Although the rioting had subsided by late on January 1, implications of the riot for a changed political culture grew steadily after that day. Those men already prominent in positions of public power saw refracted in the riot still other issues to which they assigned their particular meaning and emphasis. Unlike those who had gone to the streets, they decried not the tax but rather the government's unrestrained use of armed violence. But like the protesters, they chose hastily prepared and, for Rio in 1880, unconventional means by which to express their condemnation. As traditional political actors they transgressed previously agreed-upon forms of political behavior.

Among those critical of measures taken by the government to quell the rioting, none censured it so severely or with such influence as a group of eight Liberal senators and deputies who convened on January 3 at Senator José Ignácio Silveira da Motta's home on Carmo street in the center of Rio. The Carmo meeting included, besides Silveira da Motta, Francisco Otaviano de Almeida Rosa, Antonio Marcelino Nunes Gonçalves, Carlos Leôncio de Carvalho,

José da Costa Azevedo, Joaquim Batista Pereira, Joaquim Nabuco, and Joaquim Saldanha Marinho.[26] In time all would declare their commitment to abolitionist or republican causes—most to both —but in January 1880 no such encompassing motive drew them together.

Instead their urgent and extraordinary meeting was required, Silveira da Motta insisted, because "silence in the face of recent events would be a violation of duty."[27] In the manifesto which they released to the press, they stingingly charged that on January 1 "military forces had fired on unarmed people."[28] They further took up the accusation that military and police had prevented the people from reaching the imperial palace to deliver their petition to the emperor. Against the "arbitrariness and crimes of the government," they pledged their firm defense and protection to the "suffering people."[29] Implications of the Carmo meeting were far-reaching. The meeting powerfully represented a defiant move to take up a popular cause, unprecedented for so influential a group of men. Their defiance had, however, an additional meaning. Urban residents without established political ties, but ready to take direct political action, represented an untapped source of power.

To know more fully who the protesters and rioters were remains a nagging puzzle. Police records that might identify those who had participated apparently do not exist and perhaps never did, for accounts suggest that police singled out only a few "leaders" for arrest. Some inconclusive glimpses do indicate, however, that those who attended the rallies were not the same persons who destroyed tramcars and stabbed mules. Nor did the various motives of the different groups necessarily coincide.

Those who joined rallies to protest the tax appear to have been persons of modest but regular incomes—salaried bureaucrats or salesmen—decently dressed, literate.[30] Clearly they had cause to object to a tax that solely burdened an urban population and that fell hardest on those dependent on public transportation. In all likelihood, their protest was aimed not exclusively at the tram tax, although it was the most visible and hence easiest to attack, but at the series of new, direct taxes that made even more precarious their none-too-secure social position.[31]

Sharply in contrast to those respectable citizens, the actual rioters were identified by contemporaries as poor workers, members of the "lower class of our population," or "persons of little importance." It was widely acknowledged that the poor could not afford to ride trams regularly so that whatever grievances the rioters' action reflected they were not immediate economic ones caused by increased tram fares.[32] Further, the three men killed during the rioting were described as troublesome immigrants already wanted by the police, two for deportation.[33] Whether rioters were in fact the rough characters alleged by police or whether this was the means by which authorities attempted to discredit them is not possible to say. Clearly, however, the Vintem Riot had drawn together at least briefly several distinct conflicts, each with its own actors.

In early January the question of who would gain control of the power represented by active and outspoken city residents lay unresolved. The Carmo Liberals were astute enough to assess what was at stake. By their support, they sought to draw within their formal political control those newly displayed popular sympathies. If they acted as much from concern for their own power as from commitment to the issue of police and military violence, they also immediately recognized that henceforth politicians would have to address issues and publicly justify actions in terms that at least acknowledged the specifically urban concerns of a specifically urban population. Swiftly, irrevocably, the conduct of politics had altered in 1880 to include city dwellers heretofore silent, whose interests had been presumed, not hotly voiced nor seriously heard.

Political culture was further transformed when the eight senators and deputies, by their decision to meet, connected the significance of the Vintem Riot to the two debates that had dominated Parliament during its recently adjourned 1879 session. The first debate had turned on Liberal opposition to their own ministry's proposed electoral reform bill.[34] The thrust of the bill was toward diminishing monarchical power. The few radical Liberals who opposed it, including those who would later meet at Carmo, had done so not because it would curb the emperor's power, a move they fully supported, but because it failed to broaden the suffrage. Other Liberals opposed it merely on procedural grounds. In an improbable alliance with the Conservative party, the dissident Liberals defeated the bill despite strong support in the chamber and thus seriously weakened their own ministry's position.[35] Animosities and bitterness over the issue hung heavily in the sultry January air.

The second debate concerned Minister of the Treasury Afonso Celso de Assis Figueiredo's determined effort to bring down a balanced budget in the face of straitened economic circumstances. Retrospectively the eight senators and deputies at Carmo reversed their position regarding the tram tax and the budget of which it was a part. Not one of them had spoken against the tax or the final

budget during formal discussion in Parliament. Now in their manifesto, they referred to the "odious tax" and to the "exaggerated execution of the vintem tax."[36] Nabuco, when challenged about the
inconsistency of their stance regarding the tax, offered the limp
apology that the style of the Liberal ministry that drew up the budget had been rigidly set and opposition useless.[37] The fact was, however, that earlier they had seen no reason to oppose the budget. Not
until the government acted in ways that the Carmo group judged
brutal and repressive, and especially not until they sensed the importance of popular protest, did they take up the cause against the
tax.

By the time the Vintem exploded in January, the Liberal party
was divided and the ministry's position precarious. The Carmo
meeting exacerbated the strains already apparent. Nearly all those
present had figured among the Liberals most opposed to the electoral bill. To that extent, then, allegiance among them was accom-
plished before the Vintem dispute flared.[38] Their tenuous awareness
of common sympathies was heightened by a shared horror at the
events of the riot, and then rendered formal by the issuance of a
manifesto that projected both their outrage and their consciousness
of solidarity suddenly forged. With their opposition now sharpened,
attack against their own ministry by means of a public manifesto
denouncing its handling of the Vintem Riot dealt the government a
severe blow. The forming of a new cabinet in March 1880 came as
no surprise.

In an important respect, however, the Carmo politicians had
acted well within the dictates of conventional political behavior.
Although they had expressed their opposition in dramatic new form,
they remained, after all, elected representatives of the empire engaged in controversy directed largely against other members of
Parliament. By construing the Vintem controversy as a set of concerns tied to ministerial conduct and their own aim to replace the
ministry, they affirmed the continued and unquestioned dominance
of imperial politics over political interests at other levels. Either
they did not recognize or they chose to ignore that the Vintem Riot
had exposed long-building tension between the city of Rio and the
imperial government. In either case, they neither defended the city's
cause nor openly allied with its spokesmen.

The city was not without spokesmen of its own, however. A
second group met, like the Liberals, in hurried opposition to the
violence of January 1 with the purpose of forming a Peace Committee. Unlike the Liberal group, the committee comprised only

Rio residents, including lawyers, legislators, doctors, former government officials, and businessmen.[39] When, on January 2, the committee declared its concern to restore public order, counseling people to act with calm and prudence, it echoed the desires of the entire city. All Rio, stunned that such violence could tear so quickly at their city, sought a return to order. Committee members did more than counsel, however. They accused police of provoking the riot and fully blamed the government for the "violent acts . . . inflicted upon Brazilians and foreigners . . . and even women and children . . . in the Largo de São Francisco."[40] By this bold denunciation, they determined to impose their particular understanding of the events rather than merely reflect the views of all citizens.

Although several ministers had played a direct role in the dispute, the committee chose to meet with João Lustosa da Cunha Paranaguá, the Minister of War, because he, they insisted, was responsible for the order to fire which had resulted in the death of "unarmed citizens."[41] The conference with Paranaguá ended in stalemate. The committee urged suspension of the tax, while the minister argued that the tax was law which he was obliged to enforce.[42] To those critical of the government, its intransigence was again manifest.

Besides meeting with the Minister of War, the Peace Committee nominated its own doctors to treat the injured. Also, and more importantly, they appointed a group of city lawyers to defend without fee those who had been arrested and denied any formal statement of the charges brought against them.[43] Like the committee, the five lawyers, including Carlos Augusto de Carvalho, brother of José Carlos (one of those arrested), demonstrated keen political skill. With careful deliberation they succeeded in making the government's law-and-order stand appear preposterous. In response to orders issued for the arrest of José do Patrocínio, Lopes Trovão, Joaquim Pedro da Costa, and Ferro Cardoso—all identified by the police as organizers of the protest rallies—the lawyers quickly made public the fact that those detained had not received their legal rights. The chief of police, in tacit acknowledgement of their charge, finally agreed to recognize their petitions for habeas corpus.[44]

Certainly neither the lawyers nor the committee that appointed them represented the widest possible base of Rio interests. Nevertheless, by casting their opposition in terms of law and order they appealed to a sufficiently large section of the city's population to achieve restoration of legal rights. Although the committee lost its bid to suspend the tax, by January 9 even the cautious, often pro-government newspaper, the *Jornal do Comércio*, had joined their cause when it published a formal request to the emperor to suspend the tax until Parliament could convene to consider the matter.[45] The tax remained, but so did the political differences now sharpened by a group of Rio citizens acting independently.

Just as imposition of the tax had drawn popular protest, the subsequent riot had compelled groups to form in determined opposition against measures they viewed as severe violations of individual rights. Members of the imperial legislature denounced by extraordinary means what they judged as the government's unwarranted use of armed force, while citizens' groups, with distinctly local ties, had further underscored and condemned the government's extreme and violent methods, at the same time calling for reasoned and orderly conduct from everyone. Like the Carmo Liberals, city spokesmen had employed urgent and novel means to express their alarm. Together the two groups contributed to a new understanding by both leaders and citizens of how political opposition might be conducted.

All the more strangely, then, the Rio Municipal Council with legitimate local authority and its interests at stake elected to take no stand. On January 4 the *Jornal do Comércio* published a letter sent to the municipal council requesting that a special session of the council be "arranged urgently" to consider what statement it would make to the imperial government.[46] The signers of the letter, two of whom were members of the council, failed in their effort. The council refused to convene an extraordinary session on grounds that it did not want to exacerbate existing tensions. It did stress, however, that the imperial government, because it refused to withdraw the tax, should itself evolve means to end the "suffering" caused by the tax.[47]

The council's statement, in fact, masked long-running conflicts with the government. Because Rio served as court of the empire, its municipal council occupied the unique position of dealing directly with the imperial government rather than with an intermediary provincial one. As a result, the extent and jurisdiction of council authority frequently appeared ambiguous or clashed openly with imperial authority. The council's posture toward the government, if hostile, was also vulnerable. The council could not, as members correctly understood, be seen to endanger public order, for too easily they could be blamed for the violence and disorder caused by the riot. At the same time, they had no power to take such firm alternative action as suspending the tax. Faced with that dilemma, they remained silent. Their hesitation underscored the importance of the Vintem Riot as an instructive, shaping event.

The council's grievances became abundantly clear to Rio residents, however, largely through the prolific efforts of a contributor to the *Jornal do Comércio* who wrote under the pseudonym of "Lord Melville." In letters that appeared well before the actual rioting on January 1, "Lord Melville" identified the two issues over which council and government most abrasively clashed: revenue for the city and city authority over public improvements, especially those involving tramway operations.[48] He argued, and cogently so, that revenue derived from the tax ought to be remitted to the municipal council in order to finance city services, not to the imperial treasury. The government, in his view, was confiscating much-needed city revenue. He further charged the government with usurping council authority to administer contracts with the tram companies, matters he deemed best handled by the council acting in the city's interests.[49]

On both counts "Lord Melville" was well informed. We can see from other evidence the slow accretion of hostilities that built toward January 1880. The council's major source of revenue, the sale of municipal licenses, hardly sufficed.[50] It therefore depended on the imperial government for additional funds as well as for approval of its budget. In September 1879, for example, the government refused to grant a loan the council had requested for filling in a swamp as a sanitation measure. Tersely, a minister advised the council to avail itself of any funds that property owners, as the beneficiaries, might provide.[51] Council tempers flared on another occasion when Parliament demanded that they submit in triplicate documents concerning council expenditure, implying council incompetence and possible corruption.[52] Although the council hesitated to make known its position on the riot, its outgoing president, Adolfo Bezerra de Menezes, in his final report decried both the restrictions imposed on the council's right to conduct its own affairs and the "nearly total deficiencies" of resources needed to carry out its obligations.[53] In other instances, the government contradicted municipal authority over administration of tram company operation and, according to Menezes, the council had no way to resist government reprisals if it refused to acquiesce.[54]

The council's accommodating stance in early January, then, concealed its continuing tensions with the government. Although its own position remained tenuous, council business would no longer be ignored as the largely inconsequential concern of a privileged few. Residents now watched as what they had come to regard as their demands for services and for social order were publicly debated. If the council remained silent, newspapers and individual council members through the newspapers did not. As Rio grew in size, in power, and in wealth, the question of who would control the city became acute. The municipal council had strong reasons to want imperial governmental authority circumscribed and represented, therefore, a potentially radical challenge. The Vintem Riot proved instructive in laying those conflicts before an increasingly alert and interested public.

The noisy clash of the Vintem Riot echoed over the next several months. After the Sinimbú ministry faltered in the face of the summer's disturbances, Liberal senator José Antonio Saraiva formed a new government in March 1880 and opened a way for an end to the tram tax. Tram company directors, in April, sent representatives to the government requesting the tax be abolished. One of the Carmo politicians, Batista Pereira, presented to Parliament a project to revoke it. Saraiva himself dealt the final blow when he declared, on opening the May session of Parliament, that had he been in Rio on January 1, he too would have refused to pay the vintem tax. He formally condemned the tax in a senate speech the following September. The tax thus discredited, passengers increasingly refused to pay, until finally on September 5 the government was forced to suspend it.[55]

More distant yet persistent reverberations would be heard, however, throughout the rest of the decade. In 1881 the Saraiva government brought through Parliament an electoral reform bill that not merely limited the emperor's power but also extended suffrage to non-Catholics, naturalized citizens, and freedmen. A direct link joined the 1880 riot with the bill's eventual success, for in 1881 its most determined supporters included Francisco Otaviano de Almeida Rosa, Joaquim Saldanha Marinho, and Joaquim Nabuco— all of whom had been members of the Carmo group.[56]

Even more importantly, dissident Liberals under Nabuco's leadership formed the Brazilian Anti-Slavery Society in July 1880. By year's end still other activists from the Vintem Riot counted among those who vigorously renewed the campaign to abolish slavery. Among the society's sixteen founding members, at least six had participated in events of the riot.[57] Throughout the 1880s José do Patrocínio, named by police as an instigator of the riot and one of those denied habeas corpus, proved relentless in his determination to see slavery abolished.[58] Before the riot, abolitionist activity had been principally a legislative concern. Even there the committed Nabuco in 1879 found it necessary to introduce measures that were not boldly abolitionist but merely budgetary in nature—an increased tax on owning slaves, for example.[59] The riot had clearly demonstrated that politics played more publicly and more popularly had strength. Those who formed the newly focused anti-slavery movement understood that this new political mood could be harnessed to their cause and a larger public appealed to. A politically engaged public meant that a power external to Parliament existed, and to that public the increasingly intense, sometimes bitter, abolitionist press aimed its propaganda.[60]

Although militant republicans had figured among those most actively engaged in organizing the protest rallies, neither the rallies nor the rioting can be considered as primarily republican agitation. The one Republican in Parliament in 1880, Joaquim Saldanha Marinho, refused to define opposition to the government's handling of the riot as principally Republican in nature. "I would lead the movement [to condemn the government] myself," he declared, "were it not that that would give the movement a Republican signature that it does not have."[61] Nonetheless, 1880 signaled a turning point in Republican party strengths. Several of those most prominent in events of the Vintem Riot were later elected delegates to the First National Republican Congress, including Saldanha Marinho and Lopes Trovão.[62] One contemporary of the early republic, in 1891, explicitly acknowledged the catalytic role performed by the Riot of the Vintem. It had heralded, in his view, the essential qualities that guided formation of the republic: "popular independence, dignity, and pride."[63] Politics from 1880 had appealed to a more diverse public, consciously set to define its own interests. Those who participated in politics, newly fashioned, proved ready to challenge the empire, pushing it to its final collapse in 1889.

City politics in January 1880 portrayed the struggle for local authority. Increasingly central government was seen as unresponsive to the city's changing needs. The issue of central versus federal authority became crucial as the empire crumbled and the scaffolding of a new government was erected. Occasioned by the Vintem Riot, the play of newly defined and uniquely urban interests and of a distinctly urban political style that relied on street rallies and marches, public meetings, lectures and recitals, and a militant prcss would characterize the 1880s in Rio.[64] The crescendo would come in 1888 and 1889 with the abolition of Brazilian slavery and the overthrow of the empire.

Certainly the Vintem Riot did not directly cause those culminating events.[65] Explosion of the Vintem did, however, reveal in a few bewildering days the entrance of inexperienced actors onto the political stage; it displayed alliances recently formed or tested, it clarified issues, and it undercut conventional authority. The Vintem Riot instructed the city in an altered political style, with new rules of what it could mean to engage in political action. Reaction to the Vintem conflict, as much as the scale of the disturbances or their unusual style, indicated that change in imperial politics was occurring. Three respectable establishment groups had not, as everything about nineteenth-century politics might have predicted, joined forces to suppress it as a social threat. And if they recoiled in horror from this violent episode, it was violence done by government authorities that most shocked them. Instead they had responded to the riot as legitimate protest, defended protesters against government abuses, and finally identified with it for political purposes of their own. Seen from the perspective and understandings of those who became participants in the controversy, we glimpse the flux, the uncertainty, the blurriness of events as they sought to render them meaningful. As they shaped that meaning, they changed the emphasis of urban political life in Brazil's major city. The Riot of the Vintem marks one of those brief but decisive moments when the shared understandings of political conduct change. The emperor could not have been more wrong about the riot than when he wrote confidingly to the Countess Barral on January 2, 1880: "I do not believe that the disturbances are political."[66] From the events surrounding the Vintem Riot a new political culture was being forged.

Notes

1. A vintem was worth twenty reis or about one U.S. cent and was the smallest coin of the realm. Political culture refers to a set of socially shared understandings about political behavior as distinct from the formal institutions of government or the arrangement of political parties. For somewhat differing approaches to the study of political culture, compare Gabriel Almond and Sidney Verba, *The Civic Culture: Political Attitudes and Democracy in Five Nations* (Princeton, 1963); Lucien W. Pye and Verba, eds., *Political Culture and Political Development* (Princeton, 1965); Richard R. Fagen, *The Transformation of Political Culture in Cuba* (Stanford, 1969); or Bernard Bailyn, *The Origins of American Politics* (New York, 1968). My own usage comes closest to that suggested by Peter H.

Smith who took political culture to be the "medium or idiom through which political behavior is seen, interpreted, and understood. By imposing conceptual (and often moral) order on patterns of action, it finds significance and 'meaning' in politics. . . ." See his "Political Legitimacy in Spanish America" in Richard Graham and Peter H. Smith, eds., *New Approaches to Latin American History* (Austin, 1974), pp. 229–230. By political culture I refer to the prescriptions and limitations placed upon the ways in which political action may be expressed and by whom, and to how, those statements will then be heard and responded to. Like Smith, I focus on the cultural—on the shared, although not necessarily explicit or fully articulated, expectations and understandings of how politics ought to be conducted, and on the meanings that a society attaches to particular actions in order to render them socially intelligible. Such expectations and understandings are learned as part of the larger culture to which they belong, and they can change. Access to political culture comes not only from attending to the writings of the articulate but also by reconstructing the actions or, better, the sequences of action that make up events such as a riot. For a wonderfully provocative and tough-minded examination of the concept of culture, see Clifford Geertz, *The Interpretation of Cultures* (New York, 1973).

2. In examining the nature of politics during the Second Empire, historians have concentrated on parliamentary politics—on legislative debates, on party divisions and alliances, on disputes within ministries, and on the relationship between Parliament and the emperor. See Joaquim Nabuco, *Um Estadista do Império: Nabuco de Araújo, Sua Vida, Suas Opiniões, Sua Época* (Rio de Janeiro, 1936); Sérgio Buarque de Holanda, *O Brasil Monárquico: Do Império à República*, vol. VII of Buarque de Holanda, ed., *História Geral da Civilização Brasileira* (São Paulo, 1972); João Camillo de Oliveira Torres, *A Democracia Coroada: Teoria Política do Brasil*, 2d ed. (Petrópolis, 1964). Those historians who have sought to explain the exercise of political power in terms of economic interests have most commonly portrayed large landowners as politically dominant, for example, Buarque de Holanda, *O Brasil Monárquico: Do Império à República*. In *A Política Geral do Brasil* (São Paulo, 1930), José Maria dos Santos argues that landowners together with capitalists and merchants, in the service of landed interests, opposed liberal efforts to bring about abolition and direct elections. He never specifies which groups represented the liberal forces, although he does see them as eventually victorious. Raymundo Faóro, while not disputing that an elite controlled political power, does argue that the elite was an urban one, comprised especially of bureaucrats. See his *Os Donos do Poder: Formação do Patronato Político Brasileiro*, rev. ed., 2 vols. (Porto Alegre, 1975). In any case, the relative power of competing groups within the elite is not my debate. My point, borne out by these several histories of the empire, is simply that politics had belonged to elites who perceived scant need to justify decisions or to take up issues from outside their own circles.

3. Other disturbances did occur after 1850, perhaps most notably the Quebra-Quilos revolt in 1874–1875. Although it achieved its immediate aims, it apparently altered neither political relationships nor the cultural understandings of politics. See Roderick J. Barman, "The Brazilian Peasantry Reexamined: The Implications of the Quebra-Quilos Revolt, 1874–1875," *Hispanic American Historical Review*, 57 (Aug. 1977), 401–424.

4. I borrow the metaphor "instructive explosion" from Clifford Geertz who used it to identify those events that mark moments of decisive political change. Geertz, *Islam Observed: Religious Development in Morocco and Indonesia* (New Haven, 1968), p. 1.

5. For background on these aspects of Rio de Janeiro's economic history, see Caio Prado Júnior, *História Econômica do Brasil*, 15th ed. (São Paulo, 1972); Afonso de E. Taunay, *Pequena História do Café no Brasil, 1727–1937* (Rio de Janeiro, 1945); Richard Graham, *Britain and the Onset of Modernization in Brazil, 1850–1914* (Cambridge, 1968); Herbert S. Klein, *The Middle Passage: Comparative Studies in the Atlantic Slave Trade* (Princeton, 1978).

6. Brazil, Directoria Geral de Estatística, *Recenseamento da População do Império do Brasil a que se Procedeu no Dia 1 de Agosto de 1872, Município Neutro* (Rio de Janeiro, 1873–1876), p. 58; *Recenseamento Geral da República dos Estados Unidos do Brasil em 31 de Dezembro de 1890, Distrito Federal* (Rio de Janeiro, 1895), pp. 169, 177; *Recenseamento do Rio de Janeiro Realizado em 20 de Setembro de 1906* (Rio de Janeiro, 1907), pp. 117–118; *Synopse do Recenseamento Realizado em 1 de Setembro de 1920. População do Brasil. Resumo do Censo Demográphico por Estados, Capitaes e Municípios. Confronto do Número de Habitantes em 1920 com as Populações Recenseadas Anteriormente* (Rio de Janeiro, 1922), pp. 37, 39.

7. No genuine social history yet exists for Rio in the second half of the nineteenth century. See Fernando Nascimento Silva et al., *Rio de Janeiro em Seus Quatrocentos Anos: Formação e Desenvolvimento da Cidade* (Rio de Janeiro, 1965), especially pp. 259–298, for description of efforts to alter the city physically and to improve sanitation; Adolfo Morales de los Rios Filho, *O Rio de Janeiro Imperial* (Rio de Janeiro, 1946), sketches the city's social life. For examples of concern over slums and their inhabitants and disease see Junta Central de Higiene Pública to Câmara Municipal, Rio de Janeiro, July 17, 1879; Comissão Sanitária de Santa Anna to Junta Central de Higiene Pública, Rio de Janeiro, Jan. 24, 1880; Secretária da Polícia da Corte to Junta Central de Higiene Pública, Rio de Janeiro, Mar. 3, 1880; all in Estalagens e Cortiços, 1834–1880, Arquivo do Patrimônio Histórico e Artístico do Estado do Rio de Janeiro (hereafter cited as APHA-RJ), Códice 43-1-25, fols. 80v, 99–99v, 121; José Pereira Rego, *Apontamentos sobre a Mortalidade da Cidade do Rio de Janeiro* (Rio de Janeiro, 1878), pp. 22, 71; Presidente da Directoria da [Companhia] Praça da Gloria to Câmara Municipal, Rio de Janeiro, Apr. 11, 1874; Companhia Praça da Gloria to Câmara Municipal, Oct. 31, 1878; in Mercado da Gloria, 1844–1904, APHA-RJ, Códice 61-2-4, fols. 22, 31. For one sustained attempt to control free labor, see Rio de Janeiro (city), Câmara Municipal, *Boletim*, Aug. 29, 1885, p. 90.

8. Afonso Celso de Assis Figueiredo, *Discursos na Sessão Legislativa de 1879* (Rio de Janeiro, 1880), pp. 835–838; Lei n. 2940, Oct. 31, 1879; Decreto n. 7565, Dec. 3, 1879, *Coleção de Leis do Império do Brasil de 1879* (Rio de Janeiro, 1880), pp. 116–121, 748–751.

9. *Gazeta de Notícias*, Dec. 29, 1879, reprinted in *A Província de São Paulo*, Dec. 31, 1879, p. 1; C. J. Dunlop, *Apontamentos para a História dos Bondes no Rio de Janeiro* (Rio de Janeiro, 1953), p. 84; *Revista Illustrada*, special supplement, no. 189, 1880.

10. *Gazeta de Notícias*, Dec. 29, 1879, reprinted in *A Província de São Paulo*, Dec. 31, 1879, p. 1.

11. Ibid.; Pedro II to Countess Barral, Rio de Janeiro, Dec. 28, 1879, in Raymundo Magalhães Júnior, ed., *Dom Pedro II e a Condessa de Barral, através da Correspondência Íntima do Imperador, Anotada e Comentada* (Rio de Janeiro, 1956), p. 295.

12. *Gazeta de Notícias*, Dec. 29, 1879, reprinted in *A Província de São Paulo*, Dec. 31, 1879, p. 1.

13. J. F. de Mello Barreto and Hormeto Lima, *História da Polícia do Rio de Janeiro: Aspectos da Cidade e da Villa Carioca, 1870–1889*, 3 vols. (Rio de Janeiro, n.d.), III, 105; *Jornal do Comércio*, Jan. 2, 1880, p. 1; *A Província de São Paulo*, Jan. 4, 1880, p. 1.

14. Villa Izabel Company, report, Rio de Janeiro, Jan. 2, 1880, APHA-RJ, Códice 55-1-12, p. 26; *Jornal do Comércio*, Jan. 2, 1880, p. 1.

15. José Carlos de Carvalho, *O Livro da Minha Vida na Guerra, na Paz e nas Revoluções, 1847–1910* (Rio de Janeiro, 1912), p. 48; *Jornal do Comércio*, Jan. 2, 1880, p. 1.

16. Report from District Police Chief Carlos Alberto Bulhões Ribeiro to Chief of Police Eduardo Pindahyba de Mattos, Rio de Janeiro, Jan. 1, 1880, published in *Jornal do Comércio*, Jan. 3, 1880, p. 1.

17. Ibid.; Carvalho, *O Livro*, p. 49; Villa Izabel Company, report, Rio de Janeiro, Jan. 2, 1880, APHA-RJ, Códice 55-1-12, p. 26; São Cristovão Company to [?], Jan. 2, 1880, Jan. 3, 1880, Rio de Janeiro, APHA-RJ, Códice 55-1-16, pp. 5–6; ibid. to Minister of Agriculture João Lins Vieira Cansansão de Sinimbú, Rio de Janciro, Feb. 22, 1880, APIIA-RJ, Códice 55-1-20, p. 7; *A Província de São Paulo*, Jan. 4, 1880, p. 2; Barreto and Lima, *História da Polícia*, p. 105.

18. Report from Lieutenant Colonel Antonio Enéas Gustavo Galvão to Lieutenant General Visconde da Gávea, Adjutant General of the army, Rio de Janciro, Jan. 2, 1880, published in *Jornal do Comércio*, Jan. 5, 1880, p. 1.

19. *Jornal do Comércio*, Jan. 2, 1880, p. 1; *A Província de São Paulo*, Jan. 4, 1880, p. 1.

20. Report from Pindahyba de Mattos to Minister of Justice Lafayette Rodrigues Pereira, Rio de Janeiro, Jan. 6, 1880, published in *Jornal do Comércio*, Jan. 8, 1880, p. 1; Villa Izabel Company, report, Rio de Janeiro, Jan. 3, 1880, Jan. 5, 1880, APHA-RJ, Códice 55-1-12, pp. 27–28.

21. Report from Bulhões Ribeiro, Jan. 2, 1880, in *Jornal do Comércio*, Jan. 3, 1880, p. 1; report from Galvão, Jan. 2, 1880, in *Jornal do Comércio*, Jan. 5, 1880, p. 1; *Gazeta de Notícias*, Jan. 6, 1880, reprinted in *A Província de São Paulo*, Jan. 8, 1880, pp. 1–2; *Revista Illustrada*, special supplement, no. 189, 1880.

22. Carvalho, *O Livro*, p. 49.

23. Pindahyba de Mattos, annexo G, p. 4, in Brazil, Ministério da Justiça, *Relatório, 1880* (Rio de Janeiro, 1880).

24. *Jornal do Comércio*, Dec. 14–27, 1879.

25. Pedro II to Countess Barral, Rio de Janeiro, Jan. 1, 1880, in Magalhães Júnior, ed., *Dom Pedro II e a Condessa de Barral*, p. 303.

26. *Jornal do Comércio*, Jan. 4, 1880, p. 1.

27. Ibid.

28. Ibid.; the *Rio News* even went so far as to accuse the secret police of wantonly provoking people to violence. They further reported the charge that "the secret police were engaged, *under orders*, in . . . provoking a conflict with the soldiery," Jan. 5, 1880, p. 2. Later the paper applauded the taking of proceedings against the police *delegado* as a way of making him, as a public official, responsible for his actions, ibid., Jan. 15, 1880, p. 3.

29. *Jornal de Comércio*, Jan. 4, 1880, p. 1.

30. *Revista Illustrada*, special supplement, no. 189, 1880; newspaper articles and editorials clearly addressed a literate public. See the *Jornal do Comércio* and the *Gazeta de Notícias* from Dec. 13, 1879.

31. Lei n. 2940, Oct. 31, 1879; Decreto n. 7565, Dec. 13, 1879, *Coleção de leis do Império do Brasil de 1879* (Rio de Janeiro, 1880), pp. 116–121, 748–751.

32. São Cristovão Company to Minister of Agriculture João Lins Vieira Cansansão de Sinimbú, Rio de Janeiro, Feb. 22, 1880, APHA-RJ, Códice 55-1-12, p. 7; Report from Galvão, Jan. 2, 1880, in *Jornal do Comércio*, Jan. 5, 1880, p. 1; *Gazeta de Notícias*, Dec. 24, 1879, reprinted in *A Província de São Paulo*, Dec. 27, 1879, p. 1.

33. Report from Police Secretary, Rio de Janeiro, Jan. 6, 1880, published in *Jornal do Comércio*, Jan. 8, 1880, p. 1.

34. For a detailed, often provocative account of the bill's stormy history, see Buarque de Holanda, *O Brasil Monárquico: Do Império à República*, pp. 197–234.

35. Ibid., pp. 198, 222, 227; Carolina Nabuco, *The Life of Joaquim Nabuco*, trans. and ed. by Ronald Hilton (Stanford, 1950), pp. 42–43, 51.

36. *Jornal do Comércio*, Jan. 4, 1880, p. 1.

37. *Jornal do Comércio*, Jan. 6, 1880, p. 2; Jan. 7, 1880, p. 2.

38. Buarque de Holanda, *O Brasil Monárquico: Do Império à República*, pp. 197–234.

39. *Jornal do Comércio*, Jan. 3, 1880, p. 1; *A Província de São Paulo*, Jan. 6, 1880, p. 1.

40. Peace Committee, "Boletim," in *A Província de São Paulo*, Jan. 6, 1880, p. 1.

41. *Jornal do Comércio*, Jan. 3, 1880, p. 1.

42. Ibid.

43. *A Província de São Paulo*, Jan. 6, 1880, pp. 1–2.

44. Ibid., p. 2; ibid., Jan. 8, 1880, p. 1; *Gazeta de Notícias*, Jan. 10, 1880, p. 2.

45. *Jornal do Comércio*, Jan. 9, 1880, p. 1.

46. *Jornal do Comércio*, Jan. 4, 1880, p. 1.

47. Rio de Janeiro (city), Câmara Municipal, *Boletim*, Jan. 17, 1880, p. 3.

48. *Jornal do Comércio*, Dec. 13, 1879, p. 4; Dec. 14, 1879, p. 2; Dec. 27, 1879, pp. 2–3.

49. Ibid.

50. Rio de Janeiro (city), Presidente da Câmara Municipal, *Relatório, 1881* (Rio de Janeiro, 1881), p. 34.

51. Rio de Janeiro (city), Câmara Municipal, *Boletim*, Oct. 4, 1879, p. 4.

52. Ibid., Sept. 3, 1879, pp. 43–44.

53. Rio de Janeiro (city), Presidente da Câmara Municipal, *Relatório, 1881* (Rio de Janeiro, 1881), p. 21.

54. Ibid., pp. 62, 105, 112–113.

55. Dunlop, *História dos Bondes*, pp. 91–92; Brazil, Congresso, Câmara dos Deputados, *Anais*, Apr. 29, 1880, Sessão Extraordinária (Rio de Janeiro, 1880), I, 42–46; Carvalho, *O Livro*, p. 51; Villa Izabel Company to Minister of the Treasury José Antonio Saraiva, Rio de Janeiro, Sept. 6, 1880, APHA-RJ, Códice 55-1-12, p. 64; *Jornal do Comércio*, Sept. 4, 1880, p. 1; Sept. 5, 1880, p. 2; *Gazeta de Notícias*, Sept. 6, 1880, p. 1.

56. Buarque de Holanda, *O Brasil Monárquico: Do Império à República*, pp. 240–242.

57. Besides Nabuco, they included José da Costa Azevedo, Joaquim Saldanha Marinho, José Carlos de Carvalho, and José Ferreira de Menezes. Rebecca Baird Bergstresser, "The Movement for the Abolition of Slavery in Rio de Janeiro, Brazil, 1880–1889" (Ph.D. Diss., Stanford University, 1973), pp. 35, 48, 101–102.

58. Osvaldo Orico, *O Tigre da Abolição* (Rio de Janeiro, 1956).

59. Brazil, Congresso, Câmara dos Deputados, *Anais*, Apr. 17, 1879, Primeira Sessão (Rio de Janeiro, 1879), I, 542–552; Nabuco, *The Life of Joaquim Nabuco*, pp. 68–70; Joaquim Nabuco, *Abolitionism: The Brazilian Anti-slavery Struggle*, trans. and ed. by Robert Conrad (Urbana, 1977), especially p. 7.

60. Bergstresser, "The Movement for the Abolition of Slavery," pp. 48–98, 190–191.

61. *Jornal do Comércio*, Jan. 4, 1880, p. 1.

62. Joaquim Saldanha Marinho, Actas das Sessões do Congresso Nacional Republicano, Rio de Janeiro, June 1, 1887, Arquivo Nacional, Códice 768, pp. 1, 13–14.

63. Moreira d'Azevedo, "Imposto do Vintem," *Revista do Instituto Histórico e Geográfico Brasileiro*, 58 (1895), 326.

64. Bergstresser, "The Movement for the Abolition of Slavery," pp. 190–191.

65. Nor have I been concerned here with the complex forces that did cause the abolition of slavery or the fall of the empire. For explanations, see Robert Conrad, *The Destruction of Brazilian Slavery* (Berkeley, 1972); George C. A. Boehrer, "The Brazilian Republican Revolution: Old and New Views," *Luso-Brazilian Review*, 3 (Winter 1966), 43–57; Emília Viotti da Costa, "Sobre as Origens da República," *Anais do Museu Paulista*, 18 (1964), 53–120.

66. Pedro II to Countess Barral, Rio de Janeiro, Jan. 2, 1880, in Magalhães Júnior, ed., *Dom Pedro II e a Condessa de Barral*, p. 301.

5

The 1893 *Bogotazo*:
Artisans and Public Violence in
Late Nineteenth-Century Bogotá

David Sowell

*David Sowell is an associate professor of history at Juniata Col-
lege. His work has focused on artisans in nineteenth-century Colombia. In addition to several articles on various aspects of
working-class history, he is the author of* The Early Colombian
Labor Movement: Artisans and Politics in Bogotá, 1832–1919
(1992) and the compiler of Santander y la opinión angloamericana:
Visión de viajeros y periódicos *(1991). He is currently writing a
history of Latin American social violence as well as a study of
Miguel Perdomo Neira, a healer in the nineteenth-century Andes.*

*In the following essay Professor Sowell views the 1893 riot as
part of Bogotá's tradition of legitimate direct action, which culminated in the well-known* bogotazo *of 1948. He traces how the earlier upheaval developed from a protest by the city's leading Mutual
Aid Society against both a journalist who impugned the honor of
the working classes and the government which failed to invoke the
press law to censor him. Sowell argues that the riot was a reaction
against the deteriorating position of the working classes under a
modernizing regime and shows the importance of artisans in urban
society.*

B ogotá suffered its most severe outbreak of public violence of
the nineteenth century on 15 and 16 January 1893. Indeed, apart
from the *bogotazo* of 9 April 1948, it was perhaps the worst violence that the Colombian capital has ever experienced.[1] For twenty-
four hours the city experienced serious social disorder, which was
brought under control only by the use of regular army troops at a
cost of an unknown number of casualties. Surprisingly, the January 1893 *bogotazo* has not been subjected to serious historical

From *Journal of Latin American Studies* 21 (May 1989): 267–82. © 1989 by
Cambridge University Press. Reprinted by permission of Cambridge University
Press.

examination. The role of craftsmen in the outbreak of violence offers a window in the largely unknown course of artisan political activity in Bogotá after the decline of the Democratic Society of Artisans in the mid-century reform period. More broadly, whereas the relationship between wage labourers and violence has attracted many scholars, the propensity of the artisan class to engage in violent activities in nineteenth-century Colombia (and in Latin America as a whole) deserves more scholarly investigation. What were the causes and the nature of the 1893 riot? Were they typical of nineteenth-century urban violence? Finally, how does the 1893 riot fit within the broad sweep of Colombian collective violence?[2] Before attempting to answer these questions it is necessary to look briefly, by way of background, at Bogotá in the late nineteenth century, its economy and society, at the nature of Colombian politics and, in particular, at the role of artisans in *bogotano* politics and in earlier episodes of urban disorder.

The rapid growth of Bogotá that began in the 1870s helped shape the events of 1893. Earlier in the century, the city had experienced only relatively slow expansion. It had contained about 21,000 people in 1800; some 40,000 in 1843. The 1870 census reported just under 41,000 inhabitants, a questionable figure, but one that certainly reflected sluggish growth. Thereafter, the city's numbers increased rapidly to 95,000 in 1884, 121,000 in 1912, and 211,000 in 1927.[3] At the same time the economy and social character of the Colombian capital began to change. Through the first two-thirds of the century Bogotá's economy was based largely upon the city's function as the country's administrative centre, supported by a modest craft sector and several fledgling industries. Various service and food industries developed after 1870 and by the turn of the century, almost half a dozen substantial industrial establishments were in operation.[4] In the 1860s the well-known social commentator Miguel Samper wrote of a city suffering from a depressed economy, a contentious society, refuse-littered streets, and generally 'miserable' conditions.[5] Beginning in the 1870s, however, as the city began to increase in size, its economic climate improved, in part due to the emergence of coffee as a major export commodity. Only political strife in 1876 and 1885 disrupted the steady expansion of the city's economy. Then in the late 1880s the 'Regeneration' government began to issue large amounts of paper currency, which spawned 20 years of inflationary pressures.[6] By early 1889, pressures on wages resulted in widespread complaints against high food prices and rents, a situation that persisted through the decade of the 1890s.[7]

Nineteenth-century Colombia suffered repeated strife arising out of the fierce partisan contest for political supremacy that raged between Conservatives and Liberals. Bogotá especially felt the effects of this struggle as a result of the dislocation of the national, regional and local economies and the drain on national resources it engendered. The years of Liberal party ascendancy (1849–85) and then the period of Conservative 'Regeneration' (1886–99) were marred by nationwide wars in 1854, 1859–63, 1876–7, 1885, 1895, and 1889–1903 and by far more frequent outbreaks of regional and local fighting. Moreover, electoral violence, that often involved artisan groups, was endemic to the capital, a city with a highly politicised social life. For example, significant street brawls accompanied elections in 1867, 1870, 1879, 1882, and 1895.[8] With the end of the Liberal ascendancy in 1885, a coalition of moderate Liberals and Conservatives combined under the rubric of the National party to write a new constitution that defined the 'Regeneration'. The Nationalists, led by Rafael Núñez (President 1880–2, 1884–94), could not, however, maintain the war-induced unity of their party. By the time of the presidential election of 1891, the party was seriously divided. President Núñez, who had left the highland capital in 1888 for his native Cartagena and in doing so had made the vice president *de facto* head of the country, let it be known that he would continue to serve as titular president, but that the vice president would hold the reins of power. Nationalists proved unable to unite behind a single vice presidential candidate, as both Marceliano Vélez and Miguel Antonio Caro, the architect of the 1886 constitution, emerged as contenders for the position. Núñez finally declared for Caro, whereupon Vélez left the party to run, unsuccessfully, as the candidate of the dissident 'Historical Conservatives'. At the same time the split in the National party inspired attempts in 1892 to revitalise the Liberals, who had been prevented from recovering their losses after 1885 by various forms of restriction and repression, including a press law that prohibited slanderous statements and the so-called 'Law of the Horses' that was employed to curb loosely defined 'political crimes'.[9]

It is against this background, a rapidly growing capital city beset with economic instability and plagued with partisan political strife, that the events of January 1893 must be understood. The immediate clues to the 1893 riot are not, however, to be found primarily in the conflict between Conservatives and Liberals, but in popular reaction to the expansion and 'modernisation' of the city, and, in particular, in the status of Bogotá's artisans. The artisan class occupied an important middle level in *bogotano* society in the nineteenth century because of its relative economic independence. Moreover, many craftsmen were literate, which, together with their income and occupation, gave them in some periods the right to vote.[10] During the Liberal Reform years of 1847–54, craftsmen had formed the Democratic Society of Artisans that pursued an often contradictory policy of attempting to advance the interests of the city's craftsmen (such as the desire for high protective tariffs) while working to further the cause of the Liberal party (which desired, among other changes, to maintain reduced tariffs).[11] In the years that followed the reform period, artisan groups had organised numerous societies dedicated to the advancement of their collective interests, with mutual aid societies the most common after 1870. Inevitably these societies became embroiled in partisan issues, particularly when politicians promised increases in tariff rates in return for artisans' votes. The protectionist stance of the governments of Rafael Núñez led many prominent craftsmen publicly to support him and the Conservative 'Regeneration'.[12]

Almost twenty years before the *bogotazo* of 1893, the bread riot that had engulfed the Colombian capital on 23 January 1875 had evoked an interesting response from leading craftsmen. In the months preceding the riot, the price of bread made from wheat rose by about 20%. Although corn flour was more widely used among the lower classes, inexpensive loaves of wheat bread provided an important supplement to their diet. In the last months of 1874, a coalition of bakers drove up the price of bread and, in January 1875, the same bakers suddenly stopped the production of quarter-peso loaves, a popular-sized bread used with meals or snacks. The move caused indignation among the city's lower classes and acted as the catalyst for the riot. A widely distributed poster of 22 January that demanded 'War and Death to those who make us hungry' drew thousands of people to the Plaza de Bolívar the following day. The protesters appealed to President Santiago Pérez to force prices down, only to be told by the president that in a country with 'free' industry, such actions were illegal. The crowd then imposed its own version of justice by stoning the houses and shops of bakers allegedly involved in monopolistic practices. No one was hurt in the action, but numerous properties suffered heavy damage. In part because of a division in the Liberal party, neither the national government, the state of Cundinamarca, nor the city of Bogotá ordered their forces to act against the rioters, although a state of siege was imposed and troops were readied for possible use.[13]

In the days that followed, numerous leaflets signed by the 'artisans' of the city urged the crowd to end their acquiescence to socioeconomic abuses by asserting their collective strength. At least one observer has seen the riot and the radical leaflets as proof of the political tendencies of Bogotá's artisans. This is a misinterpretation of the event.[14] The language of the circulars and their anonymity suggest, instead, that they probably originated not among the city's craftsmen, but with students at the city's universities who in the past had attempted to manipulate 'popular' passions.[15] Prominent craftsmen of all political tendencies wrote several disclaimers to the leaflets, uniformly condemning the violence while expressing sympathy for those people who were suffering the effects of monopolist practices.[16] Artisans, then, refused to join a seemingly legitimate incident of direct action because their interests were not immediately threatened. The refusal of leading artisans to sanction public violence reveals the distance between themselves and the crowd, and demonstrates the cleavage that divided the non-élite sectors of the city. The riot against the perceived unjust speculation by monopolists illustrates that some notion of the 'moral economy' existed among the capital's populace and that the crowd's behaviour was 'popular retaliation'.[17] Complaints against high food prices in the 1880s sustain this interpretation.[18] Leading artisans, however, do not seem to have shared such an economic belief.

The 1893 *Bogotazo*

The violent events of 15 and 16 January 1893 were sparked by a four-part article in *Colombia Cristiana*, a leading pro-government newspaper supported by the bishopric, that criticised 'immoral practices' among the city's working classes. José Ignacio Gutiérrez Isaza, the author of the series, claimed that the social vices of the working classes, especially alcohol abuse and gambling, were the principal causes of the alleged family deterioration and mendicancy prevalent in Bogotá.[19] The editor of the paper apparently foresaw a potentially negative reaction to the accusations, since he added an editorial note to the final article claiming not to have read the essay before it was printed![20] *El Orden*, an important Conservative paper, came to the defence of the city's labourers, publishing a glowing account of the honour and positive economic, moral, and social contributions of Bogotá's workers and artisans, while criticising Gutiérrez as either lacking in 'Christian charity' or ignorant of the situation of the capital's labouring classes.[21]

Leading artisans promptly expressed their outrage at Gutiérrez's charges. A number of funeral orations by prominent tradesmen early in January provided the forum for the agitated defence of the artisan class and verbal attacks upon Gutiérrez. The Philanthropic Society, the oldest and largest mutual aid society in the city, publicly denounced Gutiérrez in a motion sponsored by José Leocadio Camacho, probably the most influential artisan leader of the period. The resolution vehemently rejected Gutiérrez's accusations and urged that craftsmen withdraw their support from the *Colombia Cristiana*. It also demanded that the minister of government castigate Gutiérrez for publishing material that antagonised social classes against each other, a behaviour prohibited under the press laws of the Regeneration.[22] No such action was taken by the government, even though it had frequently used the legislation to silence political opposition, undoubtedly because it had no desire to alienate the church or its officials.

In the days preceding the outbreak of violence, Gutiérrez was subjected to repeated verbal assaults and threats of violence, which led him to request police protection. The director of the police, Ignacio B. Caicedo, accordingly deployed guards at his home on Sunday morning, 15 January.[23] An estimated 300 artisans and workers gathered at the house later that day, where they shouted insults and cast stones at the author's house. Several unarmed policemen and members of the crowd suffered injuries in the mêlée, which was broken up only by the arrival of armed police reinforcements. The government ordered the closure of *chicherías* and liquor stores to calm the crowd, but to no avail. After nightfall protestors returned to the site and stone-throwing resumed, despite the presence of several high-ranking officials, including Minister of Government General Antonio B. Cuervo, who was at the time entrusted with the political leadership of the country as Vice President Caro was absent from the city. The house remained threatened until midnight.[24]

On Monday morning, 16 January, the capital city was quiet until 1.00 p.m., when a crowd gathered in front of Cuervo's home. Féliz Valois Madero, an artisan, and another craftsman requested and were granted an audience with the general. The delegation demanded that the individuals arrested the previous night be released and that Cuervo invoke the press law to censure Gutiérrez. The general informed the craftsmen that the prisoners had already been freed, but that he had no intention of invoking the press law. When the delegation informed the crowd outside of the results of the meeting, it dispersed, satisfied according to some reports and indignant according to others.[25]

In the afternoon of 16 January the city exploded in violence. Around 3.00 p.m., a large crowd, armed with rocks, sticks, and firearms gathered at Gutiérrez's house. The 35-man police guard opened fire, killing one artisan and wounding at least two others. Two policemen were injured by stones. Confrontations then broke out in several sections of the city. Police opened fire on the crowd at various sites, killing several at one plaza. Fearing escalation of the violence, Cuervo declared a state of siege, ordered the police to their barracks, and called out the regular army to restore order.[26] Another decree declared that the Philanthropic Society had incited the riot and suppressed its public and private operations. A few days later, Cuervo imposed a press blackout on the riot until the siege was lifted.[27]

Despite the strong official response to the violent turn of events, crowd violence persisted. One large mob besieged the police headquarters. Again the crowd was fired upon, causing numerous deaths and injuries. Repelled by the gunfire, the rioters moved on to other police stations, which they forced their way into and looted, taking special care to destroy all obtainable archives. In time, all but one of the capital's police stations were sacked. As night fell, the level of violence increased. Public light fixtures were destroyed to darken the streets. Barricades were raised across some thoroughfares. One group of rioters attacked the house of General Cuervo, to which they gained entrance and which they vandalised. Others went to the homes of the police inspector and the *alcalde*, which they also sacked. Later, thwarted in an attempt to mount an assault on city hall, several hundred rioters marched on the women's prison. When the crowd reached its destination on the city's outskirts, the rioters freed over 200 prisoners and looted the building.

Their passions heightened by the successful assault on the prison, the rioters returned to the centre of the city. There they encountered patrols of army troops, who were arresting all persons encountered in the streets. At least 400 people were arrested before order was finally restored around midnight. In addition to those apprehended by the army, police records show about 100 other persons were arrested. The riot left an untold number of persons wounded and between 40 and 45 dead. Only one of those killed was a policeman. During the night, the army secretly interred an unknown number of the dead in order to avoid inflaming once again the crowd's anger.

The list of wounded individuals treated in various clinics around the city offers a glimpse of the composition of the crowd. Sixteen of the 23 wounded men were skilled workers, most were single, aged 24–32, and they came from all areas of the city.[28]

An undetermined number of the arrested individuals were sent into exile by the government. A decree of 20 January, imposed under the state of siege, enabled the authorities to confine those persons deemed the 'worst offenders' to the Colombian island of San Andrés; to expel others from the capital; and to exile still others from the country.[29] Those arrested were not put on public trial, which led to an outpouring of complaints about unjust governmental behaviour. Moreover, Liberals insisted that the Caro administration had exploited the riot as a cover for the deportation of several of its leading critics, including the Liberal satirist Alfredo Greñas, a charge that appears accurate.[30] By late March, reports of hardships among the deported provoked several editors to urge that the government declare a general amnesty, especially since the collective nature of the riot had precluded identification of the particular offenders.[31] No amnesty was offered, although many men were allowed to return to the city.

The government's suppression of the Philanthropic Society was, to many, an ill-considered and hasty step. The capital's oldest mutual aid society was commonly associated with Conservative, and especially National, political leanings—a point Liberals were quick to point out in their analyses of the riot—but it had never been actively involved in partisan politics. José Leocadio Camacho protested at the action, calling it unjust. In February, Camacho petitioned Vice President Caro to allow the society to resume its meetings. The petition was approved in April, but only when the society obtained permission to meet in advance and, even then, consented to the presence of a representative of the police to monitor any 'subversive' discussion. No political discussions of any kind would be permitted in the group's sessions and the government warned that any violation of its strictures would be treated as rebellious.[32]

For the rest of the decade, the government's fear of conspiracy resulted in the close supervision of all organisations that offered a potential base for collective action. There is evidence to suggest that some of these concerns were legitimate, but most seem exaggerated. In February police informers reported that groups of Radicals (Liberals) were meeting secretly in the lower-class barrios of the city. One such reunion of 40 persons was broken up when complaints against the government and praise of Liberal politicians were overheard. The reports alleged that Féliz Valois Madero, one of the two artisans who had spoken with Cuervo on 16 January, was seen leaving the meeting and was suspected of plotting against the government.[33]

In April, after martial law had been lifted and order had returned to the city, Valois Madero founded the newspaper *El Artesano* in an attempt both to improve the tarnished image of the artisan class and to unite that class politically to enable craftsmen to pursue their own interests. Valois filled the pages of the paper with articles of interest to craftsmen, while engaging in various polemical exchanges with Liberals such as Miguel Samper and Conservatives such as Carlos Holguín.[34] During the months that followed, Valois emerged as a highly visible spokesman for the artisan class.

It is questionable, however, whether the public image of the artisan improved and certainly Valois did not escape official suspicion. In March 1894, police informers told the authorities of a workers' conspiracy to overthrow the government. On 11 March, Valois and numerous others were arrested. Most of those detained were described as artisans, who were said to have been affiliated with all political groups. In one craftsman's shop, agents reportedly found some 6,000 leaflets with the slogans 'Viva el trabajo', 'Viva el pueblo', and 'Abajo los monopolios'. A month later, in the nearby town of Facatativá, the authorities confiscated some 500 rifles and substantial quantities of ammunition. Many of those arrested, including Valois, were tried under the 'Law of the Horses', found guilty of planning a movement against the government, and sentenced to several months' imprisonment.[35]

In spite of such actions, it was the Liberal party, and not the workers, that primarily preoccupied the government. In May 1893, Liberal leader Santiago Pérez issued a ten-point programme that signalled the ideological revival of his party. In June, Marceliano Vélez, on behalf of the Historical Conservatives, supported the programme, forming an unofficial front that greatly alarmed the overly sensitive Caro government. In August, when a plot by more convinced militant Liberals to overthrow the government was uncovered, Caro closed Pérez's *El Relator*, confiscated the Liberal party funds, and exiled its leaders, including Pérez. Liberal militants responded to the repression by preparing to revolt, a course of action not supported by many party moderates. As a consequence, the revolt that began in the department of Cundinamarca in January 1895 was put down with relative ease.[36] Numerous artisans were arrested in the opening days of the rebellion in Bogotá, although there is little evidence to indicate widespread support for the insurrection among that class.[37]

Bogotá's intensely partisan press ensured that the public analysis of the violence of 15 and 16 January 1893 would be highly polemical, a debate that serves well as a point of departure for analysis of the riot's origins. All leading political factions used the riot as a pretext to expound their favourite themes. Indeed, when restrictions on the press were lifted on 24 February, editors wasted little time in offering the public the 'truth' about the riot.

Appropriately, *El Orden* initiated the polemic on 4 March in response to charges in a Medellín paper that supported the Historical Conservatives that its praise of the workers in early January had contributed to the outbreak of violence. The editors of *El Orden*, who tended to accept the Caro line, flatly refuted that accusation, claiming instead that the 'pseudo-political' philosophy of the Liberal party had led 'lower' social classes to engage in rebellious activities on numerous occasions, with the January riot only the most recent.[38] Several days later the same paper continued its condemnation of Liberal influences by reprinting an article from Cartagena's *El Porvenir*, a paper generally seen as a mouthpiece for President Núñez. The article reasoned that the January riot signalled the appearance of the 'socialist scourge' in the country, an alien menace introduced by 'free-thinking Liberals'. According to the paper, the long Liberal rule prior to the Regeneration had demoralised the Colombian people, caused them to lose their religious foundations, and develop a disrespect for legal authority. Public disorder was, for *El Porvenir*, a logical outcome of such teachings. In short, the essay concluded, 'the cupidity of those above cannot justify, but it can explain many of the storms of those below'.[39]

Colombia's leading Liberal newspaper, *El Diario de Cundinamarca*, willingly took up the gauntlet. It criticised *El Orden* for its effort to deny 'any real and direct guilt in those disgraceful acts'. Not only had the pro-government *El Orden* incited the fury of the artisans, according to the paper's editors, but other favourites of the Regeneration shared the guilt in the disturbance. The clerical *Colombia Cristiana* had, in the Liberal mind, initiated the events; *El Orden* had called the slanderous article to the artisans' attention; the Conservative artisan and avid supporter of the Regeneration José Leocadio Camacho had challenged the author and government by his resolution in the Philanthropic Society; and, finally, Conservative craftsman Féliz Valois Madero was deemed responsible for the meeting with Cuervo on the 16th that set the violent sequence of events in motion. To the Liberal daily, the January riot was not only caused by Regenerators but constituted a popular 'plebiscite' on the government, an expression of popular opposition to the 'scientific peace' of the Regeneration.[40]

A less partisan opinion presented by the moderate *El Heraldo* reasoned that the riot did not contain any overt political characteristics. Consequently, those arrested should be offered an amnesty. This approach was particularly appropriate, in its view, in light of the charges levelled by José Leocadio Camacho.[41] Camacho had alleged, in two letters to Rafael Núñez which were printed in *La Idea*, that the articles in *Colombia Cristiana* should not be seen as the cause of the riot. Rather, the craftsman wrote, the poverty of Bogotá's population, the high prices they were forced to pay for necessary goods, and unreasonable taxes on shops and food provided the real cause of the riot. Bogotá's people were fundamentally peaceful, he continued, but even good people reached a point of unbearable pressures. Camacho added that the uprising was not aimed at the church, the stores, or banks, but only at the police, the symbols of governmental authority.[42] This touched off a storm of controversy in the municipal council, on which Camacho sat as an elected member. In several sessions of heated debate, other councillors vehemently rejected his accusations as subversive. Finally, the council voted unanimously in favour of a motion of censure on its artisan member—a resolution that Camacho timidly accepted.[43]

The government's report on the 1893 disturbances declared that they had no partisan political character, which seems to be an accurate conclusion.[44] Instead of accepting blindly the charges levelled in the press, some of which do contain elements of truth, the riot is better comprehended by the examination both of the events that set off the disruptive behaviour and of the objects of the crowd's fury. The cycle of violence began with the negative portrayal of the city's popular sectors in *Colombia Cristiana*. When another pro-government newspaper criticised the paper, the unity of opinion in the Regeneration press, which had ardently defended the administration since its beginning seven years earlier, was broken. The printed indictment of *Colombia Cristiana* in *El Orden* might be seen as granting a certain 'approval' to verbal attacks on Gutiérrez by those he had defamed.

Equally importantly, and in a similar vein, members of the artisan class demanded through the Philanthropic Society's resolution

that Gutiérrez retract his comments and that the government punish him for his violation of the press law. These clamours initiated
the pressures upon Gutiérrez. On several previous occasions artisan leaders had condemned crowd violence, which, perhaps as a
consequence, never reached the magnitude of the 1893 riot. Now,
the apparent sanctioning of violence by leading artisans along with
the breach of authority by *El Orden* provided the opening through
which the various social pressures of the time could be vented.

All accounts related that food prices in Bogotá had been rising
faster than wages since the late 1880s. Municipal taxes undoubtedly aggravated that situation, but the fundamental problem lay with
the inflationary monetary policies of the Regeneration. But, while
rising food costs contributed to the tense social climate, the anger
of the crowd was not directed against food vendors or persons in
the food industry, but at Gutiérrez. The objects of the crowd's passion do not support Camacho's accusation that marketplace pressures incited the mob. Rather, the attacks on Gutiérrez indicate that
craftsmen were defending their social standing in an attempt to rec-
tify what they perceived as an injustice done to the 'good name of
the artisan'. The affront to artisan pride accounts for the demands
that the press law be enforced.

Yet the intensity of the violence, especially against the police,
suggests that more than pride was at stake and more than artisans
were involved. When the national police, in their attempt to protect
the author, killed a protester, they too incurred the crowd's anger.
Government leaders who had refused to enforce the press law were
assaulted, as were the homes of private individuals where the police took refuge. The women's jail was attacked, but not the men's.

The mob targeted the police for reprisals after the killing of
one of their number, but other factors were being played out as
well. A few years earlier, the national police had been reorganised,
which had redefined the relationship between the people and the
police. Moves to 'professionalise' the police force had included
the recruitment of a French authority charged with bringing Bogotá's
police department up to 'modern' standards. Juan María Marcelino
Gilibert had never become accustomed to the culture of Colombia's
capital and remained very much a foreigner, a point that did not
escape contemporary observers. Moreover, he had recruited officers from other areas of the country, not simply from Bogotá as
had been the previous tradition, a move that undoubtedly distanced
the police force from the local populace. It seems probable that
some of his efforts were designed to bring to Bogotá the 'civilised'

appearance of Paris. The crackdown on crime and prostitution in the second half of 1892 could be seen as an effort to define an 'ordered' capital city. It certainly aggravated tensions between the people and the police and offers a rationale for the 'liberation' of the women prisoners, who were probably perceived by the mob as having been wrongfully arrested.[45]

The January 1893 riot illustrates the complexity of Bogotá's social, political, and cultural environments. The late nineteenth-century redefinition of the urban social landscape created various fault lines that could fracture into violence. The points at which those tensions erupted into collective violence are telling. By its collective action, the crowd sought to administer justice on several levels; to censure Gutiérrez for his slander of the artisan class; to punish the police for their protection of the author, and perhaps as a further consequence of the alienation springing from the reorganisation of the police department; and, finally, to condemn officials of the government for their failure to enforce the press law and to provide a stable economic environment in which to live and work. The tensions that underlay the 1893 *bogotazo* thus emerged from a complex mixture of factors. How, then, does it fit within the broad sweep of Colombian collective violence?

In the late colonial period, public disorder, according to Anthony McFarlane, most often sprang from a violation of community and social values, usually by crown officials. A cross section of the community sought to restore traditional norms through 'purposeful and selective' violent actions; that is, the use of threatening force to impose justice upon outside agents disrupting accustomed community patterns. In the colonial setting, this type of protest was one of the few means of political participation open to New Granada's inhabitants. Significantly, these tumults seldom challenged crown authority; they instead notified public officials of violations of traditional norms.[46] Various other scholars have identified similar patterns in other areas of colonial Latin America.[47]

A similar synthesis of collective violence is lacking for Colombia (or any other Latin American country) in the nineteenth century. Some progress has been made in the examination of rural violence,[48] but urban violence awaits systematic study. The 1875 bread riot in Bogotá, it seems, constituted a popular reaction against the intrusion of the cash nexus upon the moral economy that apparently prevailed in the popular mentality.[49] Two riots in Rio de Janeiro displayed a similar violent reaction to the introduction of 'modern' urban ways. In the first, a new tax upon urban tramways that were frequently used by 'popular' sectors sparked several days of violent unrest in 1880. The tax served to reveal the tensions caused by the modernisation of the city and to reshape Rio's political culture to include, among other changes, the voices of previously non-influential groups.[50] The second, the *revolta contra vacina* of 1904, has been seen as a reaction against 'civilising' forces by the urban poor and working classes.[51] The manner by which the Bogotá crowd in 1893 reacted to changes in established urban patterns, such as the reorganisation of the police force, suggests that late nineteenth-century Latin American collective violence might well be seen as generally reactive in nature.[52] The rapid expansion of both Bogotá and Rio undoubtedly reordered social relations, adding an element of insecurity that could have sparked a violent response by an urban populace faced with threats to traditional ways of life.

The role of the craft sector in the outbreak of violence constituted a central component of the 1893 riot. Most disturbances during the colonial period had been multi-class in nature. The upper and lower sectors of Bogotá's society did not, by contrast, unite in violent expressions in the late nineteenth century. The riots of the period instead manifested the division between the 'masses', the 'élites', and the artisans, who occupied an often ambiguous middle social stratum. Artisans were at the centre of partisan disorders, which has served to draw considerable attention to their political activity. Craftsmen did not join in the 1875 tumult, a riot not rooted in the political struggle, but were integral to the events of January 1893, a riot with similar non-partisan origins. The 1893 *bogotazo* brings to our attention the importance of the artisan class as a pivotal force in urban society and suggests aspects of their value system that would precipitate extra-legal activity. Craftsmen, threatened as a class by imported manufactured goods, attached considerable significance to their public image, a point quite clearly illustrated by the 1893 *bogotazo*.[53] Insofar as the 'modernisation' of the Latin American city can be seen as creating the climate for collective violence, the examination of social groups that were threatened by that process, such as artisans, contributes to our understanding of the social history of the period.

Notes

1. The *bogotazo* of 9 April 1948 occurred in reaction to the assassination of the popular Liberal party leader Jorge Elicier Gaitán. It destroyed much of downtown Bogotá and resulted in hundreds of deaths, while igniting the nationwide

outbreak of *La Violencia*. For a recent account see Herbert Braun, *The Assassination of Gaitán: Public Life and Urban Violence in Colombia* (Madison, 1986).

2. Rural and urban violence during the colonial period, rural violence in the nineteenth century, and 'modern' incidents of collective violence have attracted considerable attention in Latin America, especially in Mexico, the Andean republics, Brazil, and Colombia. For the latter, considerable progress has been made towards a long-term understanding of collective violence. The late colonial period, especially the Comunero rebellion of 1781, is well synthesised in Anthony McFarlane, 'Civil Disorders and Popular Protests in Late Colonial New Granada', *Hispanic American Historical Review*, vol. 64, no. 1 (Feb. 1984), pp. 17–54. Various studies have sought to explain rural violence in the early national period, notably Catherine LeGrand, 'Labor Acquisition and Social Conflict on the Colombian Frontier, 1850–1936', *Journal of Latin American Studies*, vol. 16, pt. 1 (Feb. 1984), pp. 27–49. There is abundant literature on violence in twentieth-century Colombia, most of it focusing on *La Violencia* of the 1940s and 1950s. Gonzalo Sánchez offers a conceptual framework for *La Violencia* and its historiography in '*La Violencia* in Colombia: New Research, New Questions', *Hispanic American Historical Review*, vol. 65, no. 4 (Nov. 1985), pp. 789–807. See also Gonzalo Sánchez, *Once ensayos sobre la Violencia* (Bogotá, 1985). And for the urban environment, Medófilo Medina, *La protesta urbana en Colombia en el siglo veinte* (Bogotá, 1984); and Peter Winn, 'The Urban Working Class and Social Protest in Latin America', *International Labor and Working Class History*, No. 14/15 (Spring 1979), pp. 61–4.

3. Richard M. Morse (ed.), *The Urban Development of Latin America, 1750–1920* (Stanford, 1971), p. 62; Peter Walter Ámato, *An Analysis of Changing Patterns of Elite Residential Areas of Bogotá, Colombia*, Ph.D. diss., Cornell University (1968), p. 138.

4. Luis Ospina Vásquez, *Industria y protección en Colombia, 1810 a 1930* (Bogotá, 1959), passim.

5. Miguel Samper, *La miseria en Bogotá y otros escritos* (Bogotá, 1969), pp. 9, 11. See also *La Opinión*, 14 Oct. 1863, 12 Oct. 1864, 4 Jan. 1865; *La República*, 9 Oct. 1867.

6. Darío Bustamante Roldán, 'Efectos económicos del papel moneda durante la regeneración', *Cuadernos Colombianos*, vol. 1, no. 4 (1974), pp. 561–660.

7. See, for example, *El Taller*, 17 Jan., 1 June 1889; *Las Noticias*, 5 March 1889; *La Capital*, 10 Oct. 1890; *El Heraldo*, 10 Sept. 1890; *Los Hechos*, 12 June 1894; *Bogotá*, 2 May 1897; and Manuel Cotes, *Régimen alimenticio de los jornaleros de la sabana de Bogotá* (Bogotá, 1893), passim. The available serial data confirm that food prices remained generally stable from 1864 through the late 1870s, then slowly increased until the late 1880s, when they began a dramatic rise. Miguel Urrutia, 'Estadísticas de precios, 1846–1933', in Miguel Urrutia and Mario Arrubla, *Compendio de estadísticas históricas de Colombia* (Bogotá, 1970), p. 85; Bustamante, 'Efectos económicos del papel moneda', pp. 645, 647.

8. Medardo Rivas, *Obras de Medardo Rivas, Parte primera, novelas, artículos de costumbres, variedades, poesías* (Bogotá, 1883), p. 89; *El Tradicionista*, 2, 5 May 1874; *La América*, 4, 11, 18 May 1874; *La Doctrina*, 7 May 1879; *Diario de Cundinamarca*, 6, 7, 10, 13 May 1879; *El Deber*, 9, 13, 27 May 1879.

9. Helen Delpar, *Red Against Blue: The Liberal Party in Colombian Politics, 1863–1899* (University, 1981), p. 144; Charles Bergquist, *Coffee and Conflict in Colombia, 1886–1910* (Durham, 1978), pp. 37–8.

10. The 1832 national constitution allowed literate men (although literacy was not to be enforced prior to 1850) who were married, or over the age of 21, to vote

if they had an assured income and were not employed as a domestic servant or day labourer. The constitution of 1843 substituted property requirements for the earlier occupational clause, while maintaining the literacy article. The most liberal of the nineteenth-century suffrage requirements came with the 1853 document, which enabled all men who were over 21, or married, to vote. The constitution of 1863 allowed states to determine their own requirements. Cundinamarca introduced a literacy requirement at that time. Finally, the Regeneration constitution required that males over the age of 21 exercise a profession or lawful occupation and demonstrate their means of support. Local and departmental elections were open to all males over 21. William Marion Gibson, *The Constitutions of Colombia* (Durham, 1948), pp. 120, 162, 201–4, 227, 316; *El Telegrama*, 4 May 1887.

11. See David Sowell, ' "La teoria y la realidad": The Democratic Society of Artisans of Bogotá, 1847–1854', *Hispanic American Historical Review*, vol. 67, no. 4 (Nov. 1987), pp. 611–30.

12. See David Bushnell, 'Two Stages of Colombian Tariff Policy: The Radical Era and the Return to Protection (1861–1885)', *Inter-American Economic Affairs*, vol. 9, no. 4 (Spring 1956), pp. 3–23.

13. *La América*, 26, 27, 29, 30 Jan. 1875; *La Ilustración*, 25, 26 Jan. 1875; *El Tradicionista*, 26, 29 Jan. 1875; Eugenio Gutiérrez Cely, 'Nuevo movimiento popular contra el laissez-faire: Bogotá, 1875', *Universitas Humanística*, vol. 11, no. 17 (March 1982), pp. 177–212.

14. Gutiérrez, 'Nuevo movimiento popular', passim.

15. Miguel Perdomo Neira, a travelling *curandero*, sparked several days of unrest in the capital in May 1872. 'Professional' doctors took offence at the *curandero*'s popularity and challenged him to demonstrate his skills, a challenge that set off several days of stone-throwing and attacks against the doctors by the 'people'. After the incident, university students attempted to found a Democratic Society among the artisans to counter Perdomo's popularity. The editorialist 'Captuso' observed that most craftsmen refused to join the effort, seeking to avoid the political manipulation experienced by craftsmen in the 1850s. *La Ilustración*, 26 Jan. 1875.

16. *La América*, 27, 30 Jan. 1875.

17. *La Ilustración*, 26 Jan. 1875.

18. *El Taller*, 17 Jan. 1889.

19. *Colombia Cristiana*, 14, 21, 28 Dec. 1892; 4 Jan. 1893.

20. Ibid., 4 Jan. 1893. The editor, Enrique Alvarez B., made a similar statement in *El Correo Nacional*, 20 Jan. 1893.

21. *El Orden*, 11 Jan. 1893. Numerous artisans thanked Antonio María Silvestre, the director of *El Orden*, for his 'act of justice' in speaking in favour of the city's craftsmen. *El Orden*, 14 Jan. 1893.

22. *El Relator*, 17 Jan. 1893; *El Correo Nacional*, 1 Feb. 1893; *El Telegrama*, 14 Jan. 1893; *El Barbero*, 16 Jan. 1893.

23. *El Relator*, 17 Jan. 1893; *El Correo Nacional*, 17 Jan. 1893; *El Telegrama*, 14 Jan. 1893; *El Heraldo*, 25 Jan. 1893.

24. Details of the riot are drawn from various sources. Unless otherwise noted, the account that follows is a composite of information from: Archivo Histórico Nacional (hereafter AHN), República, Policía Nacional, Tomo 2, fols. 422–521r, Tomo 3, fols. 409, 625–6; *Diario Oficial*, 2, 3 Feb. 1893; *El Correo Nacional*, 1 Feb. 1893; *El Orden*, 4 March 1893; Julio H. Palacio, *Historia de mi vida* (Bogotá, 1942), pp. 186–92; and Alvaro Tirado Mejía, *Aspectos sociales de las guerras civiles en Colombia* (Bogotá, 1976), pp. 462–87. Gutiérrez published

and had distributed a leaflet on the 16th which insisted that he had not meant to hurt or insult members of the artisan class, but he did not refute his earlier comments. *El Telegrama*, 16 Jan. 1893.

25. *Diario Oficial*, 2 Feb. 1893.

26. Ibid., 17 Jan. 1893.

27. *Diario de Cundinamarca*, 24 Jan. 1893.

28. *El Correo Nacional*, 1 Feb. 1893.

29. AHN, República, Policía Nacional, Tomo 3, fols. 409, 625–6; Tirado Mejía, *Aspectos sociales*, p. 463. About 50 prisoners reportedly were sent from Bogotá to the coast by steamboat. *Diario de la Tarde*, 7, 27, 28 Feb., 6, 8 April 1893; *Diario Oficial*, 4 Feb. 1893. One report alleged that the army drafted many prisoners into its ranks. *El Telegrama*, 19 April 1893.

30. *Diario de Cundinamarca*, 7, 14, 28 March, 21 April, 12 May 1893. Alfredo Greñas, an ardent enemy of the Regeneration, had published a mild analysis of the early riot on 16 January: *El Barbero*, 16 Jan. 1893. Government officials seized the opportunity to arrest the author and expel him from the country. Greñas sought refuge in Costa Rica, from where he continued his criticisms of the Regeneration government. For a discussion of Greñas's role as a cartoonist and political commentator, see J. León Helguera, 'Notes on a Century of Colombian Political Cartooning: 1830–1930', *Studies in Latin American Popular Culture*, vol. 6 (1987), pp. 268–72.

31. *Diario de Cundinamarca*, 7, 14 March 1893; *El Heraldo*, 8, 12, 22 April 1893.

32. AHN, República, Gobernaciones varios, Tomo 28, fols. 954–5; *El Correo Nacional*, 3 April 1893.

33. AHN, República, Policía Nacional, Tomo 2, fols. 520–1r; *Diario Oficial*, 2 Feb. 1893.

34. *El Artesano*, 8, 15 April, 2, 17 June 1893.

35. *El Correo Nacional*, 20 March, 3, 7, 10, 11, 13, 19, 21, 24, 28 April 1894; *El Orden*, 17 March, 14 April 1894.

36. Bergquist, *Coffee and Conflict in Colombia*, pp. 44–45, 49; Delpar, *Red Against Blue*, pp. 149–57.

37. *El Telegrama*, 12 Jan. 1895; *Los Hechos*, 23 Jan. 1895.

38. *El Orden*, 4 March 1893.

39. Ibid., 8 March 1893.

40. *El Diario de Cundinamarca*, 10, 14, 21 March 1893.

41. *El Heraldo*, 8, 12 April 1893.

42. Ibid., 8 April 1893.

43. Ibid., 12 April 1893; *El Telegrama*, 4 May 1893.

44. *Informe que presenta el subsecretario del ministerio de gobierno de Colombia al congreso constitucional de 1894* (Bogotá, 1894), p. iv.

45. On the reorganisation, see Alvaro Castaño Castillo, *La Policia, su origen y su destino* (Bogotá, 1947), Vol. VIII, pp. 12–18; *El Correo Nacional*, 15, 16 Jan. 1892. Similar reactions to police reorganisations in the United States are described in Samuel Walker, *Popular Justice: A History of American Criminal Justice* (New York, 1980), p. 60–4 and in England in Robert D. Storch, 'The Plague of the Blue Locusts: Police Reform and Popular Resistance in Northern England, 1840–75', *International Review of Social History*, No. 1 (1975), pp. 61–90. Police officials realised that the riot in part impinged upon their organisation. In the months that followed the tumult, several changes were made in the methods of recruitment, patrols, and public comportment of officers. *El Correo Nacional*, 18 Feb., 29 March 1893. See also Oscar de J. Saldarriaga Vélez, 'Bogotá, la

Regeneración y la policía, 1880–1900', *Revista Universidad de Antioquia*, No. 211 (Jan.–March 1988), pp. 37–55.

46. McFarlane, 'Civil Disorders', pp. 31–2, 43, 50, 53–4, and passim.

47. For example, see William B. Taylor, *Drinking, Homocide, and Rebellion in Colonial Mexican Villages* (Stanford, 1979); John L. Phelan, *The People and the King: The Comunero Revolt of 1781* (Madison, 1979); and Scarlett O'Phelan Godoy, *Rebellions and Revolts in Eighteenth-Century Peru and Upper Peru* (Cologne, 1985).

48. José Escorcia, *Sociedad y economía en el Valle del Cauca*. Tomo III. *Desarrollo político, social y económico, 1800–1854* (Bogotá, 1983), pp. 86–92; Michael T. Taussig, *The Devil and Commodity Fetishism in South America* (Chapel Hill, 1980), pp. 55–65; Helguera, 'Antecedentes sociales de la revolución de 1851 en el sur de Colombia', *Anuario Colombiano de Historia Social y de la Cultura*, vol. 5 (1970), pp. 53–63; LeGrand, 'Labor Acquisition and Social Conflict', pp. 27–49.

49. E. P. Thompson notes in his seminal article that the moral economy remains in the popular mind far after the new market has in fact upset traditional economic patterns. E. P. Thompson, 'The Moral Economy of the English Crowd in the Eighteenth Century', *Past and Present*, vol. 50 (1971), p. 87, passim.

50. Sandra Lauderdale Graham, 'The Vintem Riot and Political Culture: Rio de Janeiro, 1880', *Hispanic American Historical Review*, vol. 60, no. 3 (August 1980), pp. 431–49. [Note: Graham's article is reprinted in this volume as Chapter 4.]

51. Teresa Meade, ' "Civilizing Rio de Janeiro": The Public Health Campaign and the Riot of 1904', *Journal of Social History*, vol. 20, no. 2 (Winter 1986), pp. 301–22; Jeffrey D. Needell, 'The *Revolta Contra Vacina* of 1904: The Revolt against "Modernization" in *Belle-Epoque* Rio de Janeiro', *Hispanic American Historical Review*, vol. 67, no. 2 (May 1987), pp. 233–69. [Note: Needell's article is reprinted in this volume as Chapter 6.]

52. On European collective violence in this period, see Charles Tilly, Louise Tilly, and Richard Tilly, *The Rebellious Century, 1830–1930* (Cambridge, MA, 1975), pp. 249–50, 259–64, 268–9.

53. Sowell, 'Las bases sociales para la movilización de obreros en Bogotá: 1866–1912', in Raymond L. Williams (comp.), *Ensayos de literatura colombiana* (Bogotá, 1985), p. 276.

6

The *Revolta Contra Vacina* of 1904: The Revolt against "Modernization" in *Belle-Epoque* Rio de Janeiro

Jeffrey D. Needell

Jeffrey D. Needell is an associate professor at the University of Florida. He specializes in the social and cultural history of Brazil during the nineteenth and twentieth centuries. The following essay is part of a larger study of Rio de Janeiro which culminated in his book, A Tropical Belle Epoque: Elite Culture and Society in Turn-of-the-Century Rio de Janeiro *(1988). Since then he has been working on Brazilian state formation and intellectual history from 1830 to 1940. Articles on Gilberto Freyre, Joaquim Nabuco, and Oliveira Viana reflect this new focus.*

Here, Professor Needell corrects the distorted historical accounts of the Revolta Contra Vacina, which focus on the agenda of dissident elites and ignore the popular agenda that intersected to produce the riot. Needell argues that it reflected two movements: a military revolt and popular opposition to an intrusive modernizing state. He also shows how the experiences of elites and lower classes continued to diverge in the aftermath of the riot, when elite participants escaped the vicious reprisals suffered by the lower-class rioters.

Francisco de Paula Rodrigues Alves's "modernizing" administration (1902–1906) imposed a new urban plan, portworks, and drastic measures against disease on Rio de Janeiro. In 1904, in a crisis linked to the administration's obligatory smallpox vaccination plans, a popular revolt dominated the capital and cleared the way for a nearly successful military coup. The historiography to date has either neglected this revolt or (more recently) focused on one aspect to the exclusion of the other. Here, I point to the *Revolta Contra Vacina* as the culmination and conjuncture of more general and more radical conflicts and resistance within Brazil's Old

From *Hispanic American Historical Review* 67, no. 2 (May 1987): 233–69.

Republic (1889–1930) a failed revolution against one sort of "modernization" which gives another meaning to the events and indicates another perspective on Rio's *belle époque*.

In October 1904, an opposition newspaper in Rio posted a portrait of a man suffering from a grisly tumor that had distorted his arm and chest. The paper, the *Correio da Manhã*, did this "so that our public may evaluate well what it is risking with obligatory vaccination." The daily then went on:

> And what is the reason for this shocking change? What? Simply vaccination, the great destroyer of human happiness, of human health, and of human life. Vaccination, the propagator by [*sic*] all means of illness, . . . the monster that pollutes the pure and innocent blood of our children with the vile excretions expelled from sick animals, of a nature that contaminates the system of any living being.[1]

This quotation was part of a sustained effort on the part of the opposition paper to galvanize the Carioca population to reject the obligatory vaccination program directed by Dr. Oswaldo [Gonçalves] Cruz during the Rodrigues Alves administration. Most of the press opposed *obligatory* vaccination, as did many prominent opposition politicians, professional organizations, academic institutions, and the Positivist church. By November's first week, a Liga Contra Vacina Obrigatória, explicitly modeled on an earlier British organization, had been put together by more radical leaders to rally popular resistance. Many of the same men, militant republicans, politicized army officers, and opposition journalists who figured in the Liga, also reached out to organized workers by addressing huge meetings at the Centro de Classes Operárias. In the second week of November, as word of the government's regulations for obligatory vaccination spread, the heated political milieu finally exploded.[2]

On November 10, in the aftermath of a mass meeting, a police officer arrested a few youths with whom he had had an angry exchange. On his detachment's return with the prisoners to headquarters, it was surrounded and attacked, and had to be rescued by well-prepared police cavalry, who charged and dispersed enraged crowds for the better part of the evening. The same pattern of public meetings, hostility, violent police repression, and riots marked the afternoons and evenings of the next three days.

The crowds mobbed streets and squares, broke streetlamps, and fought police sabers, revolvers, and rifles with paving stones, knives, straight razors, revolvers, and rifles of their own. Streetcars soon stopped running, since they served too well as barricades which were repeatedly thrown up in the narrow streets of the Old City, Rio's historic center, and the nearby working-class slums near the northern docks. Indeed, by November 12, the army and navy were called in to reinforce the police garrisoning strategic points in the Old City and the outlying working-class districts. The endangered positions included the local police stations, the Gazómetro (which, if taken, would leave the city's gas lighting without fuel), and, of course, the streets leading from the Old City to Catete—the presidential palace where, during the next two days, Rodrigues Alves's ministers periodically rushed to confer with the president about their vain attempts to regain control of his capital. Rio was effectively in the hands of the masses.[3]

One of the men who came to see Rodrigues Alves on the 14th angered and dismayed the president profoundly. General Olímpio de Silveira, though polite, offered the president a scarcely veiled ultimatum on behalf of elements in the army. Rodrigues Alves rejected it pointedly. On General Silveira's return to the Club Militar, traditional focus of the army's more political activities, he reported the president's response to the civilian and military conspirators awaiting him. The general's mission had been an attempt to force administration concessions under the threat of military rebellion; now it was decided to take the fatal step and compel the government's fall. Together, the military and civilian conspirators went ahead with plans hastily put together that day at the club.[4]

By late afternoon and early evening, these plans had had uneven success. The military school of Praia Vermelha, a source of youthful, violent, radical idealism for a generation, had been made ready by the conspirators, and now rose up at the call of Senator Lauro Sodré. The senator, an army officer, had been the most prominent opposition figure at the Liga and the Centro de Classes Operárias. In the Senate, representing Rio itself, he had long censured the administration and had urged the radical recasting of the republic back to its betrayed ideals. Now, joined by General Silvestre Travassos, he organized the cadets to march the short distance to Catete, to depose Rodrigues Alves, and to set up a new government, with himself as its leader.[5]

While Lauro was successful in arousing the military school, however, his agents at the tactical school of Realengo, in the North Zone of the city, suffered a complete reverse. Just when they called on the cadets to revolt, the head of the school, forewarned and aided by loyal officers, attacked and imprisoned all but one of the conspirators who were to have led the cadets from Realengo to the northwestern edge of the Old City at the Praça da República, across from the army's general headquarters. There they were to have joined those army units expected to adhere to their triumphant cause, before proceeding to help Lauro, who was to attack Catete in the South Zone. However, these two coordinated moves, one to pull in the army from the north, the other to lead the attack to depose the president in the south, were now out of step. The northern thrust had been parried—the coup's success was now to be decided wholly in the south.[6]

Precious time was lost at Praia Vermelha as cadets sought ammunition for a reserve in their attack. This search gave loyal officers time to warn the president of the uprising and to attempt to organize a palace defense and a small, mixed unit of military police and other loyal soldiers to meet the cadets en route from the military school. The president, upset at the delays and the paucity of troops sent to his defense by his generals in the Old City, then prepared, with family, staff, and ministers, to await his fate. Late that night, the cadets, with Lauro and Travassos in the van, finally began their march, strengthened by the adhesion of two other units on their way. Then, unexpectedly, they met the demoralized, exhausted loyalist forces on a dark street leading from Praia Vermelha into the residential district of Botafogo. There was less than a halfhour's exchange of fire, which brought little honor to the loyalists and disaster to the rebels. On the one hand, the government forces fled headlong in disorder, quickly spreading rumors of defeat in their rout. On the other hand, however, the charismatic leadership of the coup was eliminated—Lauro, felled by a bloody scalp wound, was unable to lead. Even Travassos, badly wounded, with his horse shot from under him, could not go on. The two rebel leaders were taken in by friends living nearby, and the cadets retreated to their school.[7]

Catete, in the immediate aftermath of the exchange, heard only the rumors of defeat brought back by the retreating loyalists. The president was urged to flee the beachfront palace to a nearby battleship; everyone in his entourage assumed Lauro's forces would soon overrun them. Rodrigues Alves refused to abandon the city. Shortly afterward, word came of the cadets' retreat; only then did army reinforcements finally arrive. The administration had survived.[8]

From November 15 to 18, the army and navy wrested the capital from its masses. The morning of the 15th was taken up with the peaceful surrender of Praia Vermelha—the next few days were more difficult elsewhere. There were industrial workers' revolts in suburban factories and street battles in town. Even while the Old City was being disputed over barricades between the military and roving groups, a more fearsome threat loomed. In one of the oldest Afro-Brazilian districts, the hilly dockside slum called Saúde, streetfighters had built an ordered series of barricades and organized a disciplined resistance, complete with military-style communications, chosen leadership, and a battle standard—the red flag. Reporters noted a great sign posted near the flag, with the words "Porto Arthur" written there. The streetfighters, mindful of the siege highlighting the ongoing Russo-Japanese War, were apparently warning of their determined resistance. Indeed, when the army began the painful task of taking Saúde back street by street, barricade by barricade, the streetfighters counterattacked, led by "Prata Preta" (Black Silver), Porto Arthur's commander. They failed. In terrible hand-to-hand combat, Prata Preta himself, isolated in the retreat, was captured, straitjacketed, and taken to jail under heavy guard (as much to protect him from the police as to prevent his escape). Porto Arthur's defenders, retreating before the army's pressure by land and threatened by bombardment from a navy ironclad positioned just off dockside, faded away into the maze-like squalor of the slums. Only sporadic street or factory conflicts, progressively contained, remained. By the 18th, the revolt was effectively over.[9] A period of repression followed, armed by an official state of siege. Imprisonment, beatings, interrogation, and internal exile were the order of the day. The trial of Lauro and a number of officers and opposition leaders took place over the next several months. The plan for obligatory vaccination, however, was put aside by the Rodrigues Alves administration. Smallpox continued to decimate the population during the course of the next few years.[10]

Contemporary response to the revolt generally fastened on its putative leadership, Lauro and his associates, and their coup attempt of November 14. Friends of the administration accused them of being dictatorial cynics, even monarchists, misleading the idealistic cadets and engaging in criminal demagoguery with regard to the masses. More neutral or opposition writers tended to decry Lauro and his followers' tactics as misguided and irresponsible, criticizing the use of violence (rather than constitutional redress), the sacrifice of the cadets, and the provocation of easily misled urban masses. What little analysis was actually spent on those masses typically turned on superficial characterizations of their actions as

the function of atavism, ignorance, criminality, and barbarism. Class
and race prejudice, redolent of the social Darwinism of the epoch,
tended to obscure any alternative approaches: the people revolted
because they were savage. The police report, attempting a more
politic and "scientific" distinction, dwelt on the central role of Rio's
marginal elements and explicitly distinguished such "prostitutes,"
"pimps," "drunks," "vagabonds," "thieves," "professional troublemakers," and "crooks" from the responsible, respectable working
class.[11]

Like some bad dreams, the revolt of 1904 was quickly repressed
and largely forgotten. It is only noted in passing by chroniclers,
and even then in a way which continues the emphasis on the coup's
leadership and its apparent political concerns—it is recorded as the
Revolta Contra Vacina. Only occasionally (or in the description of
the revolt) is the role of the common people indicated (and distorted) by using the term *quebra lampiões* (streetlamp breakers) to
designate those most active in the street violence. The fact that the
revolt's successes were (and remain) unparalleled in Brazilian history has generally gone unremarked. Nor have the underlying reasons for the revolt, even on the part of Lauro and his followers,
been given proper analytic attention until relatively recently. As
for the Cariocas who, for several days, met their enemies in bloody
combat or defied them from smoldering barricades—their story has
only recently been given the possibility of investigation.

Thus, the traditional historiography, as Nachman has observed,[12]
has left 1904 as its elite and middle-sector contemporaries be-
queathed it—a focus on the leadership; observations on the constitutional and medical issues of compulsory smallpox vaccination;
and an account of the ferocity of the popular violence and government repression (though, for the most part, blatant racial and class
prejudices have been shed or disguised). Revisionists, at least, have
pointed to the context of the revolt; but they have not explored its
origins at length. Even Melo Franco's discussion (1973), doubtless
the best published account to date, makes only the scantiest reference to the possible underlying causes for mass violence, though
he advances our understanding of the conspiracy headed by Lauro
with the greater precision possible through primary research.[13]

Since Melo Franco's work, little has been published which
breaks new ground on the revolt. In 1977, Nachman offered a brief
article demonstrating the revolt's links to the enduring tradition of
positivist radicalism in the Old Republic.[14] In 1986, Meade published a fresh account of the people's role, a focus which, while

based on exemplary research on the poor, did not allow for a fully developed contextual analysis or satisfactory handling of other elements involved.[15] For the most part, those who wish to comprehend the revolt of 1904 must turn to primary source research, recent theses and monographs touching on related problems, and Lahmeyer Lobo's statistical analysis of Rio's history (1978). The theses are, with the exception of Maram's (1972), recent indeed. Benchimol, Keremitsis, Porta Rocha, Costa, Adamo, and Meade have written theses and dissertations since 1980 focusing on urban reform, Carioca labor, public health, popular culture and resistance, the plight of people of color, and community response which give us the fragments of a framework for understanding the masses' role in the revolt. What I and others (the Casa de Rui Barbosa's Equipe de Pesquisas) are adding is the necessary comprehensive analysis of the revolt itself, generated from these and untapped contemporary records.[16]

The Carioca *Belle Epoque*

The revolt must first be placed in its immediate context—the Carioca *belle époque* of 1898–1914. This era emerged after nearly two decades of urban and national upheaval. The struggle for abolition (ca. 1880–88) and for the republic (ca. 1870–89) had brought street violence, middle-sector politicization, and elite division to the city during the 1880s. The 1890s intensified such symptoms, as the underlying struggle over the nature of the new republic and the impact of alternating policies of inflation and deflation galvanized the city. The period was one in which the nation's direction was disputed by two different groups. On the one hand, the victors of 1889—radical republicans (*jacobinos*) among the urban middle sectors and the army's officer corps, often positivist-influenced or positivists—were attempting to use the state to remake Brazil. Influential in the early republic's government, they sought an authoritarian, centralized, "modernizing" regime in which Brazil's progress would be quickened and more opportunities would be brought to the urban middle sector and working class by promoting an expanded meritocratic bureaucracy and a nationalist, paternalist industrial program. On the other hand, the badly divided traditional elites, tied to regional plantation agriculture and its associated complement of commerce and credit, were trying to regain power. They were struggling, first, to reestablish elite consensus in the wake of certain regions' agricultural decline and other regions'

increasingly clear preeminence, and, second, to reassert their traditional agroexport bias as national policy. Both tasks involved the
ouster of the radicals. The second necessarily implied an end to the
radicals' statist interventionism, and the promotion, instead, of only
limited intervention, to encourage foreign credit and, with it, facili-
tate infrastructural expansion, access to cheap labor, and foreign
investment and trade.[17]

In the mid-1890s, the leaders among the great planter interests
of São Paulo found the opening through which to lead the reorganizing agroexport elites against the *jacobinos*, who had coalesced
around the government of Marshal Floriano [Vieira] Peixoto (1891–
94). Floriano, struggling against a desperate revolt in the south,
needed Paulista support and turned to the moderate Paulista Republicans; he received the weight of their firm backing, in exchange
for allowing the "election" of a Paulista president in 1894. It was
the beginning of the end. In the next two administrations, those of
Prudente [José] de Morais [e Barros] (1894–98) and Manuel [Ferrez]
de Campos Sales (1898–1902), both Paulistas, the republican radicals were routed—broken as a power in national politics and rooted
out, with federal connivance, from all but one of those state governments where they had gained power in the early 1890s. The exception, Rio Grande do Sul, remained a beacon to Florianistas
among the military and the Carioca middle sectors, though its national representation, headed by Senator Pinheiro Machado, would,
over time, seek more to win power within the emergent structure
than leverage to remake it. Indeed, under Campos Sales, the notorious *política dos governadores* delivered the state governments
over to the local reorganized machines controlled by each state's
agroexport oligarchy, in exchange for acquiescence to the national
government's new political and economic direction (which favored,
above all, the two most powerful coffee states, São Paulo and Minas
Gerais).[18]

It is under Campos Sales that Rio began its *belle époque*. It was
clear that the nation had once again been bent to the will of the
"conservative classes." Campos Sales's political victory for the oligarchies signaled domestic stability at the expense of radical ideology and broader political participation. His personal negotiations
with Lord Rothschild brought new credit to Brazil at the expense
of a savage deflationary policy that brought recession by 1900.
Naturally, however, the return to oligarchical control and foreign
credit also brought a sense of relief and delighted anticipation to
those associated with traditional elite circles. Fashionable week-

lies began publishing light literature and society gossip. The Jockey Club and the Club dos Diários enjoyed a period of resurgence, merger, new members, and new pleasures. Indeed, when Rodrigues Alves came to power as the third Paulista president and the first without credentials earned in the early republican movement, an official ball was held at the Casino Fluminense, old seat of the monarchy's high society. It was the first such affair since the celebrated one at the Ilha Fiscal in 1889—where D. Pedro II had been the host.[19]

Personally, Rodrigues Alves was hardly interested in a renaissance in high society. He hoped to build from the secure political and fiscal base left him by Campos Sales to provide the limited intervention traditionally preferred in Brazilian liberal economic thought. He planned to promote national change along European lines by encouraging immigration, building infrastructure, and securing more foreign credit, and he focused on the reform of Rio as the centerpiece of such promotion. Rodrigues Alves proposed to dramatically strengthen Rio's role as the nation's port-capital—symbolic and functional neocolonial nexus between North Atlantic civilization and economy and a "modernizing" Brazil.[20]

There were three hinges to this portal to the future. One was the ambitious, sophisticated program of disease control and eradication directed by Oswaldo Cruz, who promised to rid Rio, Brazil's threshold, of the illnesses (yellow fever, plague, and smallpox) that had made it notorious among immigrant laborers and foreign capitalists. The second was Rio's Europeanization, by way of the building, improvement, beautification, and rationalization of the city's streets and public places according to the Parisian model synonymous with Haussmann, reforms placed in the practiced hands of Rio's prefect, Francisco Pereira Passos. The third was the construction of Rio's modern port, a practical necessity for Brazil's major entrepôt; a port, moreover, linked to the burgeoning commerce, industry, and labor of the Old City and the North Zone by Parisian-style boulevards. This last reform was undertaken by the minister of industry, transport, and public works, Lauro Müller, who delegated the complicated planning and construction to the clique of engineers and entrepreneurs associated with the Club de Engenharia and headed by [Gustavo André] Paulo de Frontin and Francisco Bicalho. This was Rodrigues Alves's dramatic "modernizing" program, one which spoke to the triumph of the traditional elites' vision of Brazil as a progressive but agroexport participant in the North Atlantic economy. It was one which rested on victories

wrested from nearly a generation of conflict; it was a program central to the meaning of the Carioca *belle époque*. This was the context of the revolt of 1904—a revolt that was the negation of the
belle époque and this particular "modernization" in political and
symbolic terms.[21]

Opposition and Radical Conspiracy

Traditional discussion and recent research alike point to the roots
of elite and middle-class opposition to Oswaldo Cruz's obligatory
vaccination. There was strong, but probably minority, resistance to
vaccination itself, and general resistance to the obligatory aspect, a
resistance obvious even in periodicals normally favorable to
Rodrigues Alves and his policies. The Positivist church, although
it never called for nor participated in violence, was the most marked
opponent to vaccination on two counts: it was especially adamant
against obligatory inoculation on the doctrinaire ground of constitutional principles, and it also mustered scientific arguments against
the practice. Individuals from the medical community, the press,
and the congress also spoke out against vaccination per se. Their
resistance to vaccination was based on misgivings (expressed sometimes soberly, often quite emotionally) regarding its safety and ef-
ficacy. It is important to recall that these were hardly a function
of obscurantism—although vaccination had become an established
method by that time, there were still international and learned debates over the practice. The more general opposition, however, was
to forced inoculation, central to Oswaldo Cruz's plan—a plan based
on foreign, successful precedent. This opposition, like that of the
positivists, was founded on constitutional grounds: the sanctity of
the individual's rights against the coercive powers of the state.
Objections on both counts were presented in the press, in congress,
and in petitions from various groups and institutions, one of which,
counting more than 10,000 names, was submitted by various unions.
It was all countered publicly by administration champions and effectively ignored by the president and his allies until far too late.[22]

The Rodrigues Alves administration presumed that such opposition was generally a cover for political sabotage of the administration and its program, or, at best, a mere misguided obstacle to
crucial reforms. It now seems clear that the administration was both
terribly wrong and correct. It was wrong in that even politically
neutral or proadministration elements opposed the measure because
of strongly felt medical fears and ideological values, or because of

a more sensitive reading of the impolitic, explosive potential of the administration's interventionism.[23] Here, in effect, one finds the roots of the general atmosphere of middle-sector and elite resistance to the policy. However, if grown in isolation, these would have flowered only in protest and anger in the press and in the congress. The roots of the revolt itself were elsewhere. For the administration was also correct in sensing that, just barely beneath much of this public outcry, there was determined political opposition seeking an issue with which to destroy the Paulista government and the forces it embodied.

It is important to remember that the *belle époque* was a victory over the radical officers and urban middle-sector elements, the *jacobinos* and Florianistas. Such men had not disappeared after 1894—they had fought rearguard actions in the form of riots, a foiled military school revolt in 1897, and, in the same year, the near assassination of Prudente de Morais, who afterward had adroitly hamstrung them politically. Thereafter, the principal *jacobino* leaders had retreated to a few congress seats or the press to maintain an energetic opposition and bide their time. Future leaders of the 1904 revolt, such as Lauro Sodré, Barbosa Lima, and Alfredo Varela, were figures of recognized polemical gifts and were closely associated with the victories and defeats of the 1890s.[24]

Lauro, above all, enjoyed a singular moral preeminence among long-time Republicans, often regardless of their political position vis-à-vis the Paulista administrations. A member of the positivist military circles who made the coup of 1889, former secretary to the "Founder of the Republic," Benjamin Constant [Botelho de Magalhães], Florianista governor of Pará, defeated presidential candidate of 1898, Lauro was generally respected as *imaculado*, a republican hero untainted by corruption or self-seeking. His birthday celebration in 1904 took on something of the quality of a national republican holiday, as he was flooded with thousands of telegrams and honored with processions and passionate speeches. He had made himself, and was recognized as, the charismatic leader of those disappointed with the administrations that followed Floriano's. Indeed, Lauro, with support in the congress and the press, championed a return to the ideal republic of which the conspirators of 1889 had dreamed, and he organized a congressional movement for constitutional reform. The senator, with the avid support of such firebrands as Barbosa Lima, was thus generally accepted as the spokesman for the radical republican forces in retreat after 1894. His natural following was the traditional one: diehard Florianistas and *jacobinos* in the military (especially the military schools in Rio) and in the economically vulnerable middle sectors (lesser bureaucrats, liberal professionals, radical polemicists, and politicized students), as well as elements of the working class (particularly a minority of government employees).[25]

There was another element in the traditional elite who backed Lauro's movement, if only for a time: the monarchists. This surprising adherence, however, was strictly opportunistic. The monarchists, though they had helped to fund the radical paper, *Comércio do Brasil* (edited by Lauro's cohort, Alfredo Varela), were hoping to add to the problems of the republic, just as they had done in the previous few years by supporting abortive workers' strikes and violence. Their game was seemingly to break the republic down in order to rebuild the monarchy. However, in the more violent phase of *Comércio do Brasil*, just before the revolt, monarchist aid evaporated. There is some proof that the restorationists declined to continue participating in the struggle when it became apparent that Lauro would not countenance their participation in the government he planned to head after deposing Rodrigues Alves. Though the police attempted to taint Lauro's coup with monarchism, it is doubtful that they persuaded anyone then, and the evidence to date would persuade no one now.[26]

The roots of the revolt of 1904, centering on the coup of November 14, thus lie in the ongoing attempts of *jacobino* military elements to retake power and destroy the regime of the Paulista-led oligarchies. From their past efforts and published positions, it is clear that these *jacobinos* hoped to institute a paternalist and authoritarian republic of national rgeneration, favoring state interventionism and protectionism, with urban middle-class and working-class support. These were not anti-"modernists"; rather, they were different "modernizers," favoring a much more radical and inclusionary path than the Paulista-led oligarchies. The latter envisioned only the relatively limited change congenial to the traditional agroexport interests; Lauro and his followers envisioned a dramatic pattern of change initiated by a strong state. They proposed to break with the old Brazil by promoting a more diversified economy, where the state not only intervened to strengthen export agriculture, but favored industry and addressed the needs and interests of the masses and the new urban groups which had been emerging since the 1850s. The authoritarian, reformist regimes men such as Lauro helped construct in various states (notably Pará,

Pernambuco, and Rio Grande do Sul) in the 1890s (regimes attempted, again, in the ephemeral *salvacionista* movement in the 1910s) give one a concrete sense of their intentions.[27]

Lauro may have begun to gather support for a coup as early as the aftermath of his unsuccessful presidential campaign in 1898. He attracted support with increasing success, especially after the election of Rodrigues Alves. Both the president and his policies were just too repellent for many old Republican purists. It was not simply that the new president, like Prudente and Campos Sales, represented the oligarchies' reascendency; it was that Rodrigues Alves, unlike the two earlier Paulistas, was a man without any link to the republican movement of 1870; indeed, he had been a stalwart of the monarchy's Conservative party and a member of the emperor's honorary council. The radical and republican milieus were fired to the point where bitter charges, conspiracy, and threats electrified the political atmosphere. Over the course of the administration, it became evident in congress and in the press that something familiar was crackling in the air again. The police, under the thoroughly "modern" administration of Dr. Antonio Augusto Cardoso de Castro, put the obvious opponents of the regime—radical, labor, and monarchist alike—under the close watch of a widespread network of police agents. What obligatory vaccination added to this situation was a lightning rod.[28]

As Nachman has made clear,[29] the principal leaders of the coup had no real animus toward Oswaldo Cruz's solution to smallpox—Barbosa Lima, for example, as the Florianista governor of Pernambuco, had even promoted obligatory vaccination. The issue, however, could be used as a fuse to ignite general opposition to the administration, and to produce the catalytic explosion of popular violence required for military cover and diversion. They also worked successfully to associate the movement leading up to the coup with symbolic celebrations and rhetoric, linking it and its leaders to the consecrated republican *golpe* of 1889. Thus, though Cardoso de Castro had frantically prepared to fend off a coup as early as mid-October (he assumed October 17, Lauro's highly politicized birthday celebration, was to be the occasion for the conspirators' move), he would have done better to remember the republican calendar. The conspirators were exploiting the issue of vaccination, the complaints of the army, and the larger issue of the regime's betrayal of the republic's ideals, gradually building toward a November crescendo. By then, after several last weeks of dcmonstrations commcmorating Lauro's birthday, celebrating the republic's founders, and recalling the events and actors linked to the Proclamation of November 15, they would be prepared to act. The coup was to be launched by participants in the military parades normally held on the 15th, the perfect date for the republic's would-be redeemers. But, as it happened, matters were taken out of the conspirators' hands by their most powerful ally. Before Lauro could seize state power, the Carioca masses had already begun to threaten it.[30]

The Carioca Masses

Recent research allows us to go beyond the word "masses" to analyze the identity and characteristics of the Cariocas who went into the streets on November 10. Even before abolition there were two main racial categories among the urban poor: the Afro-Brazilian and the fluctuating, immigrant (largely Portuguese) component. The main sources of wages, excluding suburban agriculture, were various forms of labor in the homes, in the shops and the tenements, and on the streets and docks, as domestics, artisans, vendors, unskilled heavy laborers, carriers, and stevedores—as well as unskilled and artisan labor in small factories, for Rio since midcentury had been the nation's center for (mostly secondary) industry. Another factor was locale: the working poor and the under- and unemployed lived as close to their work (or hope of work) as they could afford. Thus, some crowded into the decaying old townhouses and mansions and the slowly increasing number of new tenements that characterized shelter in the Old City and the New City, where commerce and most of the factories were. Others lived on the hillsides and on the twisted streets that lay between the city's hills and northern shoreline. These areas were near the docks that had grown up over the last century and the two main railheads (one at the shore, the other at the frontier between the Old City and the New—both connecting commerce and industry to hinterland plantations).[31]

Over the last 30 years of the nineteenth century, little had changed structurally for the poor. What did change was the impact that ever increasing numbers had on their already desperate conditions of life. Especially after abolition, the population flow into Rio was striking. About 20 percent of the city's population in 1890 was foreign-born, about 25 percent made up of native migrants. Immigrants from Portugal remained plentiful; the censuses indicate that, unlike São Paulo, where Italian immigrants tended to predominate, the Portuguese made up perhaps two-thirds of the foreigners in Rio in 1890 and 1906. In 1906, that meant that about 16 percent of the population was first-generation Portuguese. After Portugal, the single greatest source of newcomers was the rural areas of the northeast and southeast of Brazil, areas in economic decline. These regions were also the origin of most of the Afro-Brazilian portion of internal migration, and Afro-Brazilians (Carioca and migrant) made up more than a third of the city's residents in 1890 and 1906. Together with their children, Portuguese peasants and the Afro-Brazilians of the old plantation areas thus characterized the poor who swelled the population of the capital, tripling it between 1872 and 1906 from 274,972 to 811,443.[32]

The opportunities presented to these people had changed only slowly, with the relative shrinking of domestic service, the spurt in industrialization, and the continued, slow fading of agriculture. Some 117,904 people (14.5 percent) were domestics in 1906; 115,779 (14.3 percent) were industrial workers (between them, they made up about 45 percent of the economically active). Those still working the land were only 21,411 (2.6 percent); day laborers already outnumbered them, at 29,933, as did those workers who had no known "profession" (65,492, or 8 percent). Among the industrial workers, the largest categories included those involved in construction (31,800); clothing and accessories (31,710, 18,187 of whom were women), metallurgy (7,144), energy (5,301), and textiles (2,934, 1,010 of whom were women). Foreigners (including Portuguese) were numerically important in agriculture (6,313), metallurgy (2,768), food preparation (1,923 of 3,585), clothing and accessories (13,977), construction (16,954), energy (1,649), day labor (16,015), and domestic service (25,432). The industrial census of 1907 suggests that most workers labored 12 hours a day; it also notes the presence of children, with some 2,859 in 315 industries (though one assumes far more were probably involved; the figures were voluntary and child labor common enough in similar industrial situations elsewhere) and that most factories were small or medium sized—of the 726 enterprises registered, 216 had from 1 to 5 workers, 306 had from 6 to 40, and only 204 had more than 40. This industrial park, which employed roughly two times the number of people in 1907 than it had in 1890, was in fact still largely made up of small manufacturing and artisanal units with little division of labor and mechanization, although the relatively few large factories employed very large numbers of workers (e.g., the 1907 census notes that 22 textile factories employed an average of 467 workers).[33]

It was in the poor parishes of the city that industry flourished, along with commerce, construction, and day labor, so the poor continued to flood into them. Even before the 1890s, when the population and industry grew dramatically, the pattern of overcrowding had intensified steadily. Between 1872 and 1890, the Old City's population grew 52 percent, and the three poorest parishes, São José, Sant'Ana, and Santa Rita, grew 100 percent, 75 percent, and 42 percent, respectively. Benchimol cites figures showing that an average of 14.7 persons per building in 1872 had increased to 32/35 in 1890, with an obvious greater proportion of this crowding taking place in the Old City center. While the 1906 census cannot be cited in this regard because it was made after the reforms central to the discussion here, the agony of the 1890s and early 1900s may be imagined by simply noting that the city's population grew from 522,651 to an estimated 691,565 between 1890 and 1900. If one bears in mind that shelter had already been considered problematic by the 1850s, and that cheap housing and the number of dwellings in the Old City and New City were never considered adequate by any of the many commissions investigating them over the next half-century, the scope of the problem is glimpsed. Indeed, by the 1870s, the poor began to build their own shelters on the hills separating most of the city from the docks. The most famous, called Favela, was founded in the late 1890s, and would later be used as a generic name for all such shantytowns. The other solution, increasingly sought by those with better wages, was flight to the North Zone, to São Cristóvão or further, necessitating travel to work by increasingly expensive railway or streetcar.[34]

For the masses who continued to live in the traditionally poor, distinctively Afro-Brazilian districts, New City, Gambôa, Saúde, and certain Old City streets, conditions were infernal. *Casas de cômodos* (rooming houses) were made of late colonial- and imperial-period townhouses and mansions, which were converted by dividing and redividing every room into several, using wooden boards or merely lines of sacks. There, industrial workers, jacks-of-all-trades, teamsters, cashiers, laundrywomen, seamstresses, and prostitutes crowded to sleep. They used the common corridors and spaces under staircases for cooking, with the out-of-work and dirty and naked infants and young children underfoot, and prostitutes, seamstresses, and laundrywomen plying their trades close by, all in the noise and filth and hot and humid air. As for the *cortiço* (tenement), one contemporary noted its hot, low, dark rooms and relative lack of privacy, and commented that "there are *cortiços* where one penetrates with one's handkerchief over one's nose and whence one leaves nauseated."[35] As for the favelas, this same investigator reported that the homes were no higher than a man, with floors of beaten earth and walls and roofs made of opened kerosene cans, the boards from boxes, and a multitude of other odds and ends, without water or suitable space, lumped together along the narrow, winding paths up the hillside. Here were prostitutes and bullyboys and the poorest of the industrial workers. It is little wonder that such conditions, when combined with the malnutrition common to such poverty, made the traditional parishes of the poor the main killing ground of the gastrointestinal illnesses and communicable diseases common to the era, sicknesses which regularly killed infants and adults by the thousands, year in and year out.[36]

Such wretched poverty was maintained, and could worsen, with under- and unemployment. Besides the obvious impact, there is also an indirect impact of a large pool of under- and unemployed. Such a pool often helps keep wages down for the labor force as a whole, and limits the success of labor organization. This may well have been the case here, especially considering the size of such a pool in Rio. Although the 1906 census does not register unemployment as such, noting only the professions declared by working men and women, it does have certain suggestive categories. Besides those for day laborer (*jornaleiros, trabalhadores braçaes*, etc.), 29,933; there were "professions badly specified" (*profissões mal especificadas*), 6,595; "unproductive classes" (*classes improdutivas*), 27,888; and "unknown professions" (*profissões desconhecidas*), 65,492. These were all distinguished from those who were apparently not economically active ("without declared profession"—*sem profissão declarada*), comprised of those younger (182,646) and older (109,556) than 15 years of age (the older, one assumes, being women who did not work and the aged who could not or no longer had to). Setting aside this last category, a total of some 129,908 people might well be defined as without steady or full-time gainful employment. This category is larger than those employed in either domestic service or industry, the two most numerous categories, and comprised 16 percent of Rio's population and 25 percent of those economically active.[37]

Good, steady work was difficult to get. Industrial employment had steadily increased, but unevenly with respect to race, national origin, and job security. As Adamo[38] has shown, the European immigrant had a much greater chance of securing factory employment, retaining it, and, most important, being promoted, than Afro-Brazilians. Moreover, no matter where the urban poor worked, their livelihood was directly affected by the financial policies and disasters of the government, events whose impact on the city's economy was immediate and quite consequential. The last half century, with the increasing growth of urban and national commerce, urban population, urban investment, and foreign capital dependency, had increased the scope and frequency of such impact. There were major periods of inflation and capital investment in the mid-1850s and 1888–95; there were major depressions or recessions in 1857, 1875–79, and 1895–1902. The last boom-and-bust cycle had been especially hard on wage earners. Their money bought relatively less from 1888 to 1898. Although many, particularly those in construction and unskilled labor, did well in 1898–1902 and received salary increases, the more skilled workers (for example, the artisanal workers common among the industries) generally received no increases. Exchange and credit problems of the 1880s had brought much of the insecurity and hardship which plagued the urban wage earners and middle sectors, and added fire to the movements for abolition and the republic. The boom-and-bust cycle of the decade or so before 1904 was a good deal more traumatic and, in the case of Campos Sales's deflationary austerity, was correctly perceived as being the work of the administration, which left office amidst violent popular anger.[39]

It seems clear, then, that by the time of the Rodrigues Alves administration, the Carioca masses, riven by racism and beset by poor housing, constant illness and disease, precarious employment, and vagaries in the amount and value of their wages, were in a wretched, rebellious condition. To speak of political alienation and hostility is an understatement, particularly in the case of the Afro-Brazilian population. The vitality and the repression of their distinct culture, as well as the poverty and racial abuse they had suffered for generations, formed only the backdrop to the new anguish they must have endured in postabolition Rio. For, although the censuses do not specify racial distinctions, it is logical to assume that it was the most recent, native rural migrants, largely Afro-Brazilian, who, handicapped by racism, illiteracy, lack of marketable skills and urban-industrial socialization, suffered most. They doubtless made up a disproportionate number of the under- and unemployed, the marginalized people who inhabited the favelas and worse slums. We know that it was there that the Afro-Brazilian cultural traditions were maintained, and that it was from there that working people were recruited for the heaviest unskilled work of docks, streets, and factories—when they could get it.[40]

Higher ranking workers, including artisans, skilled factory workers, and shop staffs—likely Rio-born or immigrant, and less disproportionately Afro-Brazilian in origin—earned more, but were just as subject to the tenuous economic health of the city. From this relative minority, some artisans, stevedores, railroad workers, and skilled factory workers were organized into Rio's first unions. Indeed, these groups, a sort of labor elite, generally led by middle-sector organizers of confused *jacobino*, positivist, socialist antecedents, had recently become increasingly militant. It was precisely over the last decade or so, with all of the interlinked problems already noted, that workers' strikes and riots had become numerous—indeed, in 1903, the capital witnessed its first May Day labor parades and a major textile strike. The police were increasingly monitoring the largely Afro-Brazilian stevedores' union, which was elaborating international ties to the stevedores of Montevideo and Buenos Aires by 1904. They were also observing the work of Dr. Vicente de Sousa, a Bahian-born mulatto and veteran of abolitionism. This physician and professor was the most successful of the era's labor organizers; in many ways, his general background seems to be typical. Vicente de Sousa was a man of the middle sectors, of positivist, *jacobino* inclinations, who supported the coup of 1889 and who had studied socialism during the 1890s, committing himself to a reformist, multiclass perspective on the workers' plight. He then worked successfully to organize labor, promoting a sort of socialist paternalism which articulated well with his earlier perspectives. In 1902, he helped found the ephemeral Partido Socialista Coletivista. By 1903, he was president of the Centro de Classes Operárias (1902–1904) in the Old City, the great meeting place of a number of constituent workers' unions. Moreover, since neither his nor other pioneering workers' organizations noted here were the handiwork of foreign agitators, the police could not simply deport the "troublemakers." In this phase, at least, Carioca labor militancy (unlike that of São Paulo) was often the accomplishment of just such native ideologues, who organized among the poor according to their own lights, without direct ties to foreign socialist or anarchist experience.[41]

The masses' perception of the *belle-époque* program of Rodrigues Alves must be understood in this context. The changes rarely brought positive elements into their lives. Although some enjoyed temporary employment in construction and allied industries, the reforms generally worsened harsh, grinding conditions for the poor and exacerbated a rising tide of hostility and militance. In 1901, there had been riots touched off by an increase in streetcar fares and by Campos Sales's repression. In 1902, violent demonstrations had marked the end of Campos Sales's regime. In Rodrigues Alves's second year, 1903, there was the textile strike just noted, the largest strike in Brazilian history, which had spread to a general strike before suppression. That same year, there were also riots (led by civilian and military *jacobinos*) sparked by the coming of foreign-born, rather than native, Benedictines.[42] Now, over the course of 1904, Rodrigues Alves's program made life suddenly worse in a matter of months. The urban reforms and the boulevards linking the new portworks to the city quite purposely destroyed as much of the decrepit housing as was economically possible. The street widening and the new streets and boulevards that smashed through the Old City, the dockside area, and the New City destroyed a world. They snapped the shoestring economies of thousands of Cariocas and brutally uprooted them. The very poorest retreated up into the hillside shantytowns. Those who could found refuge in certain unreformed pockets of the New City. Others added to those flooding into the North Zone, where the population increased by 116.1 percent between 1890 and 1906. In the Old City and the New City some 1,600 buildings were destroyed, and an estimated 20,000 people were forced to leave, presumably with enormous difficulty and trauma for themselves and those who now had to share their small space with the refugees. For no real effort was made to find or build new dwellings. The prefect, Pereira Passos, long an advocate of authoritarian reforms to order and sanitize working-class housing, did build some multiple residences to accommodate workers—but they were so few (and their residents so select) as to be ridiculous. The poor, as usual, had to take care of themselves.[43]

If the poor had reason to look on such administration policies with less than a sanguine eye, the same can be said with respect to the administration's related program of disease control. The two phases (yellow fever and plague eradication) completed before obligatory vaccination goaded the population mercilessly. For example, Oswaldo Cruz's plans for yellow fever (derived from the model of U.S. success in Cuba) turned on a strategy of dramatic and authoritarian tactics, carried out with precise military-style organization and in conjunction with the housing destruction. Despite the obvious benefit to the population, the doctor's prescription doubtless fostered bitterness and suspicion. Cruz divided the city into sections and then, armed with the appropriate legal dispensations, sent in teams of officials and sanitary police to inspect every building, force the cleanup of mosquito breeding grounds, and designate which buildings were too amenable for such breeding to be allowed to stand. These were promptly torn down. The procedure for plague eradication was similar: it involved rat killing and unannounced visits to buildings to ensure that the residents maintained the required conditions and, as with yellow fever, registered the diseased. In both cases, then, the poor were physically forced to stand aside while the public physicians, sanitary police, and public health officials entered and ransacked their homes, designating some for destruction and reserving the rest for periodic invasions, threats, and meddling.[44]

With the smallpox vaccination campaign, even worse was threatened. It was not simply that one's home was to be invaded by police and other agents. Now, every man knew that he would be forced to allow these strangers to inoculate the women of his household; modesty was sure to be outraged. Barbosa Lima, in a scandalous speech in the Chamber of Deputies, asked the aged gentleman presiding what his response would be to obligatory inoculation in the buttocks. If this mortified Barbosa Lima's associates, one can barely imagine the indignation and fear even the thought aroused in the poor men and women who had no reason whatever to expect discretion or respect from Dr. Oswaldo's squads. Moreover, as the editorial at the beginning of this essay indicates, the opposition radicals exploited the fears and ignorance of the poor with inflammatory articles. They focused skillfully on the vaccination's purported ill effects and on antivaccination arguments of the elite and middle classes, which appealed to constitutional principles and more forcefully, surely, to the norms of an unchallenged patriarchal tradition of masculine protection. Nor, apparently, was mendacity neglected. During the revolt, supposedly, a few of the streetfighters interviewed testified that they had heard that the vaccination serum was to be injected into their women's groin area and that it was drawn from the bodies of rats.[45]

Impoverished, overcrowded, poorly and irregularly employed, wracked with disease, profoundly alienated from the governing elite, traumatized by migration, the loss of home, and government abuse, and now, finally, threatened in the integrity of their wretched households with the violation of women, it is little wonder that the Carioca masses turned to violence in 1904.

After all, it was not the first time. Violence among the poor in Rio was endemic; in many of the forms that came into play in 1904, it was also traditional. The papers reported daily the seemingly pervasive violence that punctuated life in the favelas, bars, and streets. Indeed, sensationalist coverage of crimes of passion, bar fights, personal disputes, muggings, and random murder and mayhem, with brief moralistic (or cynical) commentaries, was apparently the delight of the literate population there and then, as it is here and now. What is worth remarking is that there were certain sorts of people who traditionally specialized in violence, some of whom were well known individually, and that public violence against authority had a long history in the city.

Certain figures repeatedly surface in the popular press in bar fights, election-day intimidation, and so on: men known by colorful sobriquets (Poxface, Kid Johnny, and the like) and given the traditional designation *desordeiro* (disorderly). Such men were dangerous with the club, the knife, the straight razor, and their feet, hands, and head; they practiced the delicate, dangerous, deadly moves of Rio's traditional Afro-Brazilian martial art and folk ballet, *capoeira*. To be sure, the *capoeiragem* of 1904 was not the highly organized gang warfare of the monarchy. Then, the city's parishes had often had distinct, secret societies of *capoeiras* (the term signified both the art and its practitioner), each gang, or *malta*, belonging to one of the two old divisions of Nagoas and Goyamas. Such *maltas* had not only fought and danced with one another in public, but had hired themselves out to the great political chiefs of the day as bodyguards and bullyboys, especially during election struggles in the city parishes. Now, such public organization and traditional connections were in decline. Many *capoeiras* had been organized to defend the monarchy (and, thus, to attack republican open meetings) in 1889, and were recruited into the Black Guard. In 1890, the new republic's provisional government attempted in turn to liquidate the *capoeiras*, and the police rounded up the most noted. By 1904, then, *capoeiragem* still existed, but without the public prominence and well-known traditional Afro-Brazilian trappings. Petty parish politicians, not imperial party chiefs, called them out for municipal elections. The rumor of gangs worked its way intermittently into the press, but now the emphasis was on the personal reputation of individual *desordeiros*, not *maltas* and their parish wars.[46]

Other forms of violence were also traditional to Rio. The earliest period of national history was punctuated with terrible riots that the police were unable to stifle. In some of these, *capoeiras* played a part, but not the major one. Numerous periods of political tension ignited in riots in which the Carioca multitude fought pitched street battles against the police, building trenches and barricades as shelter against their traditional, better armed foe. The records indicate that such events were well known in the First Reign. In the Second Reign street violence, under republican and abolitionist auspices since the 1870s, became a common threat again. The hardships of the lower middle class and the working masses gave new strength to the street violence of the 1880s, and continued to feed that of the 1890s. In that last decade, some *jacobinos* cultivated popular fury and directed it against Portuguese workers, shopkeepers, merchants, and native-born monarchists alike—and now, not only civilian firebrands but young officers joined in the rioting.[47]

It is legitimate to ask whether immigration from Portugal and rural Brazil might have diluted the strength of this Carioca tradition of street violence by bringing in population foreign to it. The answer is initially ambiguous: the poor Portuguese immigrants might definitely undercut such a tradition, while the Afro-Brazilian might strengthen it. We have no direct evidence either way, and must rely on inference. A Portuguese, for example, might understandably refrain from joining traditionally Lusophobic *jacobinos* and more reasonably hope for the real relative opportunity for social mobility present in the case of white workers. He might also be counting on familial or old-country village relations to help him advance in commerce, traditionally dominated by his countrymen through just such patterns of mobility. Finally, Portuguese immigration had slowed dramatically by 1900. Those already in Rio were probably in a relatively more stable, upwardly mobile position than recent immigrants; certainly, their relative strength in, say, the industrial work force was dropping. Matters for the Afro-Brazilian migrants, who were still flooding in, remained different and harsh. Such migrants more likely took more of the economy's body blows and might well respond to *jacobino* nativism in a racial and economic situation favoring European immigrants. They might also be prone to embrace the established patterns of Carioca violence because it was something born of an environment whose values they quickly assimilated. It is important in this regard to recall that the Afro-Brazilian migrants generally came from the same areas, generation after generation, and lived in the same urban districts on arrival, where they would undergo shared hardships and doubtless respond in shared ways as they were absorbed into the preexisting Afro-Brazilian community. This was something of a world apart, with its distinct cultural heritage sharply distinguished from the European immigrants' and the urban elite's Europhile ways. Coming to the city in wave after wave, migrants constantly reinforced that milieu's rural, African, and servile origins, while learning the community's response to sufferings such new and old city-dwellers bore alike: accentuated racism, poverty, oppression, petty violence, and socioeconomic instability. Moreover, it is central to underscore that the last ten years exacerbated the problems and fed the Carioca tradition of violence, this time fortified by political and labor militance. Thus, although there is no way to prove it, one may reasonably conclude that while many Portuguese in the working class may have held back from the revolt, the Afro-Brazilians were almost certainly in its vanguard.[48]

Finally, one cannot neglect the fact that violent individuals and violent mass response were not only traditional in Rio but reinforced by state violence. On the one hand, the army provided a school for mayhem. Its ranks were generally made up of poor criminals and the unemployed, brought to the colors by press gangs. Violent recruitment, training in violence, and constant billeting close to, or within, the favelas and tenements of the city made the army's recruits and veterans a constant pool of violent potential among the Carioca masses. On the other hand, the police provided this multitude with both a goad to violence and a traditional enemy. Although recruited from the poor themselves, they showed no mercy; they were notorious as being among the city's most violent thugs and *capoeiras*. Uniformed or plain-clothes agents, they commonly acted as just another gang of bullyboys, but one licensed to beat, maim, rob, extort, and kill. At constant war with the *desordeiros* and preying on the masses among whom the *desordeiros* had their place, the police were hated by the Carioca poor with good reason and a terrible passion.[49]

So neither tensions, traditions, nor training were lacking in 1904. The masses, both the elite of organized workers and the larger group of under- and unemployed, had reasons, experience, and their own leaders for battle. What made 1904 different from years gone by was a larger vision of the possibilities of violence and the hope of effecting social change. These would both be provided by the conspirators linked to Lauro Sodré.

Achievements of a Failed Revolt

All the evidence agrees on the revolt's leadership: Lauro, Barbosa Lima, Alfredo Varela, and Vicente de Sousa. The generals, other officers, and civilians who met at the Club Militar on November 14 were tools of these men, trusted agents, or ambitious opportunists. It is safe to assume that Lauro, deciding to use the disruptive potential of mass street violence, a potential evident since 1880, agreed to ally his cause to that of his old comrade, Vicente de Sousa. As noted, the latter, like Lauro, was associated with 1889 and was a man of positivist, *jacobino* background. Now, his unprecedented achievement as the founder of the Centro de Classes Operárias, joining industrial artisan, railroad, and dockworker unions into one umbrella organization, provided the conspirators with a new weapon against the oligarchs' republic. The roles of Barbosa Lima and Alfredo Varela focused on middle-sector and elite agitation. Each seconded Lauro in increasing the tensions in congress; Varela added to this the editing of his extremist opposition paper. The others, as suggested, joined either out of loyalty to the old cause or for reasons of thwarted or whetted ambition, and were involved in the mechanics of the coup.[50]

Sousa and his Centro provided the crucial link to the masses. By October 1904, all the pieces were in place, and the leadership, building the pressure and heightening the tensions, used the vaccination issue to ready the middle sector for opposition and the military, radicals, and urban poor for action. The Centro was the staging area for that action. In public meetings there the leadership played to the public with the inflammatory speeches and tactics that precipitated violence. The founding of the Liga Contra Vacina at the Centro on November 5 was the penultimate step. It formally linked the leadership to cadets, middle-sector radicals, students, and organized workers in an organization of legitimate opposition that provided the oratorical platform for launching the revolt. The last step was short—from the call for violent resistance, out the Centro's door to the agitated thousands of *jacobino* militants and desperate throngs in the hall and the streets.[51]

There, in the streets, the revolt was entirely within the Carioca tradition; what varied was its scope and success—and the latter was the result of the former. Public meetings, heckling, hostility, and armed clashes—these were nothing new; nor were the locales— Cariocas had always massed at the plazas and then stormed down the main streets of the Old City, building barricades and pitting themselves against the police. The *desordeiros*, often leading the action now, were commonly the most terrible antagonists in such mélées, and streetcar barricades were a part of Carioca rioting since at least 1880. What was different now was the numbers involved and their determination.[52]

Some 4,000 people attended the last league meeting of November 12, immediately before 500 or 600 marched on Catete and other groups of hundreds began widespread violence and rioting in the Old City. More than 24 streetcars were destroyed that day. By the 13th, whole sections of the Old City's center were barricaded and held. Groups of a thousand or more were cited in action on other days of the revolt. Groups were attacking parish police stations and taking streets not only in the Old City but on the hillsides and in other working-class parishes. After the 14th, strikes and violence broke out in factories in the South Zone at the Gâvea and Laranjeiras, and large sections of the North Zone became battlegrounds.

Then, too, the violence was hardly the complete anarchy often recorded afterward. It often mixed strategic and symbolic violence and, to a great extent, was clearly purposeful within a larger plan. As a rule, the only passersby who were robbed, beaten, or shot were victims of the police; the streetfighters generally reserved their stones for the carriages of the ministers and officials most responsible for repression. Many of the stores sacked were those stocked with food and liquor, arms and kerosene. On one occasion, wealthy commuters from the elite resort of Petropólis, on docking at their ferry building, were received by a mob—but the latter touched none of the wealthy physically; they apparently wanted symbolic vengeance. They allowed the rich to leave unmolested, but attacked the property of the ferry company. Other destruction was just as symbolic, though it often served practical military purposes as well. Property associated with the police, public transportation, the administration, and the urban reform construction seems to have been singled out for attention. Although streetcars were probably a special target as the property of the hated companies that the North Zone workers blamed for the high cost of transportation, they also made excellent barricades. As for the constant destruction of streetlamps, telegraph and telephone wires, and the attacks on the Gazómetro, these were tactical; without light, the streetfighters were safer; without telephone and telegraph, the authorities were less able to coordinate repression.[53]

It also seems clear that the streetfighters, who were, after all, occasionally joined by uniformed army officers, and who cheered the army whenever its units appeared (ostensibly to aid the police), saw themselves in alliance with the military. They apparently expected the coup that the speeches and the obvious military links of the leadership made patent. It is worth noting here that, indeed, the army, though its units were sent to defend positions against the streetfighters on the 12th, was rarely trusted with offensives against them until after the cadets' failure signaled the coup's collapse. On those occasions when they were sent against the masses before the 15th, they proved unenthusiastic, if not sympathetic. More indicative still is one memoir which recalls seeing many important officers waiting hidden near the military school on the 14th, to see which direction the fortunes of war might blow. Rodrigues Alves's own dismay at the lack of military support sent him by the generals on the evening of the 14th has already been noted.[54]

The violence of the streetfighters, then, although it obviously corresponded to their own particular hatreds and anger in many details, was directed toward a larger goal. As evident from their actions and the context just noted, their mission was to distract, divide, and tire the government's loyal forces and thus provide the military and psychological milieu propitious for Lauro's coup. In this, they were successful. Indeed, too successful; they apparently forced the leadership to change plans. By taking over the city streets and neutralizing the police, the streetfighters placed the government in an emergency situation in which the armed forces had to be called on and the military parade celebrating the republic's proclamation on November 15 had to be canceled. This parade, as noted earlier, was going to be the crucial medium for launching the planned coup. Now, the conspirators, meeting at the Club Militar, had to figure out how to bring the military out against Rodrigues Alves from their barracks or, worse, from the field, where they were now deployed against their popular allies. They seemingly fell back on the paradigm of November 15, 1889. Then, the cadets of Praia Vermelha and regular troops from the North Zone, organized by republican, positivist militants, had come out at the call of a

general of great personal prestige and struck together at the imperial government in the person of its prime minister and his cabinet.
Now, after organizing among both cadets and the military, the conspirators again turned to the military school cadets; once again, a
combination of the cadets' militance and army solidarity would
launch attacks north and south against the government, in the person of its president and his assembled ministers. If only the cadets
of Praia Vermelha (not to mention those of the Realengo school or
the wavering army units in the Old City) had been able to strike
quickly, matters might easily have gone Lauro's way. If the cadets
had had their proper arms and ammunition and had marched immediately, all the evidence suggests that they might well have reached
Catete unopposed, indeed, quite possibly reinforced, and have received the surrender of the palace's demoralized defenders. The
army might well have gone over completely at such a juncture, and
the day been won. But though the *desordeiros*, radicals, workers,
and marginalized Cariocas had made this feasible, it was not to be.
They were, in the end, dependent on Lauro's success, and Lauro
failed.[55]

By November 14, the streetfighters began fortifying sections
of the hillside shantytowns and dockside slums. These preparations,
it will be recalled, centered on the Afro-Brazilian district of Saúde,
where they called their barricaded trenchworks "Porto Arthur." They
obeyed the commands of a well-known *desordeiro*, Horácio José
da Silva, "Prata Preta," who had been elected to command. He did
so with military precision; possibly he and others were veterans.
Behind the barricades, cornets sounded, mock-up cannon were set
up, and dynamite bombs were prepared (some real, some fake, for
effect, like the cannon). And it was all done under the red flag the
streetfighters unfurled, doubtless to signify adherence to the kind
of socialist sindicalism men like Vicente de Sousa had injected into
the Carioca milieu over the past decade. Until the ironclad turned
its big guns against them, and until their hoped-for ally, the army,
began its street-by-street attack, the streetfighters seemed to have
maintained their readiness for battle. In the end, however, after Prata
Preta's failed counterattack, they decided against striking the pose
of some sort of tropical commune, with its terrible bloodbath: they
left Porto Arthur. Unhappily, Rodrigues Alves was quite willing to
play out the roles of 1870 Paris—if the *desordeiros* abandoned the
role of communards, the president, as will be shown, was quite
willing to take up something of the role of Thiers.[56]

The Triumph of the *Belle Epoque*

The so-called Revolta Contra Vacina was, in essence, two revolts against the Paulista regime and its "modernizing" policies, each with distinct participants and agenda; two revolts, one of which consciously, and the other perhaps unconsciously, fought under the useful banner of a constitutional and medical issue of little real moment. The leadership launched their coup to remake the republic; the streetfighters among the masses, as far as we can discern, fought for a new social order or, at least, fought back against their immediate oppressors. Ostensibly, both leadership and masses won—obligatory vaccination, after all, was abandoned for several years. In reality, both lost. And each lost to the "modernizing" oligarchs' regime in separate ways which are worth noting.

The radical opposition lost in its bid for power and was further marginalized politically. They would never offer another real challenge to the Old Republic and its oligarchies—at least, not in Rio. Though Rodrigues Alves was bitter to see Lauro and other surviving conspirators and cadets amnestied in 1905, the larger questions of power had been answered in favor of the forces he represented. Save for vaccination, his policies triumphed. Rio became "modern," trade, immigration, and investment were successfully cultivated, and "progress" and "civilization" were assured. The *belle époque* had triumphed.[57]

If the leadership and cadets paid a small price for their failure, the poor paid terribly for their success. There was no amnesty for them. Hundreds arrested in the fighting were sent to the Ilha das Cobras compound just offshore, in a process of capture and imprisonment involving fearful beatings. After the revolt was smoldering and then cold, the police took their vengeance and the *belle époque* its toll. The police swept through the favelas, "beating" their target areas the way beaters flush out English sportsmen's quarry. There, and in raids in the various refuges to which the *desordeiros* fled, the police selected their enemies and the most dangerous-looking unemployed and sent them, along with beggars, poor prostitutes, and noted pimps to the Ilha das Cobras. Under the state of siege that an accommodating congress granted the administration thrice in succession, the rights of such prisoners could be trampled on, and they were. The wealthy foreign dealers in the white-slave trade were deported. For the native sons, Rodrigues Alves's government took a page from the French bourgeois who triumphed over the

Paris commune. The streetfighters, beggars, unemployed, and prostitutes were sent to a kind of Brazilian Devil's Island—the recently acquired Territory of Acre, in the steaming tropical rain forests drained by tributaries of the Amazon. The newspapers record that between 539 and 855 or more prisoners—men and women—were sent there in three or four levies between the end of November and the first week of January, on coastal packet boats the opposition would later aptly compare to the slaveships of the Middle Passage. Rio had been purged of the dangerous and the unsightly; the government had singled out people for elimination, just as it had eliminated so much of old Rio, the traditional, Afro-Brazilian port capital—both were condemned by the values and needs of the elite's vision of modernity.[58]

The Brazilian-dominated unions that survived or succeeded those of 1904 would be moderate in their politics; indeed, like the radical leadership of 1904, native-born workers would generally no longer offer a substantial threat to the status quo. Their great struggle soon became unknown to most Cariocas, successfully captured and dismissed by middle-class and elite chroniclers as a kind of tropical Luddite reaction to the blessings of "modern" science— savage, barbaric, the work of political opportunists and atavistic masses.[59]

We have seen that it was far different and far more. The revolt of 1904 was a coordinated effort by at least two distinct groups to remake the Brazilian path: to destroy the oligarchical government, to strike back at its oppression and the savage attrition of its works, and, possibly, to erect an authoritarian, inclusionary, paternalist order dedicated to "modernity" without marginalization or the continued hegemony of the agroexport elites. But this unique attempt, mercilessly crushed, left no trace, no tradition. The alliance between ideological middle-sector leaders and the workers, marginalized, and *desordeiros* bore no fruit—only a distorted memory.

Each of the two elements went its separate way. After the amnesty that freed Lauro, his colleagues, and the cadets, there was tremendous acclaim for the senator—he was lionized by elements of the city's elite and middle sectors opposed to the particular policies of Rodrigues Alves (though none acclaimed the use of violence, nor the failed revolt). On his release, he enjoyed a fevered reception at the Teatro Lírico, traditional social center for the elite and the stage of the fantasy triumphs of opera. A subscription had raised the money for a sword of gold, which was presented to Lauro on that occasion.

One wag remembered, however, someone whom everyone else at the theater was apparently trying to forget. This wit observed that Lauro's sword would have been more fitting if it were made of silver—of *prata*. In two generations, this acid allusion to Prata Preta and the streetfighters of Saúde would go unnoticed.[60] The last contemporary reference I found to the *desordeiro* leader formed part of what its author described as a "Dantesque nightmare." In December 1904, a proadministration paper recorded this description of a group of those exiled to Acre. It says more, perhaps, about the "modernizers" than about their *desordeiro* enemy:

> From below decks of the ship came muffled sounds, shouts, curses, blasphemies. . . . There, piled up in the greatest promiscuity, were children and old people, blacks and whites, native-born and foreigners, some lying down, others standing, with both hands bound securely to the cable-heads, trying to breathe, making superhuman efforts to take in the pure air of the exterior, which penetrated through only with difficulty. . . . The 334 convicts, almost all naked, fought with the enormous rats in the dark, who attacked them boldly and covered them with bites . . . without support, the prisoners rolled over one another, hurting themselves and slipping in the nauseating mud of feces and vomit. . . . Next to the hatches, riflemen pointed their weapons below, maintaining the respect of the miserable. Thus passed the first day, but other days followed and nothing changed the situation of the unhappy; on the contrary, their evils were aggravated with the sinister apparition of a terrible black, Prata Preta—a true demon. This black, tall, muscular, among the strongest present, immediately took a certain supremacy, taking on the office of chief below decks. Armed with a thick piece of rope, he began to beat his companions in misfortune bestially, ferociously, only stopping when the blood ran in jets.[61]

Plainly, Afro-Brazilian Rio was being exorcised in 1904—the city was "civilizing itself"[62] indeed.

Notes

1. "Perigos de vaccina," *Correio da Manhã* (hereafter, *CM*), Oct. 13, 1904, p. 1.
2. The Oswaldo Cruz campaign is discussed below. On the opposition, see, e.g., Gil Vidal, "A terceira discussão," *CM*, Oct. 1, 1904, p. 1; "Vida operária,"

CM, Oct. 1, 1904, p. 3; "¿Preparativos para a violencia?," *CM*, Oct. 6, 1904, p. 1; "Vaccina ou morte," *CM*, Oct. 7, 1904, p. 1; "Vaccinação obrigatória," *CM*, Oct. 10, 1904, p. 1; "Apelo ao povo contra a vaccinação obrigatória," *CM*, Nov. 5, 1904, p. 1; "Liga Contra a Vaccinação Obrigatória," *CM*, Nov. 6, 1904, p. 1; "O dever do povo," *CM*, Nov. 7, 1904, p. 1; "Liga Contra a Vaccinação Obrigatória," *CM*, Nov. 9, 1904, p. 2; *Gazeta de Noticias* (hereafter, *GN*), Nov. 12, 1904, p. 1; Menelau, "Croniqueta," *A Avenida* (hereafter, *AA*), Oct. 29, 1904, p. 2; *AA*, Oct. 29, 1904, p. 5; Vital do Valle, "Notas e apanhados: Vaccinação obrigatória," *AA*, Nov. 12, 1904, p. 15; "A vaccina," *Rua do ouvidor*, July 16, 1904, p. 2; ibid., Aug. 13, 1904, p. 2; José [Araujo] Vieira, *O boto abaixo: Crónica de 1904* (Rio de Janeiro, 1934), 84-86, 88–89.

3. This synthesis is based on the analysis of the era's four major dailies: *O Paiz* (mass circulation, progovernment); *O Jornal do Comércio* (elite circulation, progovernment); *Gazeta de Noticias* (mass circulation, progovernment); and *Correio da Manhã* (mass circulation, opposition).

4. *Jornal do comércio* (hereafter, *JC*), Nov. 16, 1904, p. 2; *O Paiz* (hereafter, *OP*), Nov. 17, 1904, p. 2; Dr. A. A. Cardoso de Castro, chefe de policia do Distrito Federal, "Relatorio apresentado ao Exmo. Snr. Dr. J. J. Seabra, Ministro da Justiça e Negocios Interiores," in Ministerio da Justiça e Negocios Interiores, *Relatorio apresentado ao Presidente da República dos Estados Unidos do Brasil pelo Dr. J. J. Seabra, Ministro . . . em Março de 1905* (Rio de Janeiro, 1905), I, 18–19, 36–39, 40; Francisco de Paula Rodrigues Alves, "1904: Movimentos de novembro," ms. quoted *in toto* in Afonso Arinos de Melo Franco, *Rodrigues Alves: Apogeu e declíneo de presidencialismo*, 2 vols. (Rio de Janeiro, 1973), I, 408–409; Dantas Barreto, *Conspirações* (Rio de Janeiro, 1917), 11–14.

5. *JC*, Nov. 20, 1904, p. 2; General Lobato Filho, *A última noite da Escola Militar da Praia Vermelha (Contribuições para a história)* (Rio de Janeiro, 1945), chs. 1, 2, 6, 7 [N.B. Lobato Filho was a rebel cadet]; Cardoso de Castro, "Relatorio," 13, 18–19, 20–21, 34–43, passim; see *CM* citations in n. 2 for a record of Lauro's activities before the rising.

6. *OP*, Nov. 15, 1904, p. 2; *JC*, Nov. 15, 1904, p. 1; Cardoso de Castro, as cited in n. 5; "O ano politico: Brasil," in *Almanaque brasileiro Garnier para o ano de 1906*, 314–315; Lobato Filho, *A última noite*, 96–98.

7. *OP*, Nov. 15, 1904, p. 1; *JC*, Nov. 15, 1904, p. 1; *GN*, Nov. 15, 1904, p. 2; Lobato Filho, *A última noite*, 91–113; Rodrigues Alves, "1904," 410–412; Emmanuel Sodré, *Lauro Sodré: Na história da República* (Rio de Janeiro, n.d.), 89–90.

8. Rodrigues Alves, "1904," 411–412. Cf. Vital do Valle, "Notas e apanhados," *AA*, Nov. 26, 1904, p. 3.

9. *OP*, Nov. 15, 1904, p. 2, Nov. 16, p. 2, and Nov. 17, p. 2; *GN*, Nov. 15, 1904, pp. 1–2, Nov. 16, 1904, pp. 1–2, and Nov. 17, pp. 2–3; *JC*, Nov. 15, 1904, p. 2, Nov. 16, 1904, p. 2, Nov. 17, 1904, p. 2, and Nov. 18, 1904, p. 2.

10. The repression began even earlier; *CM* was suspended Nov. 16–17 and Nov. 18–Dec. 14, 1904. Arrests of principal suspects began before Nov. 18 (see *CM*, Nov. 18, 1904, p. 2 and Dec. 28, 1904, p. 2; *GN* as cited in n. 9). On the immediate repression thereafter, see *JC* or *OP* through early Jan. 1905. On the subsequent smallpox toll, see Nancy Stepan, *Beginnings of Brazilian Science: Oswaldo Cruz, Medical Research and Policy, 1890–1920* (New York, 1976), 90, who reports some 9,000 dead of smallpox in 1908 alone.

Note that the rising in Rio was echoed by an abortive revolt in Salvador's ninth battalion on Nov. 18 (see *JC*, Nov. 20, 1904, p. 1; *OP*, Nov. 19, 1904, p. 1).

11. See, e.g., *JC*, Nov. 16, 1904, p. 2; *OP*, Nov. 15, 1904, p. 1, Nov. 17, 1904, p. 1, and Nov. 19, 1904, p. 1; *GN*, Nov. 16, 1904, p. 1; "Notas e noticias: Agitação inutil," *GN*, Nov. 13, 1904, p. 1; O. B., "Crónica," ibid.; "Notas e noticias: Os acontecimentos de hontem," *GN*, Nov. 14, 1904, p. 1; "Notas e noticias: Tentativa malograda," *GN*, Nov. 16, 1904, p. 1; "Notas e noticias: A lição dos factos," *GN*, Nov. 20, 1904, p. 1; Sancho Alves, "Comentários," *Kósmos*, 2:3 (Mar. 1905), 1–2; Vital do Valle, "Notas e apanhados: Vaccinação obrigatória," *AA*, Nov. 12, 1904, p. 15; Til do Tal, "Sabatinas," ibid., Nov. 19, 1904, p. 2; Vital do Valle, "Notas e apanhados: Prevenção d'*A Avenida*," ibid., p. 3; "O ano politico: Brasil," *Almanaque brasileiro*, 314–315; Cardoso de Castro, "Relatorio," 12, 14, 16–17; "Crónica politica," *Os Annaes*, 1:17 (Nov. 24, 1904), 110.

12. Robert G. Nachman, "Positivism and Revolution in Brazil's First Republic: The 1904 Revolt," *The Americas*, 34:1 (July 1977), 20.

13. Melo Franco, *Rodrigues Alves*, I, 392–436, especially 395–404. Nachman ("Positivism and Revolution," 20–21, nn. 1–4) lists these traditional and revisionist sources: Glauco Carneiro, *História das revoluções brasileiras* (Rio de Janeiro, 1965), I, 136–150; Lobato Filho, Dantas Barreto, and João Cruz Costa, *O positivismo na República* (São Paulo, 1956), 37–44; João Camilo de Oliveira Torres, *O positivismo no Brasil* (Petrópolis, 1934), 282–286; Edgar Carone, *A República Velha (evolução política)* (São Paulo, 1971), 196–221; José Maria Bello, *A History of Modern Brazil, 1889–1964*, J. L. Taylor, trans. (Stanford, 1966).

14. Nachman, "Positivism and Revolution," especially pp. 22–37, discusses the position of the Positivist church and analyzes the relationship of the foremost conspirators and positivist republican militancy. He also points to the impact of the urban reforms on the masses as crucial to the revolt, although he does not explore the issue (21–22, 25–26).

15. Teresa Meade, "Civilizing Rio de Janeiro: The Public Health Campaign and the Riot of 1904," *Journal of Social History*, 20:2 (Winter 1986), 301–22. Meade's contribution is in excellent archival research and a good discussion of the plight of the poor.

16. See Sheldon Leslie Maram, "Anarchists, Immigrants, and the Brazilian Labor Movement, 1890–1920" (Ph.D. diss., University of California, Santa Barbara, 1972); Eulália Maria Lahmeyer Lobo, *História de Rio de Janeiro (do capital comercial ao capital industrial e financeiro)*, 2 vols. (Rio de Janeiro, 1978); Jaime Larry Benchimol, "Pereira Passos—Um Haussmann tropical: as transformações urbanas na cidade do Rio de Janeiro no início do século XX" (M.S. thesis, Universidade Federal do Rio de Janeiro, 1982); Eileen Keremitsis, "The Early Industrial Worker in Rio de Janeiro, 1870–1930" (Ph.D. diss., Columbia University, 1982); Oswaldo Porto Rocha, "A era das demolições: Cidade do Rio de Janeiro, 1870–1920" (M.A. thesis, Universidade Federal Fluminense, 1983); Nilson do Rosário Costa, "Estado e políticas de saúde pública (1889–1930)" (M.A. thesis, Instituto Universitario de Pesquisas do Rio de Janeiro, 1983); Samuel C. Adamo, "The Broken Promise: Race, Health, and Justice in Rio de Janeiro, 1890–1940" (Ph.D. diss., University of New Mexico, 1983); Meade, "Community Protest in Rio de Janeiro, Brazil, During the First Republic, 1890–1917" (Ph.D. diss., Rutgers University, 1984). See also Boris Fausto, *Trabalho urbano e conflito social (1890–1920)* (São Paulo, 1977), 13–62, passim; Nicolau Sevcenko, *Literatura como missão: Tensões socials e criação cultural na Primeira República* (Rio de Janeiro, 1983), 51–68 and his pamphlet, *A revolta da vacina: Mentes insanas em corpos rebeldes* (São Paulo, 1984); Jeffrey D. Needell, "Making the Carioca *Belle Epoque* Concrete: The Urban Reforms of Rio de Janeiro

Under Pereira Passos," *Journal of Urban History*, 10:4 (Aug. 1984); and José Murilo de Carvalho, "A revolta da vacina" (preliminary draft presented in the Seminário Rio Republicano, Rio de Janeiro, Oct. 4, 1984) [ms. photocopy in author's possession through authors' exchange]. Sevcenko's suggestive pamphlet, as such, lacks the documentation so notable in his book; more important, its focus skirts the role of the conspirators and their linkage to the masses and blurs some simple facts. Murilo de Carvalho's work, focusing on the workers' role and making apt comparisons with nineteenth-century Parisian revolts, is complementary to mine. Murilo de Carvalho, heading one group of the Equipe de Pesquisas of the Centro de Estudos Históricos, Fundação Casa de Rui Barbosa (Rio de Janeiro), has brought sophisticated methodology to bear on his team's extensive primary source research.

17. See Needell, "Making the Carioca *Belle Epoque* Concrete," 399–400, 405–406 and "The Origins of the Carioca *Belle Epoque*: The Emergence of the Elite Culture and Society of Turn-of-the-Century Rio de Janeiro" (Ph.D. diss., Stanford University, 1982), 45–68. With respect to the *jacobinos* and positivism, it must be noted that such radical positivists were distinct from members of the Positivist church. The latter was a formal organization, whose members refrained from political partisan activity per se—*jacobinos* were positivists as individuals, and were very partisan indeed.

18. Ibid.; Sevcenko, *Literatura como missão*, 41–51, 63–65; June E. Hahner, *Civilian-Military Relations in Brazil: 1889–1898* (Columbia, SC, 1969), 125–134, 140–144, ch. 7; Joseph L. Love, *Rio Grande do Sul and Brazilian Regionalism, 1882–1930* (Stanford, 1971), 99–105, 151–152. Rio Grande radicals were distinguished by integration with one faction of the state's divided oligarchy (ibid., ch. 2, p. 75).

19. Needell, "Origins of the Carioca *Belle Epoque*," 62–68, 115–128, 132–133, passim; Melo Franco, *Rodrigues Alves*, I, 241; Luiz Viana Filho, *A vida de Rui Barbosa* (São Paulo, 1943), 209.

20. Needell, "Making the Carioca *Belle Epoque* Concrete," 400, 405–406.

21. Ibid., 400–406. For the dominant concept of "modernization," and the *belle époque* in Rio, see 403–410 and also Needell, "Rio de Janeiro at the Turn of the Century: Modernization and the Parisian Ideal," *Journal of Interamerican Studies and World Affairs*, 25:1 (Feb. 1983), 83–103.

22. For contemporary responses to obligatory vaccination, see the citations in n. 2, above. For traditional analyses, see, e.g., Bello, *A History of Modern Brazil*, 181–182; Lobato Filho, *A última noite*, 68; Carneiro, *História*, 136–138; Melo Franco, *Rodrigues Alves*, I, 390–395, 417–420; Sodré, *Lauro Sodré*, 85–87. For recent research, see Nachman, "Positivism and Revolution," 21–24; Stepan, *Beginnings of Brazilian Science*, 88–91; Costa, "Estado e políticas," 75, 78–79, 82, 84–87; and Meade. See also Donald B. Cooper, "Brazil's Long Fight Against Epidemic Disease, 1849–1914, With Special Emphasis on Yellow Fever," *Bulletin of the New York Academy of Medicine*, 51:5 (May 1975), 672–696 and his "Oswaldo Cruz and the Impact of Yellow Fever on Brazilian History," *The Bulletin of the Tulane University Medical Faculty*, 26:1 (Feb. 1967), 49–52.

23. See, e.g., regarding neutral or proadministration opposition, the case of the establishment lawyer, Villela dos Santos, seeking a writ of habeas corpus against obligatory vaccination in *GN*, Nov. 12, 1904, p. 1; the reasoned arguments against the legislation on political grounds in Menelau, "Cróniqueta," *AA*, Oct. 29, 1904, p. 2; cf. ibid., p. 5 (provaccination); the provaccination, antiobligatory comments in "A vaccina," *Rua do Ouvidor*, July 16, Aug. 13, 1904, p. 2. See also Nachman's review of the Positivist church's position, "Positivism and Revolution," 22–23.

24. Melo Franco, *Rodrigues Alves*, I, 390–399; Nachman, "Positivism and Revolution," 23–37. Again, note the distinction that must be made between these men, often positivist or positivist-influenced, and members of the Positivist church, which abstained from politics and violence.

25. Melo Franco, *Rodrigues Alves*, I, 399–400; Nachman, "Positivism and Revolution," 33–35; Sodré, *Lauro Sodré*, 34–66, 69–99; Lobato Filho, *A última noite*, 69–86; *CM*, Oct. 18, 1904, pp. 1–2. On the *jacobinos* and Florianistas, see Hahner, "Jacobinos versus Galegos: Urban Radicals versus Portuguese Immigrants in Rio de Janeiro in the 1890s," *Journal of Interamerican Studies and World Affairs*, 18:2 (May 1976), 131–133, 135–139; and Sevcenko, *Literatura como missão*, 63–64; Benchimol, "Pereira Passos," 365–371.

26. Melo Franco, *Rodrigues Alves*, I, 396, 403–404; Nachman, "Positivism and Revolution," 27–30; Edgar Carone, *A República Velha, I: Instituições e classes socials (1889–1930)*, 4a ed. (São Paulo, 1978), 386–388; Cardoso de Castro, *Relatorio*, 9, 11–12, 14–15, 18, 41–42, 45–46; *JC*, Nov. 19, 1904, p. 2; *OP*, Nov. 19, 1904, p. 2.

27. See the speeches and editorials given full play in *CM* during Oct. and Nov. 1904. See also Lobato Filho, *A última noite*, 69–73, 82–86; Hahner, "Jacobinos versus Galegos," 131–132, 142; Nachman, "Positivism and Revolution," 31–37; and his "Positivism, Modernization, and the Middle Class in Brazil," *Hispanic American Historical Review*, 57:1 (Feb. 1977), 7, 10–16, 22–23; but cf. Sodré, *Lauro Sodré*, 55–57, 58–59, 65–66. Note, especially, Lauro's Pará administration (see Sodré, 54–74, passim, and Nachman, "Positivism, Modernization, and the Middle Class," 10–16, passim). Nachman points to links between Brazilian positivism and post-1920 ideology, from Plínio Salgado's *integralismo* to Getúlio Vargas, in both of his pieces. On the *salvacionista* movement, see Love, *Rio Grande do Sul*, 156–157, 159, 163.

28. "Os Acontecimentos," *Os Annaes*, 1:7 (Nov. 24, 1904), 111–112; Cardoso de Castro, *Relatorio*, 8–13, 15, 34–40; Lobato Filho, *A última noite*, 67–73. On the police, see also "Dr. Cardoso de Castro," *Rua do Ouvidor*, May 2, 1903, pp. 1–2. Rodrigues Alves's election was the work of Campos Sales, who, although he recognized the importance of "historical" republican credentials (as did Rodrigues Alves), writes that he preferred a successor he could trust to carry on his financial policies through competent administration, above the partisan considerations of the 1890s; see Campos Sales, *Da propaganda á presidencia* (São Paulo, 1908), 366–368. Cf. Dunshee de Abranches, *Como se faziam presidentes: Homens e fotos do início da república* (Rio de Janeiro, 1973), 304–307, 322, 326–328, 334–335, 341, 343–347, who relates that Rodrigues Alves, then governor of São Paulo, was indicated by northern politicians and São Paulo's machine principally to avoid the candidacy of a certain northern political chief, and was then embraced by Campos Sales, who wished to take the credit and had become personally uncomfortable with the most obvious alternatives.

29. Nachman, "Positivism and Revolution," 32–33; Sodré's son tells us that his father had had the family vaccinated but opposed *obligatory* vaccination (*Lauro Sodré*, 85).

30. For opposition articles on vaccination, see n. 2; for the rest, see, e.g., "Pelo exercito: É demais," *CM*, Oct. 2, 1904, p. 1; "A miseria no exercito," *CM*, Oct. 4, 1904, p. 2; "¿Preparativos para a violencia?" *CM*, Oct. 6, 1904, p. 1; "Campanhas de assassinato," *CM*, Oct. 10, 1904, p. 1; "Eleições e governo," *CM*, Oct. 11, 1904, p. 1; "¿Que será?: ¿Greve?—¿Revolução?—¿Agitação policial?—O Sr. Cardoso de Castro em campo—Promptidão absoluta," *CM*, Oct. 18, 1904, p. 1; "A Bernarda," *CM*, Oct. 19, 1904, p. 1; "Escravidão," *CM*, Oct. 21, 1904, p. 1.

See also the coverage of the "civic pilgrimage" celebrating Benjamin Constant [Botelho de Magalhães], *CM*, Oct. 19, 1904, pp. 1–2. On the conspiracy, see n. 28 and Carneiro, *História*, 148–149; Nachman, "Positivism and Revolution," 24–36, passim; Melo Franco, *Rodrigues Alves*, I, 394–403.

31. See Benchimol, "Pereira Passos," chs. 4, 7, and especially pp. 144, 145, 147, 151, 153, 165–172; Keremitsis, "The Early Industrial Worker," ch. 2, especially pp. 17, 24, 28, 50, 54; Lahmeyer Lobo, *História do Rio*, I, 227–231. Note that slaves made up a fifth of the work force in 1872, with most involved in agriculture, domestic service, and artisanal activities (Lahmeyer Lobo, *História do Rio*, I, 231). A study of domestic labor can be found in Sandra Lauderdale Graham, "Protection and Obedience: The Paternalist World of Female Domestic Servants, Rio de Janeiro, 1860–1910" (Ph.D. diss., University of Texas, 1982).

32. See Adamo, "The Broken Promise," 7, 11, 13–15, 18, 21–24 and ch. 1, passim. The 1906 census did not pick out race: Adamo estimated it by computer extrapolation (see pp. 11–12, n. 14). The reliability of the apposite censuses is discussed on p. 9. The basis for extrapolation was censuses in which respondents identified themselves racially; in a racist society, one should expect respondents to "whiten" themselves, hence these figures are probably too low. See also República dos Estados Unidos do Brasil, Diretoria Geral de Estatistica, *Recenseamento do Rio de Janeiro (Distrito Fededal): Realisado em 20 de setembro de 1906* (Rio de Janeiro, 1907), 388–389; Lahmayer Lobo, *História do Rio*, II, 469; Benchimol, "Pereira Passos," 339–341.

33. *Recenseamento . . . 1906*, 104, 236–237; Lahmeyer Lobo, *História do Rio*, II, 508, 572; Benchimol, "Pereira Passos," 345, 388–389. In the 1870 census, of the urban population of 235,381, there were 53,160 domestics (23 percent); 13,560 people employed in agriculture (*lavradores*) (6 percent); and 41,381 people (18 percent) employed in *manufactura, artes e oficios*—some 80,717 (34 percent) were *sem profissão conhecida* (*Recenseamento . . . 1906*, 100). In comparing the figures and proportions, bear in mind that the commercial and professional-liberal sectors of the economy had grown significantly by 1906 (see Benchimol, "Pereira Passos," 350, 351–352), and that the category *manufactura, artes e oficios* includes artisans and the like, as well as industrial workers per se. The 1907 industrial census is in Lahmeyer Lobo,. *História do Rio*, II, 572–576. One supposes the great difference between the figures for textile employment in 1906 and 1907 has to do with census categories; 1906 distinguishes "textiles" from "clothing and accessories"—1907 apparently includes much of 1906's clothing and accessories in its "textiles" category.

34. Porta Rocha, "A era dos demolições," 92, 101–102; Benchimol, "Pereira Passos," chs. 7, 9, pp. 359–364, passim; Adamo, "The Broken Promise," 31–40; Keremitsis, "The Early Industrial Worker," 41–53; Sevcenko, *Literatura como missão*, 51–59. Beyond the commission reports, analyzed in Benchimol, an excellent contemporary description is Everardo Backheuser, "Onde moram os pobres," *Renacença*, 2:13, 2:15 (Mar., May 1905), 89–94, 185–189.

35. Backheuser, "Onde moram," 92. More graphic descriptions made Alusío de Azevedo's novel, *O cortiço* (1890), a naturalist classic.

36. Backheuser, "Onde moram," 92–94; on illness, beyond Cooper, Costa, Benchimol, and Stepan the best quantitative and medical analysis is Adamo, "The Broken Promise," chs. 3, 4.

37. *Recenseamento . . . 1906*, 104. On the impact of the under- and unemployed on Rio's labor force, see Fausto, *Trabalho urbano*, 26–28.

38. Adamo, "The Broken Promise," ch. 2.

39. Sevcenko, *Literatura como missão*, 59–61; Lahmeyer Lobo, *História do Rio*, I, 209–222, II, 453–468, 471–508; Rebecca Baird Bergstresser, "The Movement for the Abolition of Slavery in Rio de Janeiro, Brazil, 1880–1889" (Ph.D. diss., Stanford University, 1973), chs. 1–3, passim; Hahner, "Jacobinos," 129–130; Francisco de Assis Barbosa, "A presidência Campos Sales," *Luso-Brazilian Review*, 5:1 (1968), 3–26.

40. On the repression of cultural expression and the disproportionate hardships of the "nonwhite" population, see Adamo, "The Broken Promise," chs. 5, 6, and passim; and Alison Raphael, "Samba and Social Control: Popular Culture and Racial Democracy in Rio de Janeiro" (Ph.D. diss., Columbia University, 1979). On the African quality of this culture, see Needell, "Making the Carioca *Belle Epoque* Concrete," 385, 408–410. Note also the cumulative impact of the African slave trade, which continued to Brazil until 1855; as late as 1872, the number of Africans in Rio and the Province of Rio de Janeiro was *at least* 67,235 (6.4 percent of the total); in Rio alone, there were 10,973 (3.9 percent of the city's total); see Stanley J. Stein, *Vassouras: A Brazilian Coffee County, 1850–1890* (New York, 1970), 296; and Robert Conrad, *The Destruction of Brazilian Slavery: 1850–1880* (Berkeley, 1972), 287. Surely, bearing in mind the traditional, rural, African roots of Bahian and Fluminense Afro-Brazilian culture, central to popular culture in turn-of-the-century Rio through migration, to speak of a distinctive culture and alienation or hostility among the emancipated or the children and grandchildren of slaves vis-à-vis the Europhile, urbane elite is not an exaggeration. On the cultural aspects of Afro-Brazilian resistance, see Porto Rocha; on the culture per se, see, e.g., Raphael, "Samba and Social Control," Ary Vasconcelos, *Panorama da música popular brasileira na belle époque* (Rio de Janeiro, 1977), or José Ramos Tinhorão, *Pequena história da música popular* (Petrópolis, 1974).

41. Fausto, *Trabalho urbano*, 14–15, 26–27, 31–32, 35–37, and especially 41–62, shows, in his discussion of Paulista labor and Carioca "*trabalhismo*," the way in which Carioca workers were often organized by déclassé intellectuals, often Florianistas or self-taught "socialists," in unions or clubs of ephemeral influence and impact. Cf. Hahner, "Jacobinos and Galegos," 136–140. Maram, "Anarchists," 3–5, 10–13, 16, 17–18, 21–23, 54–55, 57–58; as in his "Labor and the Left in Brazil, 1890–1921: A Movement Aborted," *Hispanic American Historical Review*, 57:2 (May 1977), 254–255, 259–260, 268, 270–271; and in his "The Immigrant and the Brazilian Labor Movement, 1890–1920," in *Essays Concerning the Socioeconomic History of Brazil and Portuguese India*, Dauril Alden and Warren Dean, eds. (Gainesville, 1977), 179–180, 182–185 n. 15, 186–188, 189, 191, tends to focus on the post-1906, immigrant-led anarchist movement, yet still provides an idea of the weaknesses besetting the nascent Carioca industrial proletariat. Murilo de Carvalho ("A revolta da vacina," 41–42) claims an important element among Carioca industrial workers, organized in the Federação das Associações de Classe (FAC), was anarchist in orientation (cf. Fausto, *Trabalho urbano*, 120–121) and suggests that its actions in 1904 were separate from those of Vicente de Sousa's Centro de Classes Operárias (CCO). This has not, however, been documented. It is also unclear that the FAC's membership was of a wholly distinct origin compared to the CCO's. Although the FAC was largely made up of artisan and factory workers, it did include dockyard workers, and, while the CCO was linked to government employees and dockyard workers traditionally associated with *jacobino* union organization, it also had artisan and factory worker elements. On women in the work force, see Hahner, "Women and

Work in Brazil, 1850–1920: A Preliminary Investigation," in *Essays Concerning the Socioeconomic History*, 87–117, especially 100–117. For contemporary accounts, police activities, and the stevedores, see, e.g., M. Curvello, "O movimento socialista no Brasil," *Almanaque brasileiro . . . 1905*, 272–277; Cardoso de Castro, "Relatorio," 13, 16, 18, 37; and his "Relatorio apresentado ao Exmo. Snr. Dr. J. J. Seabra, Ministro da Justiça e Negocios Interiores pelo Chefe de Policia do Distrito Federal. . . ," in Ministerio da Justiça e Negocios Interiores, *Anexos ao relatorio apresentado ao Presidente da República dos Estados Unidos do Brasil pelo Dr. J. J. Seabra . . . em março de 1904* (Rio de Janeiro, 1904), 15, 29–30; "Vida operária," *CM*, Oct. 1, 1904, p. 3; "Vida operária," ibid., Oct. 7, 1904, p. 2; "Os estivadores," ibid., Oct. 19, 1904, p. 3; "O estivadores," ibid., Oct. 22, 1904, p. 2; "Vida operária," ibid., Nov. 1, 1904, p. 1; *GN*, Nov. 17, 1904, p. 2.

42. See Lahmeyer Lobo, *História do Rio*, II, 503–504, 505–506; Carone, *República Velha*, I, 219–220; Maram, "Anarchists," 54–55; "Augmento de passagens," *CM*, Oct. 11, 1904, p. 1; Cardoso de Castro, "Relatorio" (1904), 16–22; F. de A. Barbosa, "A presidência Campos Sales," 16; Murilo de Carvalho, "A revolta da vacina," 22, 39–40.

43. See Needell, "Making the *Belle Epoque* Concrete," 401–403, 408; Backheuser, "Onde moram"; Benchimol, "Pereira Passos," 359–364, ch. 14, passim, and 592–609; Porta Rocha, "A era das demolições," ch. 4. I differ here from Murilo de Carvalho ("A revolta da vacina," 44–45) on the impact of the economic situation and housing.

44. Costa, "Estado e políticas," 68–79. Murilo de Carvalho points out that the issue of "invading the hearth" was central to the signed petitions against vaccination sent to congress by thousands of organized workers ("A revolta da vacina," 7, 23).

45. Costa, "Estado e políticas," 79, 82, 84–87; Vieira, *O boto abaixo*, 170; "A terceira discussão," *CM*, Oct. 1, 1904, p. 1; "Vida operária," ibid., p. 3; "Vaccinação ou morte," ibid., Oct. 7, 1904, p. 1; "O dever do povo," ibid., Nov. 7, 1904, p. 1; Menelau, "Croniqueta," *AA*, Oct. 29, 1904, p. 2; *GN*, Nov. 15, 1904, p. 2.

46. Elisio de Araujo, *Estudo historico sobre a policia da Capital Federal: 1808–1831* (Rio de Janeiro, 1898), 56–62, 113, 123, 133–135; Thomas Flory, "Race and Social Control in Independent Brazil," *Journal of Latin American Studies*, 9:2 (Nov. 1977), 203–204; L. C., "A capoeira," *Kósmos*, 3:3 (Mar. 1906), 56–57; Dunshee de Abranches, *Actas e actos do governo provisorio* (Rio de Janeiro, 1907), 361–366; Medeiros e Albuquerque, *Minha vida: Da infancia a mocidade: Memorias: 1867–1893*, 3a ed. (Rio de Janeiro, 1933), 123–129; R. Magalhães Junior, *Deodoro: A espada contra o império*, 2 vols. (São Paulo, 1957), II, 182–187; on contemporary response, see, e.g., "Grande conflito," *CM*, Oct. 10, 1904, p. 2; "Reclamações," ibid., Oct. 26, 1904, p. 3; Menelau, "Croniqueta," *AA*, Oct. 29, 1904, p. 2.

47. Araujo, *Estudo historico*, ch. 5, passim, 135–137; Mello Moraes Filho, *Factos e memorias* (Rio de Janeiro, 1904), pt. 4, ch. 10, and pt. 5, ch. 11; Bergstresser, "Abolition of Slavery," chs. 1–3, passim; Sandra Lauderdale Graham, "The Vintem Riot and Political Culture: Rio de Janeiro, 1880," *Hispanic American Historical Review*, 60:3 (Aug. 1980), 431–449 [Note: Graham's article is reprinted in this volume as Chapter 4]; Hahner, "Jacobinos versus Galegos," 128, 132, 140–141, 143; O. B., "Crónica," *GN*, Nov. 13, 1904, p. 1. The basis for Lusophobia lay in the traditionally dominant Portuguese role in Carioca commerce and the active sympathy the Portuguese government appeared to show for the fallen Braganza dynasty's cause.

48. On the Portuguese, cf. Maram, "Labor and the Left," 257–258, and his "Immigrant and Brazilian Labor," 190–191; Hahner, "Jacobinos versus Galegos," 126–128, 130, 139, 148. Murilo de Carvalho ("A revolta da vacina," 35–37, 55n.) notes Portuguese participation in 1904, despite the alienation from Carioca traditions of violent resistance I suggest here. Indeed, as Maram notes, the Portuguese-dominated workers' movement in Santos was quite militant; Santos, however, did not have the ongoing, violent tradition of Lusophobia noteworthy in Rio. Indeed, regarding the 1904 events, it may well be impossible, even given the superb research done by Murilo's Equipe de Pesquisas, to ever know precisely the extent of Portuguese involvement or that of any other group. For example, both my own research and Murilo's comments suggest that the police arrest records are hardly a record of activism in the revolt, since the police arrested whomever they pleased, especially after the 18th. Neither do reports of the dead and wounded necessarily prove Portuguese involvement in the revolt. Although they do detail nationality, one cannot presume casualties are proofs of participation—the papers regularly report the damage done to passers-by during the disorders. As for occupation, the list of 90 casualties, dubious for the reason just noted, is hardly helpful—the occupations of fewer than 50 are noted. The best indications are in the analysis of the workers' petitions in Murilo de Carvalho, which suggest the participation of organized labor. However, such petitions are not the sort of thing the marginalized or the *desordeiros* were likely to sign. On the urban Afro-Brazilian culture, see the references in n. 40, above. I found no reference to Lusophobia in the *published* propaganda of the movement; thus, this paragraph deals with the putative memory, or "unofficial" expression, of such prejudice in *jacobino*-mass relations.

49. Frank D. McCann, "The Nation in Arms: Obligatory Military Service During the Old Republic," in *Essays Concerning the Socioeconomic History*, 217–219; José Murilo de Carvalho, "As forças armadas na Primeira República: O poder desestabilizador," in *História geral da civilização brasileira*, tomo 3; *O Brasil republicano*, Boris Fausto, ed., 2 vols. (São Paulo, 1977), II, 189–191; Adamo, "The Broken Promise," 188–194; cf. Cardoso de Castro, "Relatorio" (1904), 5–7; *AA*, Oct. 29, 1904, p. 26.

50. Cardoso de Castro, "Relatorio" (1905), 18, 38–39; *JC*, Nov. 16, 1904, p. 1; *OP*, Nov. 17, 1904, p. 2; Lobato Filho, *A última noite*, 68–69, 70–80; Dantas Barreto, *Conspirações*, 12–15; Nachman, "Positivism and Revolution," 24–33; Fausto, *Trabalho urbano*, 43–51 and passim; "Vida operária," *CM*, Oct. 7, 1904, p. 2.

51. See the elements involved in the first meeting of the league and the speech in which Lauro made clear the larger political issues: "Liga Contra a Vaccinação Obrigatória," *CM*, Nov. 6, 1904, p. 2; see also the introductory "Apelo ao povo," ibid., Nov. 5, 1904, p. 1. An excellent analysis of the actions of the mass participants vis-à-vis urban workers is Murilo de Carvalho, "A revolta da vacina," 35–42 and passim.

52. See, e.g., O. B., "Crónica," *GN*, Nov. 13, 1904, p. 2; Graham, "Vintem Riot," 436–437.

53. On these last two paragraphs, see *CM*, Nov. 13, 1904, p. 1, Nov. 14, 1904, p. 2, and Nov. 15, 1904, p. 2; *GN*, Nov. 13, 1904, pp. 1–2, Nov. 14, 1904, pp. 1–2, and Nov. 15, 1904, pp. 1–2; *JC*, Nov. 15, 1904, p. 2. My interpretation here owes something to the studies of mass and urban violence appearing in *Past and Present* since the 1950s and associated with E. J. Hobsbawm, E. P. Thompson, George Rudé, et al. Meade and, especially, Murilo de Carvalho are more heavily indebted to this approach, since they focus on the masses' role.

54. See the accounts in *CM* cited in n. 53, above; the "fictional" memoir of Vieira, *O boto abaixo*, 171–172; on the waiting officers, Dantas Barreto, *Conspirações*, 41; and Rodrigues Alves, "1904," in Melo Franco, *Rodrigues Alves*, I, 409–411.

55. On the conspirators' expectations and strategy, see Cardoso de Castro, "Relatorio" (1905), 36–39; Lobato Filho, *A última noite*, 79–81, 98, 100. Cf. the contemporary accounts and memoirs of the coup of 1889 in Ernesto Senna, *Deodoro: Subsídios para a história* (Brasilia, 1981). Murilo de Carvalho, "A revolta da vacina," 41–42, argues for a clearly disassociated factory revolt after Nov. 15, distinct from the larger movement of the CCO. I agree that, after that date, the various components of the Carioca masses continued with their several agendas, but I disagree that this proves they were without earlier links to Vicente de Sousa or Lauro's hopes.

56. The *CM* being closed down, the best coverage of Porto Arthur is in *OP*, *GN*, and *JC*. See *JC*, Nov. 15, 1904, p. 1, Nov. 16, 1904, p. 2, and Nov. 17, 1904, p. 2; *OP*, Nov. 15, 1904, p. 1, Nov. 16, 1904, p. 2, and Nov. 17, 1904, p. 2; *GN*, Nov. 15, 1904, p. 2, Nov. 16, 1904, p. 2, and Nov. 17, 1904, pp. 2–3.

57. The amnesty occurred at the end of 1905, largely as a maneuver to embarrass the president by elements who were successfully undermining his personal power; see Melo Franco, *Rodrigues Alves*, 427–435.

58. The repression is covered in the progovernment dailies, which uniformly accepted the measures as salutary: see, e.g., *OP*, Dec. 11, 1904, p. 2, Dec. 16, 1904, p. 2, Dec. 21, 1904, p. 2, Dec. 30, 1904, p. 2, and Dec. 31, 1904, p. 2; *JC*, Nov. 20, 1904, p. 2, Nov. 21, 1904, p. 2, Nov. 23, 1904, p. 2, Dec. 24, 1904, p. 2, Dec. 25, 1904, p. 2; *GN*, Nov. 26, 1904, p. 2, and Nov. 27, 1904, p. 2; cf. Melo Franco, *Rodrigues Alves*, I, 424–426.

59. Post-1904 labor militance was largely immigrant anarcho-syndicalist in origin; see the references in n. 41. On the memory of 1904, see the responses cited in n. 13; cf. Bello, *A History of Modern Brazil*, 181–183 or Melo Franco, *Rodrigues Alves*, I, 391–393.

60. Melo Franco, *Rodrigues Alves*, I, 434. I have the cited comment from a quotation Melo Franco takes from Rodrigues Alves's notebook, where the president apparently took pleasure in the jibe. Melo Franco, however, seems not to understand the point—Porto Arthur and Prata Preta do not appear in his narrative.

61. "Os degregados do Acre," *CM*, Dec. 28, 1904, p. 1, quoting *A Noticia*, Dec. 27, 1904. Prata Preta was apparently on the first packet boat sent out.

62. This is a reference to Figueiredo Pimentel's celebrated contemporary phrase, "O Rio civiliza-se" and to the elite fears and hopes linked to the urban reforms which Figueiredo Pimentel championed. See Needell, "Making the Carioca *Belle Epoque* Concrete," 403, 410, 421.

7

"¡Viva México! ¡Mueran los yanquis!": The Guadalajara Riots of 1910

Avital H. Bloch and Servando Ortoll*

*This essay is written jointly by Avital Bloch, an Israeli historian, and Servando Ortoll, a Mexican sociologist, who met and married while earning their doctorates at Columbia University. Professor Bloch specializes in the intellectual history of the United States and has published articles on American culture, particularly since the 1950s. She directs the American Studies Program at the University of Colima, Mexico. Professor Ortoll is the author of numerous articles on Catholic organizations in Mexico's national politics and international diplomacy during the first half of the twentieth century. He teaches history and sociology at the University of Guadalajara. Together they have written articles on the history of the states of Colima and Jalisco.

This essay analyzes two nights of rioting in Guadalajara, Mexico. Although the disturbances occurred shortly before the outbreak of the Mexican Revolution, Professors Bloch and Ortoll conclude that they did not merely presage the new social movement. Instead, the 1910 riots are part of a long local tradition of anti-American protests heightened by anti-Protestant fervor. Like the riots of 1765 and 1828 (studied in Chapters 1 and 2), these disorders demonstrate that popular nationalism has deep roots in Latin America. In this case, the xenophobia of the urban masses was clearly at odds with the far more conciliatory official line.

*We gratefully acknowledge the critical and enthusiastic comments about an earlier version of this paper by Silvia M. Arrom, Felipe Castro Gutiérrez, Robert L. Cohen, and Barbara Hoekje. Martha Gabriela Ortoll and Fabiola Zúñiga helped us with additional research, while Gabriela Ulloa and Sergio Camarena worked on the map reproductions. We also thank Regina Marie Klemas, who reviewed the English syntax of this text. A University of Guadalajara grant helped to cover the minor expenses that we incurred in the completion of this article. To achieve stylistic unity, we have corrected minor spelling errors in the original documents. An earlier version was published in Spanish as "Xenofobia y nacionalismo revolucionario: Los tumultos de Guadalajara, México, en 1910," *Cristianismo y Sociedad* 86 (1985): 63–76.

Two nights of massive rioting were directed against American targets by the residents of Guadalajara, the capital of the Mexican state of Jalisco, on November 10 and 11, 1910. These riots were initially ignited as a protest against a highly provocative incident in Rock Springs, Texas, where, on November 4, a twenty-year-old Mexican, Antonio Rodríguez, had been burned to death by an enraged mob for the alleged rape and murder of an American woman.[1] But the disturbances were more than that. The Guadalajara riots have not received the attention they deserve because they were overshadowed by the outbreak of the Mexican Revolution ten days later. A few scholars have referred to them in passing as precursors to the Revolution, although Charles C. Cumberland declared that they were not revolutionary. "In fact," he wrote, "the revolts were the result of a deeply rooted hostility against foreigners in general and against Americans in particular, and did not derive from any anti-American propaganda broadcast by Madero or his followers."[2] After studying the riots in detail, we agree with Cumberland that there was no linkage between them and revolutionary leader Francisco Madero's call to arms. The two days of protests should be studied apart from the Revolution.

Indeed, this "deeply rooted hostility against . . . Americans" that Cumberland registers was traditionally vented on the eve of Independence Day celebrations every September 15. The 1910 riots should be seen as part of this tradition and should be analyzed for what they tell us about popular ideology. Feelings of anti-Americanism among the different urban classes, including students, were an important component of a very old and profound popular nationalism that challenged Mexico's official stance toward foreigners. In this essay, we emphasize xenophobia, particularly anti-Americanism mixed with anti-Protestantism, as a unique political expression that predated revolutionary radicalism.

A Political Paradox?

To make sense of the sequence of events that brought about the November 1910 occurrences and to understand various emotional responses in Guadalajara toward Americans, we will discuss the antecedents of the riots as revealed in the September 1910 Independence Day celebrations. Unlike previous years, when Americans were the victims of the xenophobic attacks on the eve of Independence Day, in 1910 they were invited for the first time to participate actively around the country in the festivities commemorating the Centennial of Mexican Independence. President Porfirio Díaz took advantage of the holiday to highlight his country's prosperity in the eyes of the world. The Centennial was also an opportunity for his administration to emphasize its official, friendly stance toward foreigners, in particular Americans.[3] "In the month of September the Mexican government celebrated with great pomp and magnificence the Centennial of Independence," Ambassador Henry Lane Wilson wrote in his memoirs:

> Preparations for this event were made upon an elaborate scale and the energies of the federal and state governments were given up to it. Large sums of money were expended in publicity and in securing the presence of notable and distinguished people at this supposed crowning event in the career of President Díaz. Almost every government in the world was represented by delegates with sonorous titles who came thither with trains and suites and participated in the festivities for the better part of the month. . . . There followed days of fiestas, dedications, memorials, and diplomatic oratory which . . . marked the distinct impression which Mexico had made upon the world under the Díaz administration.[4]

Given the tenor of the Centennial, local government officials were bound to align themselves with national politics. In Guadalajara, for the first time as well, Mexicans and Americans celebrated as one the nation's Independence: prominent foreigners, together with the Mexican rich, renowned intellectuals, trustworthy politicians, and other respectable government officials participated in organizing these celebrations. On September 16, amid the commotion of firecrackers, whistles, and the excitement of the crowds, the American colony in Guadalajara contributed a float to the enthusiastic parade taking place in the city. A coordinating committee of prominent American residents, under the leadership of Carlos B. Carothers—a tall and strongly built Saltillo-born individual of American origins, a U.S. citizen by choice, a real estate broker, an active member of the colony, and one of its wealthiest—organized a track and field competition on the turf of the West End Realty Company. This firm was the largest real estate agency, dealing in huge tracts of land, which Carothers administered and possibly partially owned, and its properties were located at the westernmost section of the city. "This event, with which the honorable and hard working [American] colony contributed to our festivities," a government-sponsored brochure reported, "was widely attended, and it pleasantly impressed all of us who hung around it."[5]

The described feelings of friendship and mutual understanding suffusing the American-sponsored events during this month of celebrations would make the anti-American riots only six weeks later appear paradoxical. A close examination of the snapshots taken at the tournament that the American colony organized, however, shows that the event itself was not so well attended by locals as the official pamphlet claimed.[6] As it turned out, Americans and foreigners had been invited to participate in the Centennial celebrations without the approval of the people. Thus, despite official expectations, popular, deep-rooted anti-American and anti-Protestant sentiments had not evaporated and were expressed thus during the commemorations: Guadalajarans simply chose not to attend the tournament in the fields of the West End Realty Company. When news arrived in Guadalajara about scheduled anti-American demonstrations in Mexico City in reaction to the Rock Springs incident of November 4,[7] many Guadalajarans thought that it was their duty to synchronize their discontent with that of Mexico's capital city.

The first anti-American demonstration took place in Mexico City on Tuesday, November 8. According to Ambassador Wilson, it was "composed largely of university students, small shopmen, and the better class of artisans," and it followed a series of "violent and inflammatory" anti-American articles written by editors "closely connected to the Mexican government."[8] The leaders of the disturbances in the capital brought to the fore, and capitalized on, a dormant but long-standing anti-Americanism that had existed prior to the burning to death of Rodríguez. But the two full days that it took to organize the Mexico City demonstrations after news of the incident reached the capital attest to the lack of spontaneity of the riots: after two days of denunciations, university students assaulted American stores, businesses, and private homes on November 8 and 9.[9]

After the second night of rioting in Mexico City (and following the jailing of fifty-one men "under charge of acts of vandalism" and the tough patrolling of the capital city's streets,[10]) rumors circulated in Guadalajara that similar demonstrations would take place there in the following days. In spite of the alarming reports, the local civil and military authorities did nothing to prevent these demonstrations.[11] As before, they chose to let Guadalajarans protest, undisturbed, against Americans throughout their city. Their plan was simple: to have the police and military troops monitor the demonstrations and only allow city residents to shatter a few windows of American homes and commercial sites. In fact, Samuel E. Magill, the American consul in the city, reported that Brigadier General Clemente Villaseñor, commander of the Military Zone, did not veto the announced demonstrations "in view with his experiences with mobs here in former times."[12]

Notwithstanding the acquiescence of the military commander and suspecting serious difficulties, Magill asked local authorities for special protection, which he received: "Rumors of trouble were frequent in the morning of yesterday [Thursday, November 10] and I stated the case to the Commander of this Military Zone as well as to the local police authorities with the result that the Consulate was well protected, although several times the mob tried to pass the guards in order to attack the building."[13] The American Consulate, at 585 Placeres Street, had been guarded but, oddly, the local authorities were unprepared for other disturbances yet to come.

The First Night of Rioting

Anti-American demonstrations in Guadalajara began during the early evening hours of November 10. Following the actions of students in Mexico City, Guadalajara's law, medical, and high-school students called for a meeting to present a "formal" and "dignified" protest against the burning to death of Rodríguez. Believing in the truly nationalistic tenor of this protest, many thought that it was their duty to respond to the call. Congregationalist missionary Sara B. Howland described the discussions among students from her school, the Colegio Internacional, who asked for permission to attend the meeting: "It was quite a question. There would be a high pressure of feeling, to say the least, and the boys were excited; but, on the other hand, they were Mexican citizens, they firmly believed that their 'country' had called them, and for an American to keep them 'shut in' would be unwise." John Howland, her husband, cautioned the students to be "wise and prudent" before letting them go. "They went off with a shout," wrote Mrs. Howland, "and I confess my heart sank within me."[14]

There was plenty of tension in the air on the afternoon of November 10. Fearing that something unexpected would happen, peaceful inhabitants of the city deserted the central streets in town. Unidentified organizers called a protest meeting against the Rock Springs incident in the Plaza de Armas, the central square, at 8:00 P.M. Shortly before, people began gathering in the *portales*, or

arcades (on the western and southern perimeters of the square facing the Government Palace), and nearby streets.[15] Their objectives
were American institutions, businesses, and private residences.

The direction that the demonstrators took confirms the hypothesis that their targets were Americans and the buildings known to
be owned by or associated with them.[16] Hundreds of Guadalajarans
walked from the *portales* to University Square and from there to
Juárez Street (see First Night of Rioting map).[17] They next proceeded west toward the Consulate, screaming and throwing stones
on their way to American commercial buildings.[18] They turned left
at the corner of San Cristóbal Street. Shouting "¡Viva México!"
and "¡Mueran los yanquis!," they marched two blocks south, arriv-
ing at the corner of San Cristóbal and Placeres, on the eastern side
of the Consulate. "The mob was met by mounted *gendarmes* at the
entrance of the block in which the Consulate is situated," stated the
Mexican Herald, "and the police prevented the turbulent body from
reaching the building."[19] A unit of the 10th Regiment, in charge of
defending both the east and west flanks of the Consulate, was responsible for blocking the way for the approaching demonstrators.[20]
"In the meanwhile the crowd behind the line of *gendarmes* grew
rapidly, and anti-American speeches were made."[21] In addition,
someone tore, spat on, and burned an American flag while the crowd
cheered.

The demonstrators continued east in the direction of Galeana
Street, where they turned north. On Galeana and López Cotilla,
they stoned the clinic of American dentist George Purnell, a University of Maryland graduate and a "specialist in fine gold crowns
and extractions without pain or danger."[22] The stoning of the
dentist's office at this point seems the isolated action of individual
protesters and did not yet define the character of the demonstration
as a whole. They walked one more block, turned east again, and
went to University Square, where other demonstrators joined them.
Together they continued to Pedro Moreno Street, where, in front of
the American Club, they held a "peaceful" demonstration, shouting "Vivas" to Mexico. Most participants were still calm at this
time. Subsequently, the demonstrators walked to the Government
Palace, where they ran into the jefe político.[23] Believing that this
was one more round of the yearly anti-American displays, he did
not react to the demonstrators' shouts. The evening paper, *El Correo
de Jalisco*, reported on the following day that the jefe político had
asked the demonstrators to behave as "civilized men." Most participants were still calm, but, as was the case with Brigadier

FIRST NIGHT OF RIOTING

A) CATHEDRAL
B) GOVERNMENT'S PALACE
C) UNIVERSITY SQUARE
D) STATE PENITENCIARY
E) AMERICAN CONSULATE
F) RAILROAD STATION
G) CAROTHERS HOUSE
H) AMERICAN CANDY STORE
I) INSTITUTO COLÓN
J) DR. GEORGE PURNELL
J) COLEGIO INTERNACIONAL
K) HOTEL GARCÍA
L) HOTEL COSMOPOLITA
M) WEST END REALTY CO.
N) JALISCO TIMES

→ RIOTERS ROUTE

Drawn by Gabriela Ulloa and Sergio Camarena, based on H. Grant Higley's map "La cuidad de Guadalajara" (ca. 1908), in Archivo Histórico del Estado de Jalisco.

General Villaseñor, the jefe político did nothing to prevent the approaching violence.[24]

The demonstrators moved on to San Francisco Street, where they reportedly spent time "stoning several houses, breaking windows, and destroying numerous signs."[25] As they went south four blocks toward San Francisco Square, someone stoned the National Candy Company, a conspicuous target believed to be an American establishment. However, the store, also known as the American Candy Company, was owned by a Mexican who had purchased it from the original American owners and had retained its English name.[26] Tension was increasing. At San Francisco Square some demonstrators attacked an American passerby, while the rest of the rioters stoned the nearby West End Realty Company building on Colón Street, the business run (or partially owned) by Carothers. The imposing two-story structure, with a heavily carved stone facade, symbolized the economic success of one of the most affluent members of the American colony and was singled out as such to inflame the fury of the mob. Next, they moved on toward the Hotel Cosmopolita, owned by an American citizen, and threw rocks at it. They smashed windows at the nearby railroad station as well.

The rioters (as the protesters can be defined from this point on because of their increasingly violent behavior) then went to the offices of the *Jalisco Times*, the city's English-language newspaper, where, outside, they angrily denounced Americans and their newspaper, listened to anti-American speeches, and stoned the building. They subsequently wandered to the northeastern corner of Placeres and Maestranza streets, to the site of the Hotel García, which used to lodge American guests, and stoned it.[27] The rioters were agitated. They continued eight blocks on Placeres Street, turned south at the intersection with San Cristóbal (on the eastern flank of the Consulate), and walked west on Prisciliano Sánchez, heading for the American colony, where most U.S. citizens resided.[28] They threw rocks at other buildings on the way. For example, the *Mexican Herald* reported that "at a Mexican house near the Consulate, where a wedding was in progress, the musicians refused to play the National [Anthem] at the behest of the mob, and the house was stoned."[29]

The federal cavalry, trying to stop the rioters, further enraged them by attacking them with drawn sabers. The incensed agitators approached the American colony while shouting and stoning nearby houses. Americans, fearing for their lives, started shooting. Some protesters were ready to reciprocate but were prevented by the timely arrival of the 10th Regiment, whose commander, Major Enrique A. López, helped avoid further mayhem by ordering the cavalry to stop its aggression against the multitude. In spite of all the shouting, shooting, and stoning, the demonstrators managed to reach their targets. They had given up lesser objectives in the downtown area for those in the wealthy suburb. There they smashed windows of houses known to be owned by Americans. Their foremost target, again, was Carothers, whose mansion lay on the southeastern corner of Prisciliano Sánchez at the crossing with Camarena Street. Carothers's case deserves closer examination. Magill, the American consul, explained that he was "a very genial man, has real estate interests here, [and] has a host of friends among both Mexicans and Americans,"[30] yet Carothers associated himself primarily with wealthy Americans and led a life-style similar to theirs.[31] Besides, he was the treasurer of the American School in Guadalajara.[32] There is no doubt, therefore, that he personified what the rioters were protesting against, and their resentment toward him certainly caused them to attack both his business office and home.[33]

The other objectives of the rioters were the two Protestant educational institutions in the colony run by Americans: the Instituto Colón (on Tolsa and Libertad streets), which was the Southern Methodist girls' school, the "only English graded school in Guadalajara,"[34] considered also the "best piece of property" that Methodist Episcopal women owned in Mexico;[35] and the Colegio Internacional, the Congregationalist school for boys.[36] The crowd did not attack the American School, only two blocks away from the Instituto Colón, perhaps because it was nondenominational.[37] The mob first moved toward the Instituto Colón,[38] which had previously been a focus for anti-Protestant antipathy. At the time of the attack, "six American lady teachers and one hundred Mexican girl students" were inside.[39] The rioters "broke down a strong stone and iron fence in front of the building, smashed many windows, and then attempted to rush the building."[40] As soon as the rioters posed a serious threat to the occupants,[41] the federal cavalry, which had remained a neutral witness, intervened, driving the stormers away from the Instituto Colón.[42] This move made the Colegio Internacional, only a few blocks away, the next target.

The headmistress, Mrs. Howland, who was at the Colegio Internacional, described in detail the turmoil: "From the college . . . the noise was terrible; [there were] shots and crashing of heavy plate glass windows in the houses of our American neighbors; and we expected an attack every moment, waiting, with doors and windows closed, till our turn came. What was our relief when the sounds became fainter and fainter and we realized that we had been passed by, for that time at least."[43] The people at the Colegio Internacional were luckier, apparently, than those of their sister mission because a group of the Colegio's students, who had been following the rioters, "took a car and arrived at the corner of the college just as the mob was preparing to turn down the road, and by good generalship succeeded in keeping them away, and the building was untouched."[44] With the Methodist school's fence seriously damaged and the Congregationalist school left untouched, the two missionary institutions, in this section of town, emerged relatively unharmed after the first night of disturbances.[45]

Once the rioters had satisfied their anti-American passions, and thanks to some local políticos who made conciliatory speeches to calm them,[46] they abandoned the American colony. Subsequently, they went east toward the downtown area, passing once more near the American Consulate. "At about 10 P.M. another attempt was made on the Consulate," wrote Magill. "Threats were made to kill the Consul and destroy the Consulate, but the troops prevented any such acts and at about 11 P.M. all was quiet over the city."[47]

The Second Night of Rioting

On the morning of November 11, Consul Magill resumed his efforts to protect U.S. citizens and their institutions. He contacted both the jefe político and the commander of the Military Zone, who pledged to better protect Americans and their property.[48] The consul had to rely on Brigadier General Villaseñor for civil order, since the previous night's experience had taught him that the local police were "unable, unwilling, or incompetent"[49] to provide Americans with the necessary security: "It now looks that, if the local police are no more efficient than they were last night, graver harm will result from the work of the mob which has no fear for or of the police."[50]

There were other practical problems. Villaseñor did not have enough people in the federal cavalry to control the anticipated riots. He informed Magill that "having less than 500 cavalry at his disposition he could not possibly send a guard to each house without so scattering his forces as to render them useless in case of a combined attack by a mob on any one point."[51] The most that Villaseñor could do was to assure the consul of "ample protection" for the Consulate and the Instituto Colón,[52] which Magill—recognizing that because of its female student population, it was possibly perceived in the imagination of the male mobs as a tempting and easy target—"feared would be the center of the disturbances."[53] Many individual Americans also looked for help. Carothers, for example, requested in writing from the jefe político special guards for his house; he also wrote the American consul "asking for federal troops to protect him."[54] But Carothers, like many others, did not receive any protection. In view of the lack of guarantees for their lives and property, many Americans took refuge in the Consulate, the American Club, and other places that were heavily guarded. Mrs. Howland wrote about the fear that she shared with others: "Yesterday and last-night were anxious times as there was great excitement in the city and a great many stories reached us about the expected attack last evening. A large number of Americans took refuge in the house of the American Consul which was guarded by troops in the Street and on the roof, and the streets were filled with soldiers who were ordered to break up the excited group of *peones* as fast as they formed."[55]

The second night of demonstrations followed a pattern similar to that of the previous evening (see Second Night of Rioting map). Between seven and eight o'clock, hundreds of Guadalajarans met at the Plaza de Armas, facing the Government Palace, where they occupied all the benches, as if preparing themselves for a regular Friday night musical program, even though the local authorities had suspended the traditional *serenata* for that evening. Around eight o'clock, those sitting on the benches or meandering nearby went to University Square. A loud explosion was suddenly heard, and people became petrified, certain that someone was shooting, but it was only a firecracker detonated by one of the demonstrators.[56] Afterward, the rioters took San Francisco Street and walked south three blocks to San Francisco Square, stoning once again the American Candy Company.[57] Next, the demonstrators went to the railway station, where they broke some windows. They tried to get to the *Jalisco Times* building—by now an indisputable target—but the municipal policemen kept them at bay. By the time they reached Colón Street, the crowd was three or four blocks long. From López Cotilla, Placeres, and Prisciliano Sánchez streets, the police and cavalry squads that had been blocking both sides of the intersections managed to break up the demonstration momentarily. The rioters, however, reorganized at López Cotilla Street and moved eight streets west. A group of policemen followed them and, managing to get ahead of them, blocked their way at the corner of Penitenciaría

SECOND NIGHT OF RIOTING

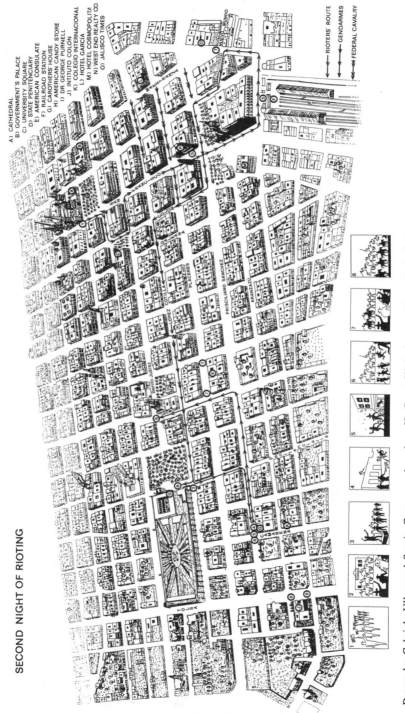

A) CATHEDRAL
B) GOVERNMENT'S PALACE
C) UNIVERSITY SQUARE
D) STATE PENITENCIARY
E) AMERICAN CONSULATE
F) RAILROAD STATION
G) CAROTHERS HOUSE
H) AMERICAN CANDY STORE (PROPERTY OF CAROTHERS)
I) DR GEORGE PURNELL
J) INTITUTO COLÓN
K) COLEGIO INTERNACIONAL
L) HOTEL GARCIA
M) HOTEL COSMOPOLITA
N) WEST END REALTY CO
O) JALISCO TIMES

→ RIOTERS ROUTE
→ GENDARMES
→ FEDERAL CAVALRY

Drawn by Gabriela Ulloa and Sergio Camarena, based on H. Grant Higley's map "La cuidad de Guadalajara" (ca. 1908), in Archivo Histórico del Estado de Jalisco.

and López Cotilla streets, at the southeastern corner of the state penitentiary, thus forcing the demonstrators to disperse by breaking up into smaller groups.[58]

One of these contingents, "made up of very few people," went south to Prisciliano Sánchez Street and turned two blocks west, stopping at the southeastern corner of Prisciliano Sánchez and Camarena. These people were told that an American lived there, and they proceeded to stone Carothers's home once again![59]This assault was more ferocious than the one that had taken place the previous night: "The rioters broke more windows, shots were fired at the house and Carothers . . . fired over the heads of the mob to frighten it and the men scattered, but being harangued and urged [on] by a well-dressed man, they renewed the attack with stones and pistols and tried to break the fence, to which Carothers replied [by] killing one youth and wounding a policeman."[60] "If the shot which wounded the policeman was fired by Carothers," the American consul wrote reflectively a few days later, "then the officer must have been in the mob." The policemen had sided with Guadalajarans, apparently testing the limits of superior orders: "After the shooting, Carothers and his *mozo* [servant] saw three policemen shoot [at] the house, but Carothers did not again shoot either at the policemen or at the mob." He "went to where his wife and children were hiding and remained with them until the jefe político came in person with a large guard." Carothers then went under "protection to the police station and afterward to the penitentiary."[61]

That evening he was fortunate. Cavalry and military squads patrolling the neighborhood managed to keep the infuriated rioters from breaking into his house and lynching him. In fact, the shooting attracted to Carothers's home the municipal policemen and federal cavalry. The policemen were those who had prevented the rioters from approaching the American colony at the intersection of López Cotilla and Penitenciaría; they had already been on their way east, toward the Consulate, believing that they had done their duty, when the shooting brought them back to the corner of Prisciliano Sánchez and Camarena. They backed up half a block to let the cavalry, led by Commandant Vicente Barragán, go by and block the intersection. The 10th Regiment also arrived there promptly, helping the federal cavalry control the infuriated mob.

According to *La Gaceta de Jalisco*, after Carothers had come out on the rooftop with a small rifle in his hand and shot Jesús Loza, one of the crowd, José García, pulled out his gun and shot back at Carothers. García was arrested immediately afterward while

the newly arrived policemen surrounded the whole block to pre
vent Carothers's getaway.[62] "After the boy was shot," reported the
Mexican Herald, "the mob cried out for revenge, and made a rush
at Carothers's residence, but the soldiers held the infuriated crowd
at bay and prevented the lynching of Carothers, and, probably, his
family."[63] The timely intervention of those armed officials undoubtedly saved Carothers's life.[64]

As Magill wrote, only "after this regrettable incident the police
commenced to do something." With the help of the federal cavalry,
the crowd "was dispersed and again attempted the Consulate reaching only the cavalry line to the west of the building." "Within an
hour after this," Magill informed Washington days later, "the city
was quiet, and has so remained notwithstanding all sorts of rumors
about additional attacks planned."[65] Loza's death, caused by
Carothers, terminated the anti-American riots. "It is believed," wrote
the consul, "that the cessation of rioting after Friday night was due
to a proclamation issued by the local police authorities in which it
was announced that if any further demonstration was made and more
property damaged or lives threatened, the perpetrators would be
summarily dealt with."[66] The authorities finally took measures to
restore public peace and safety.[67] On Monday, November 14,
Mrs. Howland wrote that, as of the previous day, the Mexican government had the city under control: "Notices were published to the
effect that all groups of more than *five* persons were to be broken
up, and that anyone raising any kind of a 'cry,' though it be only
'Viva México,' should be placed under arrest. All places of amuse-
ment were closed, theatre, bull-fight, even the *serenatas* in the *plaza*,
and complete silence reigned."[68] Days after the riots, Consul Magill
still reported numerous cases of abuse against Americans. The military curfew, all witnesses seem to conclude, put an end to the rioting but not to the intense anti-Protestant and anti-American feelings
of Guadalajarans.[69]

Anti-Americanism and Anti-Protestantism

The Díaz administration was characterized by its policies of economic and industrial development of Mexico. Throughout, but most
particularly during the closing quarter of the nineteenth century,
Porfirio Díaz's government devised plans for the expansion of rail-
roads, mines, and manufacturing, plans that deepened the country's
dependency on foreign know-how and investments, especially
American. Through different means, capital from the United States

was attracted to Mexico so that American investment grew from $200,000 in 1887 to $1 million by 1911. As part of this growth, Guadalajara expanded and transformed itself from a provincial capital into an industrial city connected through railways with national and international markets. Generally considered by historians as the bulwark of staunchest conservatism, both political and religious, Guadalajara emerged at the turn of the century as the commercial capital of the west. Not only did it control most of the rudimentary business operations emanating from (and directed abroad through) the port of Manzanillo, but, as of 1908, the year that the railroad operations from Mexico City to the port were inaugurated, Guadalajara also became the unequaled mercantile leader in the region.[70]

A considerable number of American investors and businessmen would soon arrive in the city, which had grown in size and population. Indeed, the composition of its foreign populace (American, German, French, and Spanish) changed drastically over a short time span. While in 1881 there were 115 foreigners in Guadalajara, by 1900 there were 740, of whom 275 were American. By 1910 the American colony in Guadalajara—the cradle of wealth resulting from several trading, real estate, and building ventures, among which the railroad construction stood out as its most forceful symbol—already reached a total of 500 people, including Protestants who established missionary schools and churches in the city. Americans clearly penetrated the city's industrial and commercial class and replaced the traditional urban elite and its prosperous leaders.

Affluence in Guadalajara, however, was soon uncovered as a treasure of the few: primarily Americans and those connected with them in all types of operations, all of whom aroused the hatred of the many. Those who seemed to be particularly hurt because of the changes in the structure of the merchant elite were the middle sectors. As historian Friedrich Katz has argued: "A dissatisfied middle class which resented the fact that it was excluded from political power, that it seemed to garner only the crumbs of Mexico's economic boom, and that foreigners were playing an increasingly important role in the country's economic and social structure existed in most parts of Mexico."[71] Writing about the dissatisfaction of the middle class, Ambassador Wilson explained on the last day of October 1910:

> This class, while not an evil, is a danger. . . . All over the Republic a class of sturdy tradesmen, usually of Indian blood, has developed. This class is industrious, intelligent, takes an acute interest in public affairs, is impatient of existing conditions, and

is constantly exerting a stronger and wider influence. Usually this class is opposed to the present Government and bitterly hostile to the group of men supposed to be its moving force. It may easily be supposed that in the event of a crisis the vast majority will rise to the support of ambitious men offering remedies for present evils.[72]

Feelings of displacement had certainly worsened during the last years of the Díaz administration when Mexico, despite its perceived and widely broadcast prosperity, underwent a profound economic depression. The "enormous growth in foreign investment after 1900 . . . the adoption of the gold standard by Mexico in 1905 . . . and the cyclical crisis that occurred in the United States during 1907–8 had a devastating effect on Mexico."[73] Guadalajara, like other old Bajío towns, was severely hit as markets and old industries declined.[74] Artisans and smaller merchants affected by the crisis became victims of the new, worsening conditions as their economic status began to slide. Such groups and, along with them, middle-class university students, anxious that their lot should improve but perhaps aware of the tough economic realities, became notably frustrated. These middle-class groups thus were susceptible to unrest, which could be translated effortlessly into mass upheaval by any provocative situation. It became, indeed, almost a routine in those years for these sectors to lead the disruption of the public order when they felt offended.

Unsurprisingly, the economic discontent and uncertainty of the middle class were easily directed toward foreigners. Xenophobia and anti-Protestant sentiments toward Americans grew because they symbolized the economic influence and cultural arrogance of outsiders. The following words, depicting the "pronounced anti-American feeling which exists throughout the Republic and is not confined to any class," come from Ambassador Wilson: "This sentiment of hostility is partially due to the memories of the [Mexican-American] war of 1846, partially to race antipathy, but in a larger measure to resentment of American commercial aggression and envy of American property and thrift."[75]

Anti-American manifestations became a common reaction, most notably during the yearly anti-American demonstrations—in which a few windows were broken here and there—when Mexicans celebrated Independence Day. "It has been the habit here for years after the celebration of the '*Grito*' at 11 o'clock P.M. of every 15th of September," wrote Magill, "for the mob, which had gathered to hear the '*Grito*,' to parade the streets and shout: 'Long live

Mexico!' and 'Death to the Yankees!,' or Spaniards, as the spirit moved it, after smashing windows of foreigners' stores or houses as a vent to its feelings."[76] The authorities, despite their official pro-American policies, had discovered that the easiest way to calm the latent discontent of angry Guadalajarans was to condone such actions. While these xenophobic performances were far from achieving social and economic equilibrium, at least politically (and symbolically) they served the purpose of appeasing the local urban population. And everything seems to indicate that the periodic victims of the exalted nationalism of the multitudes had learned to live with these recurrent displays in exchange for tranquility during the rest of the year.

Another element that added fuel to local anti-Americanism was the success achieved by Protestant missionaries while converting Guadalajarans to their religious persuasion. The following quotation demonstrates how violently the editors of an ardently pro-Catholic organ, exasperated at the missionaries' activities, fomented anti-Protestant feelings among Guadalajarans: "We have been warning parents so that, regardless of the promises [that Protestant missionaries] make them, they do not register their children at the Instituto Colón or the Instituto Corona. We notice with sorrow, however, that there are many girls in the [Instituto Corona,] located in front of the church of San Diego. . . . And we know, also, that on Sundays the ugly and sterile *gringas* [Yankee women] take young women and little girls to sing in the temple, situated in front of Núñez Square."[77]

The Catholic paper raved in such an anti-Protestant reaction probably because Mrs. Norwood E. Wynn, of the Methodist Episcopal Church South, had recently sent converted Mexican girls from the Instituto Colón into a proselytizing street campaign: "Our girls who were already Christians . . . walked the streets, giving out invitations, tracts, and portions of the Scriptures . . . the people (many of them) came to the meetings, and a number were converted."[78] It is evident that Guadalajara's Catholics wanted to stop the Protestant invasion since they feared that Protestants were out to impinge upon their local supremacy. Certainly, their concern was legitimate. Minnie Varner, suspecting that she would have to give up her missionary work because she suffered "a good deal from nervousness" following the attack on the Instituto Colón, stated in her annual report: "We have met with a great many problems this year [1910], some being caused by the unsettled political condition. We are not discouraged, but look forward with glad expectation to the time when Mexico shall acknowledge Christ as her Lord and Master, and the people shall pattern their lives by His blessed example. I am sure that the Catholic religion will have a hard death, but it *must* die to give way to the teachings of our Saviour."[79]

Another pretext for the local Catholic press to attack the Instituto Colón was the fact that its building, constructed by a Dr. Kellogg, had formerly been a sanatorium for consumptives. After a series of articles in several Catholic publications requesting that the school be closed, the local authorities ordered a health investigation. Anti-Protestant feelings among the local population, offended by the visible Protestant missionary work in the city, were easily awakened by official Catholic propaganda and made the Instituto vulnerable. Thus, its building was not only one of the main targets that the mob chose to attack on the first night of rioting in Guadalajara, but it was also selected for further attacks later that month. "There was a bomb found back of the girls' school of the M. E. Church South," an American Protestant woman residing in Guadalajara wrote on November 23.[80] Anti-Protestantism, an important, albeit underlying, element during the riots, was nourished by missionary determination.

Conclusions and Implications

Because xenophobic outbursts were perceived as an accepted practice, the November 1910 events at first almost passed unnoticed in the eyes of local authorities. On Thursday and Friday evenings of November 10 and 11, hundreds of Guadalajarans ran into the streets and rioted against the Americans living in their city. Several factors, however, made these mass actions distinct. First, the riots were initially ignited as a protest against a specific incident, the burning to death of Antonio Rodríguez in Rock Springs, Texas.[81] Second, unlike previous occasions of turbulent Independence Day festivities, the disturbances were the sequel to two nights of rioting in Mexico City in response to the Rodríguez episode. Third, these riots were far more violent and destructive than ever before: the two nights left one demonstrator dead and at least one policeman seriously wounded.[82] This time, therefore, local authorities did suppress the riots and arrest rioters.[83] Fourth, there was a strong anti-Protestant feeling that had been incited before by the work of missionaries and verbal attacks by Catholics on their activities. And fifth, these riots took place immediately before the outbreak of the

Revolution so that, in a sense, they announced the coming of the Revolution without being part of it.[84]

The 1910 riots were an outgrowth of officially permitted, traditional Independence Day acts of vandalism against foreigners in Guadalajara, yet the recent disturbances were different from previous ones in significant ways. They lasted longer and were clearly more intense and violent than earlier anti-American demonstrations in the capital of Jalisco. The fact that the only death resulting from these events was that of a rioter did not erase the terror that the demonstrations produced in those attacked. Certainly, the riots highlighted the incapacity of the local authorities to prevent violence and the declining ability of the Porfiriato to impose its pro-foreigner politics on the urban masses.

The rioting was characterized by certain noteworthy patterns. The attacks seemed to be calculated, clearly directed, and obviously focused. In these aspects the rioters displayed a rational and structured mass behavior. They knew who their victims were, and they collectively channelled their discontent and feelings of resentment into definite targets: wealthy and/or Protestant Americans. The protestors also knew where to find their victims and could, as locals, easily identify and locate what obviously belonged to them: their homes and institutions. Thus, the rioters stoned and damaged sites that visibly symbolized the ostentatious American presence and arrogant dominance, which were the focus of their anger. At the same time the protestors aimed their fury at those sites which they recognized as unprotected: private residences, businesses, and missionary schools. So they proceeded, not along a prearranged route, but rather along a circuit that was unspokenly premeditated and that resulted from the logic of their aims. The combination of the mob's clarity of purpose with its knowledge of the city's layout enabled the rioters to organize and mobilize rapidly and to move rationally even without individually recognized leaders.

While the protesting urban populace was visibly multiclass in its character, incorporating all sectors in society, middle-class elements seem to have provided the initial leadership to the rioting. Prominent among these were students: educated young people who represented the aspirations of the city's middle sectors but who faced the anxiety and frustration of possibly unmet socioeconomic expectations. Together with these disenchanted individuals there were others, from different layers in society, who were more easily identified by their staunch Catholicism. "If word came [that] Pres. Díaz was blown up by a bomb," wrote an American Protestant woman, "I believe there is a class here which would believe they were earning their entrance to heaven by killing the *protestante*. . . . This city is one of the most fanatical, and they will take great interest in doing what they believe a duty. . . . We have faithful and loyal friends among the Catholics, but the macheto class [*sic*] is the class to be feared."[85]

Considering the socioeconomic profile of the participants in the riots, therefore, the protests can be seen as popular, attracting multitudes who acted collectively, although petit-bourgeois interests reigned. The traditional deference of Guadalajara's residents to the upper class explains, in part, why they blamed their difficulties on Americans rather than on their own Mexican elite. The intriguing aspects of the American presence, urban concentration, and cultural differences, in addition to their uninhibited Protestant missionary campaigns, fomented the open anger of the Guadalajaran populace.

By leaving in peace the local aristocracy, the rioters were able to ally themselves with certain elements of the security forces who shared their antiforeign sentiments and economic dissatisfaction. The municipal police in Guadalajara were a telling example. It seemed that the policemen were active against the mob only in extreme cases of violence. More often, they helped the rioters actively or passively, as reported in various instances, because as lower-middle-class civil servants the municipal forces shared many grievances with the crowd.[86] The federal troops, on the other hand, sometimes sympathized with the American victims. Distant from the local population and its hardships, they were more loyal to the central regime.

When the local ruling class is too powerful or too well protected, the fury of the protesters is usually vented against a traditional scapegoat. In this case, they chose visible symbols of American wealth and dominance. Therefore, although the middle class and other members of society did not rise up against Guadalajara's traditional elite—still feared before the Mexican Revolution—the anti-American attacks, as symbolic class actions, could have signified at the same time dissatisfaction with the city's aristocracy.[87] A weak economy and unstable politics in the prerevolutionary years shook lower- and middle-class political loyalties. Anti-American discontent could have camouflaged what might have been dissatisfaction with basic political and social structures that, in general, characterized the Porfirian regime. The middle sectors in particular wished to reverse social processes that had hurt their status and life-style, but they were not alone in their discontent. Other members of society had suffered the inconveniences of a poorly directed economy.

The Guadalajara disturbances, which occurred just days before the Revolution, should be understood as part of the anti-American and anti-Protestant prerevolutionary scene. Furthermore, what had started in Guadalajara in November 1910 as a protest against the collapsing Porfirian regime's stated xenophilia[88] was substituted by an official nationalist xenophobia at the service of the revolutionary ideal. The disturbances in Guadalajara were scattered and fundamentally unorganized and, as such, were not absorbed into the political theater of the Revolution. But the leaders of the Revolution did utilize the Guadalajaran spirit of protest as an authentic popular force against the Díaz administration and as a way to consolidate the revolutionary regime in years to come.

Significantly, urban violence across the country showed that prerevolutionary protest was not restricted to peasants and organized workers, as has been usually assumed, but included agitators from all sectors of Mexican society. Urban populations were not apathetic, and in some cases the revolutionary leaders were able to integrate their discontent and tradition of mass action into the political struggle of the period. Although anti-Americanism was exploited in the Revolution and continued to be "an important ingredient of Mexican nationalism,"[89] it is the role of urban popular action that has remained as the historically significant legacy of the prerevolutionary years.

Notes

1. For additional studies of anti-American protests see Frederick C. Turner, "Anti-Americanism in Mexico, 1910–1913," *Hispanic American Historical Review* 47 (1967): 502–18; idem, *The Dynamic of Mexican Nationalism* (Chapel Hill: University of North Carolina Press, 1968), 202–53; and Servando Ortoll, " 'Turbas' antiyanquis en vísperas de la revolución del diez," *Boletín del Archivo Histórico de Jalisco* 1 (1983): 2–15.

2. See Charles C. Cumberland, *Madero y la Revolución Mexicana* (México: Siglo XXI, 1984, first English ed.: 1952), 145. (Our translation.) We do not accept, therefore, a recent interpretation by historian John Mason Hart, who concludes that the Guadalajara riots were direct revolutionary acts as part of the larger insurrection plans of the Maderistas. See Hart, *El México revolucionario* (México: Editorial Patria, 1990, first English ed.: 1987), 343. In this connection, it is interesting to note the words of A. A. Graham, a Kansas attorney and the American consul in San Luis Potosí: "You will observe that the [Maderista] disturbances at Puebla were directed against the authorities, and those at the City of

Mexico and Guadalajara, against Americans." A. A. Graham to secretary of state, San Luis Potosí, November 14, 1910, Department of State, Record Group 59, 812.00/39, National Archives, Washington, DC (hereafter cited as RG, NA).

3. "It is believed that the Centennial celebration in a small way was instrumental in creating a better feeling between the Mexican people and the Americans," wrote the American consul in Tampico. See Clarence A. Miller to assistant secretary of state, Tampico, September 19, 1910, RG 59, 812.00/347, NA.

4. Henry Lane Wilson, *Diplomatic Episodes in Mexico, Belgium, and Chile* (New York: Doubleday, Page and Company, 1927), 189–90.

5. *El centenario de Independencia* (Guadalajara: n.p., ca. 1910), 24, 26. (Our translation.)

6. See, for example, the picture taken at the field competitions on the property of the West End Realty Company in ibid., 18.

7. Telegram from Henry Lane Wilson to secretary of state, Mexico City, November 9, 1910, RG 59, 812.00/357, NA; and Turner, *The Dynamic of Mexican Nationalism*, 216.

8. Wilson to secretary of state, Mexico City, November 10, 1910, RG 59, 812.00/385, NA.

9. For two views of the Mexico City anti-American riots see Ortoll, " 'Turbas' antiyanquis," 6–8; and Turner, *The Dynamic of Mexican Nationalism*, 216–17.

10. Telegram of Wilson to secretary of state, Mexico City, November 10, 1910, RG 59, 812.00/360, NA.

11. Jalisco Governor Miguel Ahumada was out of town during these two days of rioting. See Samuel E. Magill to secretary of state, Guadalajara, November 15, 1910, RG 59, 812.00/438, NA; Magill to Wilson, Guadalajara, November 13, 1910, in RG 84, Guadalajara, Jalisco, Mexico, Consular Post Files, Official Correspondence with United States Embassy, January 1, 1910, to June 30, 1911, 96, NA.

12. Magill to secretary of state, Guadalajara, December 24, 1910, RG 59, 812.00/615, NA.

13. Magill to Wilson, Guadalajara, November 11, 1910, in RG 84, Guadalajara, Jalisco, Mexico, Consular Post Files, Official Correspondence with United States Embassy, January 1, 1910, to June 30, 1911, 90, NA. While the Consulate was well guarded, however, other well-known American places around the city and the American colony, in particular, were not.

14. Quoted in "Letters from the Missions," *Missionary Herald*, January 1911, 33.

15. We reconstructed the demonstrators' movements based on a report that appeared in *La Gaceta de Jalisco*, November 11, 1910, and derived some additional information from the American consul's writings.

16. The 1910 edition of the *Directorio Toussaint de la Ciudad de Guadalajara* was probably the best source available on the rioters' potential victims, since it disclosed the names and addresses of most members of the American colony. Consult the *Directorio Toussaint de la Ciudad de Guadalajara* (Puebla: Carlos V. Toussaint Ed., 1910), under the heading "Directorio de Colonias Extranjeras," notably under "Colonia Americana," 202–5.

17. Some of the locations of buildings that were stoned are approximate, given that most of them have been torn down in recent years.

18. "There are about sixty-five to seventy-five residences in this city occupied by Americans," wrote Magill, "of which eleven had some windows broken." About commercial and other establishments, he summarized: "Of thirty-two places of business, hotels, churches, etc., nine had windows broken." Magill to secretary

of state, Guadalajara, December 24, 1910, RG 59, 812.00/615, NA. Since the specific names of all American businesses or residences stoned by the rioters were not mentioned in the missionary letters or in the consular reports to Washington, we have considered here only the most conspicuous sites cited in these sources. At any rate, a total of twenty seems to be a small number of buildings stoned, if we are to believe the newspapers' reports on that night of rioting.

19. *Mexican Herald*, November 10, 1910. *Gendarme*, the French word for policeman, was widely used at the time in Guadalajara.

20. Regarding the protection that the local authorities granted the American Consulate on the first day of the disturbances, Magill reported: "A guard of two policemen came . . . to the Consulate as early as 2 P.M. Thursday and at 7:30 P.M. a troop of federal cavalry was placed on the street corners at either end of the block in which this Consulate is located." Magill to secretary of state, Guadalajara, November 15, 1910, RG 59, 812.00/438, NA.

21. *Mexican Herald*, November 10, 1910.

22. See his advertising in the *Directorio Toussaint de la Ciudad de Guadalajara*, 119 (authors' translation).

23. "The power of [the jefes políticos]," the American ambassador wrote years later, "sometimes exceeds that of the governor." The jefes políticos, according to him, were a powerful "retinue of personal agents and the chief executive." See Wilson, *Diplomatic Episodes*, 195.

24. See *El Correo de Jalisco*, November 11, 1910.

25. *La Gaceta de Jalisco*, November 11, 1910 (authors' translation).

26. *Mexican Herald*, November 11, 1910.

27. It is interesting to note the similarities between the facades of the Hotel García and the West End Realty Company office. Both buildings were probably designed by the same architect.

28. "The Americans have built out in the suburbs," wrote an anonymous Protestant woman residing for twenty years in Guadalajara, "and are open to attacks on all sides." Excerpt of a letter written by a "thoroughly well poised woman, not at all nervous or in any sense an alarmist," and sent to Edward B. Leigh, president of the Chicago Railway Equipment Company, from Guadalajara, November 23, 1910. See Edward B. Leigh to secretary of state, Chicago, December 1, 1910, RG 59, 812.00/531, NA.

29. *Mexican Herald*, November 12, 1910.

30. Magill to secretary of state, Guadalajara, November 15, 1910, RG 59, 812.00/438, NA.

31. His brother was an American consular agent in the city of Torreón. See Magill to G. C. Carothers, Guadalajara, November 15, 1910, in RG 84, Guadalajara, Jalisco, Mexico, Consular Post Files, Official Correspondence with Officials of the United States in General, January 1, 1910, to December 31, 1911, 84, NA.

32. Excerpt of a letter written by an anonymous Protestant woman and sent to Leigh, Guadalajara, November 23, 1910. See Leigh to secretary of state, Chicago, December 1, 1910, RG 59, 812.00/531, NA.

33. The *Mexican Herald* reported that "during the time the demonstration near the Consulate was taking place, rioters smashed plate glass windows of the American Banking Company. . . . Windows in the Masonic Hall, West End Realty Company, American Drug Company, and National Candy Company were also broken." *Mexican Herald*, November 11, 1910. Mexico City's Catholic daily, *El País*, reported that the Guadalajaran police were guarding all businesses with English names. *El País*, November 11, 1910.

34. See James Ervin Helms, "Origins and Growth of Protestantism in Mexico to 1920" (Ph.D. dissertation, University of Texas at Austin, 1955), 413.

35. Sara Estelle Haskin, *Women and Missions in the Methodist Episcopal Church, South* (Nashville, TN: Publishing House of the M.E. Church, South, 1920), 155.

36. The Congregationalist girls' school, the Instituto Corona, was "situated outside of the storm center," according to Sara B. Howland, who also stated that "the ladies of Corona Institute are well and the school has had no interruption." *Missionary Herald*, January 1911, 34.

37. The American consul suspected a "religious incentive" at work because, on the night that the mob attacked the Instituto Colón, it left the American School intact. See Magill to secretary of state, Guadalajara, December 24, 1910, RG 59, 812.00/615, NA. A reporter informed Mexico City's daily, the *Mexican Herald*, that "the American School which was closed Friday [November 11] will be opened again tomorrow [November 14]. The school was not attacked by rioters, but guards have been provided for the building." *Mexican Herald*, November 14, 1910.

38. Some students from the Colegio Internacional mingled with the rioters and tried to divert them from the Instituto Colón, but they did not succeed. They went to the rear of the building where the female Methodist teachers, recognizing them, asked for help in safeguarding the children. See *Missionary Herald*, January 1911, 33.

39. These are the figures that the American consul provided. The *Missionary Herald* reported the presence of only eighty-five children together with their teachers. See *Missionary Herald*, January 1911, 33.

40. Magill to secretary of state, Guadalajara, November 15, 1910, RG 59, 812.00/438, NA. In another report written by Magill in the middle of the turmoil, he stated that the demonstrators succeeded in "wrecking the iron fence which surrounded [the Instituto Colón] as well as breaking as many windows as could be reached causing much damage to windows and endangering the lives of the occupants." Magill to Wilson, Guadalajara, November 11, 1910, in RG 84, Guadalajara, Jalisco, Mexico, Consular Post Files, Official Correspondence with United States Embassy, January 1, 1910, to January 30, 1911, 90, NA.

41. "The policy of the authorities of the city," Magill reported weeks later, "seemed to have been to let the mob's desire for revenge be gratified by the breaking of a few windows rather than opposing it and cause bloodshed." See Magill to secretary of state, Guadalajara, December 24, 1910, RG 59, 812.00/615, NA.

42. Magill complained later that while the cavalry had successfully driven the rioters away from the Instituto Colón, it had allowed them to "continue their depradations on American houses in that vicinity and elsewhere and on American banks and business houses in the business district." See Magill to secretary of state, Guadalajara, November 15, 1910, RG 59, 812.00/438, NA.

43. Sara B. Howland to Dr. James L. Barton, Guadalajara, November 14, 1910, Papers of the American Board of Commissioners for Foreign Missions (hereafter cited as ABCFM), Houghton Library, Harvard University, Cambridge, Massachusetts. Howland's letter was printed in the *Missionary Herald*, January 1911, 33. Servando Ortoll acknowledges Professor John Womack's generosity in informing him of the existence of these archives so crucial to the history of Protestantism in Latin America.

44. Letter from Mrs. Howland reproduced in the *Missionary Herald*, January 1911, 33.

45. This is what the *Missionary Herald* printed based on information sent by Mrs. Howland from Guadalajara: "Some of the students in the boys' college did good service during the rioting in guarding the girls' school; other assisted in protecting the premises of the Methodist Mission, while still others were effective in turning aside the mob by mingling with them and diverting their attention from the mission buildings." *Missionary Herald*, December 1910, 545.

46. *La Gaceta de Jalisco*, November 11, 1910; Magill to secretary of state, Guadalajara, December 24, 1910, RG 59, 812.00/615, NA.

47. Magill to secretary of state, Guadalajara, November 15, 1910, RG 59, 812.00/438, NA. *La Gaceta de Jalisco* reported that the disturbances ended that evening around 11:30 P.M. See *La Gaceta de Jalisco*, November 11, 1910.

48. On that same day Magill informed the American ambassador in Mexico City that "rumors are about that another attack will be made tonight or this afternoon both on the Consulate and on the Instituto Colón which latter building is threatened with complete destruction." Magill to Wilson, Guadalajara, November 11, 1910, in RG 84, Guadalajara, Jalisco, Mexico, Consular Post Files, Official Correspondence with United States Embassy, January 1, 1910, to June 30, 1911, 90, NA.

49. Magill to secretary of state, Guadalajara, November 15, 1910, RG 59, 812.00/438, NA. At a later date, Magill stated that "when the intent to demonstrate against the Americans became known on the 10th of November, . . . the authorities presumed it would only amount to the smashing of windows, and the police acted as if their instructions were to permit that much and to only interfere to prevent bodily harm, for the police accompanied the mob and made no effort whatever to prevent window smashing, but rather encouraged it or remained passive." Magill to secretary of state, Guadalajara, December 24, 1910, RG 59, 812.00/615, NA.

50. Magill to Wilson, Guadalajara, November 11, 1910, in RG 84, Guadalajara, Jalisco, Mexico, Consular Post Files, Official Correspondence with United States Embassy, January 1, 1910, to June 30, 1911, 90, NA.

51. Magill to secretary of state, Guadalajara, November 15, 1910, RG 59, 812.00/438, NA.

52. Magill reported that at 7:30 P.M. on Friday, November 11, Villaseñor sent 105 federal cavalry and 9 foot soldiers to the Consulate: "At my request [Villaseñor] left only 9 unmounted and 16 mounted to guard this place; sent 9 to specially guard the Instituto Colón, . . . and the balance in two or three groups to patrol the streets and districts west of the Consulate where the damage to American residents had been greatest on Thursday night. This was thoroughly done by the federal cavalry and the Instituto Colón was not again attacked." Magill to secretary of state, Guadalajara, November 15, 1910, ibid.

53. Magill to Wilson, Guadalajara, November 12, 1910, in RG 84, Guadalajara, Jalisco, Mexico, Consular Post Files, Official Correspondence with United States Embassy, January 1, 1910, to June 30, 1911, 92, NA. The Southern Methodists at the Instituto Colón, taking advantage of the military protection accorded them by the Guadalajara authorities, began proselytizing among the soldiers. Mary E. Massey disclosed months later: "Our school work came near being interrupted by the mob which so cruelly stoned our house on the night of November 10th. For several weeks conditions were somewhat unsettled, but we did not lose a single day. During that time our house was under military guard several days, and we had the opportunity of giving tracts and Bibles to the soldiers, which they read with a great deal of interest." *First Annual Report of the Woman's*

Missionary Council of the Methodist Episcopal Church, South for 1910–1911 (Nashville, TN: Publishing House of the Methodist Episcopal Church, South, 1911), 332.

54. Magill to secretary of state, Guadalajara, November 15, 1910, RG 59, 812.00/438, NA.

55. Mrs. Howland to Barton, Guadalajara, November 12, 1910, ABCFM. During the following days there were rumors of continuing disturbances. Fearing for their lives, Americans organized themselves in various ways. The *Mexican Herald*, for instance, reported that "Americans, and in fact, most of the foreigners, have been buying arms and ammunition all day today [Saturday, November 12]. Several meetings have been held quietly, by the foreigners, to discuss what steps should be taken for defense, in case of another attack, which all fear is coming tonight." *Mexican Herald*, November 13, 1910. Mrs. Howland wrote the following about that Saturday: "All through the day alarming reports were circulated and the excitement was intense. Towards evening an American gentleman came to the house saying that he had come as a representative of the American Club to ask us to go down to the center of the city to sleep, as there was to be an attack on the colony and it would be better to be under guard and all together. The Consulate was already full, but the houses of the ex-consul and others were open to all and the hotels were thoroughly guarded." Mrs. Howland to Barton, Guadalajara, November 14, 1910, ABCFM.

56. A reporter from *La Gaceta de Jalisco* followed the demonstrators' march around the city. Most of the information about the second night of rioting comes from his account. See *La Gaceta de Jalisco*, November 12, 1910.

57. When the second attack on the American Candy Company came, the owner, Juan Montoya, still had not changed the store's name to one more suitable for a Mexican anti-American audience. Several merchants, aware of the nationalist overtones of the rampage, displayed Mexican banners in their shop windows. This maneuver, according to one source, stopped several rioters from stoning their stores. See *La Gaceta de Jalisco*, November 12, 1910. It is evident that the wisdom of Mexican nationalism provided the riot with its own logic; the multitude knew what its motivations for rioting were.

58. Unaware of the size of the demonstration at its origin, Magill wrote of the second night that "there did not appear to be so large a mob out [Friday] night as [the] one Thursday night, but those composing it were more vicious." Magill to Wilson, Guadalajara, November 12, 1910, in RG 84, Guadalajara, Jalisco, Mexico, Consular Post Files, Official Correspondence with United States Embassy, January 1, 1910, to June 30, 1911, 92, NA.

59. From the reporter's account, it seems that the rioters had no idea that they were stoning, for the second time in two successive nights, Carothers's home. See *La Gaceta de Jalisco*, November 13, 1910.

60. Magill to secretary of state, Guadalajara, November 15, 1910, RG 59, 812.00/438, NA. (The wounded municipal policeman was Prudencio Chávez, while the fourteen-year-old boy killed by Carothers was Jesús Loza, a neighbor from the Barrio de Analco. Loza had worked in a shoe store and was a member of the Hidalgo Society's band. Possibly other society members also participated in the attack on the American colony that night. See Ortoll, " 'Turbas' antiyanquis," 11.) A few days later, Carothers described in greater detail what had happened on the second night of anti-American rioting: "Having renewed the breaking of windows and the shooting at his house having commenced, [Carothers] shot three times quickly into the air which caused the crowd to scatter so that the street was cleared. A well-dressed man then called the mob together and addressed them

urging the mob to again attack the house. Up to this time [Carothers] had seen no police and with the renewal of the attack he shot into the mob with the result that a youth was killed and a policeman was wounded." Magill to Wilson, Guadalajara, November 17, 1910, in RG 84, Guadalajara, Jalisco, Mexico, Consular Post Files, Official Correspondence with United States Embassy, January 1, 1910, to June 30, 1911, 110, NA.

61. Magill to Wilson, Guadalajara, November 17, 1910, ibid. Carothers was released a few days later. No charges were pressed against him.

62. See *La Gaceta de Jalisco*, November 12, 1910.

63. *Mexican Herald*, November 13, 1910.

64. See *La Gaceta de Jalisco*, November 12, 1910.

65. Magill to secretary of state, Guadalajara, November 15, 1910, RG 59, 812.00/438, NA.

66. Ibid.

67. "In pursuance with your two messages of yesterday," wrote the governor of Jalisco to Wilson, "I have proceeded to take all necessary precautions to evade scandals and to guarantee the safety of American citizens. Last night the scandalous demonstration against Americans was repeated and two Mexicans were wounded as a result. I am already taking necessary measures to avoid the repetition of such disorders tonight." Translation of letter from Governor Miguel Ahumada to Ambassador Wilson, Guadalajara, November 12, 1910, Enclosure with letter from Wilson to secretary of state, Mexico City, November 25, 1910, RG 59, 812.00/518, NA.

68. Mrs. Howland to Barton, Guadalajara, November 14, 1910, ABCFM.

69. Magill wrote:

Since the anti-American demonstrations, there has been reported to me only the following: On his way to conduct service at the Union Church (Congregational) in this city, at about 10:45 A.M. of Nov. 24th, Thanksgiving, some persons threw a stone fiercely at Rev. Robert C. Elliot. He was not struck. Americans attending that service were whistled at as they entered the edifice, and the writer heard "¡Mueran los!" as he approached the building. During the services stones were thrown at the windows but none was broken as all are protected by wire netting. At a native Methodist Church, on the same date in the evening, rocks were thrown at the building, people going and coming were yelled at and insulted, and a bomb or *cohete* was thrown in the room and exploded during service. At five o'clock A.M. of Nov. 25th, a rock was hurled through the window of the residence of H. L. Baumgardner with whom reside his wife's parents, Mr. and Mrs. Gunnell. No damage was done.

Magill to Wilson, Guadalajara, November 28, 1910, in RG 84, Guadalajara, Jalisco, Mexico, Consular Post Files, Official Correspondence with United States Embassy, January 1, 1910, to June 30, 1911, 123–24, NA.

70. Information on economic, social, and demographic changes in the Jalisco region is found in Chapters 5, 6, and 7 of Ellen McAuliffe Brennan's dissertation. See Ellen McAuliffe Brennan, "Demographic and Social Patterns in Urban Mexico: Guadalajara, 1876–1910" (Ph.D. dissertation, Columbia University, 1978).

71. Friedrich Katz, *The Secret War in Mexico: Europe, the United States, and the Mexican Revolution* (Chicago: University of Chicago Press, 1981), 30.

72. Special and Confidential letter from Wilson to Philander C. Knox, secretary of state, Mexico City, October 31, 1910, RG 59, 812.00/355, NA.

73. Katz, *The Secret War in Mexico*, 30.

74. See Alan Knight, *The Mexican Revolution*, 2 vols. (Lincoln: University of Nebraska Press, 1990), I: 214.

75. Special and Confidential letter from Wilson to Knox, Mexico City, October 31, 1910, RG 59, 812.00/355, NA. "In commenting on the basic Mexican hostility toward the United States, the American vice-consul in Mexico City stated that the anti-American rioting was not so much a protest against the Rodríguez burning as it was a sign of 'jealousy of American success' and the fact that Americans had come to control some of Mexico's most productive industries and lands." See Turner, *The Dynamic of Mexican Nationalism*, 217.

76. Magill to secretary of state, Guadalajara, December 24, 1910, RG 59, 812.00/615, NA. The *"Grito"* that Magill refers to is the "Cry" of Independence shouted by the highest local authority echoing the words of Miguel Hidalgo in September 1810.

77. See *La Chispa*, November 17, 1910. (Our translation.)

78. See Mrs. Norwood E. Wynn's Report for 1909 in the *32nd Annual Report of the Woman's Board of Foreign Missions of the Methodist Episcopal Church, South for 1909–1910* (Nashville, TN: Publishing House of the Methodist Episcopal Church, South, 1910), 83.

79. April 1911 meeting in St. Louis, Missouri, at St. John's Church. *First Annual Report of the Woman's Missionary Council of the Methodist Episcopal Church, South for 1910–1911*, 334.

80. Excerpt of a letter written by an anonymous Protestant woman sent to Leigh, Guadalajara, November 23, 1910. See Leigh to secretary of state, Chicago, December 1, 1910, RG 59, 812.00/531, NA.

81. See Turner, "Anti-Americanism in Mexico," 504–5; and idem, *The Dynamic of Mexican Nationalism*, 216–17.

82. A Mr. Mordough, who had been in Guadalajara one of the two nights of rioting, declared to an American Embassy officer that "he, personally, with his daughter and granddaughter, saw many of the depredations committed; they, themselves, on leaving a restaurant in the *portales*, en route to their hotel through some back streets in order to avoid the mob, ran directly into it, and they would have been assaulted, but that a Mexican . . . took them into his house and protected them and afterwards escorted them to their hotel." See enclosure with letter from Wilson to secretary of state, Mexico City, November 15, 1910, RG 59, 812.00/450, NA.

83. Writing on December 24, Consul Magill stated: "Numerous arrests of rioters were made during the demonstrations, but I find it impossible to get definite information as to the number punished, as those arrested for aiding in the proposed revolution immediately following the anti-American demonstrations were treated with the former and no record of each separate [arrest] is obtainable. There were probably between fifty and sixty sent to the army as a punishment." Magill to secretary of state, Guadalajara, December 24, 1910, RG 59, 812.00/615, NA.

84. This position contradicts the way that President Díaz depicted the causes of the riots. In an interview that the American ambassador held with Porfirio Díaz, Wilson was told that "the real cause of the disturbance was not the anti-American sentiments of the people, but that a number of politicians adverse to the government had taken advantage of the unfortunate affair which happened in Texas to excite young students and men of the laboring classes in order to dis-

credit the government by such disturbances as occurred here [in Mexico City] during the past week." See Wilson to secretary of state, Mexico City, November 15, 1910, RG 59, 812.00/450, NA. In what appears to be a second report on the same interview with President Díaz, Wilson was told that "the anti-American disturbances . . . had been brought about by persons antagonistic to the government; that the students had been used as a tool to discredit the government and that the crime committed in Rock Springs, Texas, had served as a pretext to arouse the young men into unlawful action." See "Interview with the President," enclosure with letter from Wilson to secretary of state, Mexico City, November 16, 1910, RG 59, 812.00/447, NA. These two diplomatic reports most likely have influenced the way that some historians have viewed these riots and connected them with the impending Maderista uprising of November 20, 1910.

85. Excerpt of a letter written by an anonymous Protestant woman sent to Leigh, Guadalajara, November 23, 1910. See Leigh to secretary of state, Chicago, December 1, 1910, RG 59, 812.00/531, NA.

86. A telling example of this situation is what the anonymous Protestant woman whom we have quoted above said about Carothers and his pregnant spouse: "His wife is a Mexican so it cannot be said he is fanatical. The first night [of rioting] his wife called to a policeman: 'I am a Mexican, protect me.' He answered: 'You married an American, you don't deserve protection.' Mr. Carothers reported the policeman next day and he was arrested; for that reason his home was attacked." Ibid.

87. The hypothesis of this being partially a class war riot seems confirmed when we take into consideration that the rioters left untouched other Protestant institutions in Guadalajara located in poorer sections of town.

88. In a letter from the Mexican president to Wilson, Díaz explained that "the great majority of the Mexican people, as well as its Government, maintain cordial and good relations of friendship for the people and Government of the United States and that only a few political agitators were the ones who had taken advantage of this incident and acted in a violent manner, inciting the students, who under the impression made on them by the crime committed in Texas against the Mexican Antonio Rodríguez, had acted imprudently pursuant to evil suggestions." Translation of letter from Díaz to Wilson, Mexico City, November 15, 1910. Enclosure with Wilson to secretary of state, Mexico City, November 25, 1910, RG 59, 812.00/516, NA.

89. Turner, *The Dynamic of Mexican Nationalism*, 248.

Conclusion: Contention and the Urban Poor in Eighteenth- and Nineteenth-Century Latin America

Charles Tilly

Charles Tilly is University Distinguished Professor at the New School for Social Research, where he directs the Center for Studies of Social Change. Trained as a sociologist, he has focused over the past four decades on large-scale social change and its relationship to popular collective action, especially in western Europe. He has published hundreds of articles and numerous prize winning books, including The Vendée *(1976),* The Contentious French *(1986),* Coercion, Capital, and European States, A.D. 990–1990 *(1990),* European Revolutions, 1492–1992 *(1993), and* Popular Contention in Great Britain *(1995).*

In this essay Professor Tilly shows what can be gained from placing the Latin American riots in a comparative perspective. He reviews the findings of European works on popular contention, proposes a new framework for analyzing these incidents, and suggests a future research agenda for Latin American historians. He ends with a selection of recent works on European and U.S. history for those who want to explore the topic further.

Successive maps of urban population in the Western Hemisphere tell a remarkable tale. In A.D. 800, cities of 20,000 inhabitants or more concentrated heavily in Central America but reached down the Andes into South America; they bore such names as Tula, Tikal, Tumbes, and Tiahuanaco. In 1500, when the definitive European penetration of the Americas was just beginning, the urban map greatly resembled the distribution of A.D. 800, except that South America's west coast had nurtured such cities as Chanchan and Pachacamac, while North American populations had built up Chillicothe and Nanih Waiya into places of more than 20,000. Nevertheless, the dominant cities clustered inland: Tenochtitlan (perhaps 80,000 inhabitants), Utatlan (60,000), and Cuzco (45,000); at that point, Tenochtitlan did not match China's Peking (some 672,000) or India's Vijayanagar (500,000), but it would have ranked among Europe's ten largest places, at the approximate magnitude of Lyon, Lisbon, and Bruges. Invading Europeans stumbled onto one of the world's great urban systems, or—if the Inca empire really operated in isolation from those to its north—two of them.

In a way, I am recapitulating the European penetration of Latin America, coming from a base in studies of European conflicts for a quick tour of their counterparts south of the Rio Grande. Like many tourists and invaders, I undoubtedly misunderstand much of what I see, interpreting people, places, and events according to European codes. Nevertheless, the casting of European eyes on Latin American scenes can help scholars of the region in three ways: 1) by identifying features of Latin America's experience that are puzzling in European perspective, and therefore point to distinctive features of its history; 2) by asking questions that are standard in European historiography but less common in Latin America—some such questions are likely to be worth asking in both continents; and 3) by calling attention to the intense interaction between Europe and Latin America during the eighteenth and nineteenth centuries, an interaction that surely had significant effects on the character of urban conflicts on both sides of the Atlantic. This essay therefore aims to identify topics for further inquiry, not to lay down a definitive scheme.

Seen from Europe, then, what shape has the history of Latin America? The changing configuration of cities provides some idea of what was distinctive about Latin American social change. By 1600, Europe's violent visitors—*conquistadores* and calamitous diseases—were taking their toll. Silver-bearing Potosí then towered above all other American metropolises at 148,000 people, while Mexico City followed at 75,000, but elsewhere urban centers had fallen into ruin. Even so, in 1750 all of America's large cities except Boston and Philadelphia still lay in regions of Spanish or Portuguese conquest, in Latin America.

Only during the nineteenth century did the American urban map take on something like its present configuration, with a large share of its cities scattered across the north and its large southern cities situated disproportionately along the coasts in such export centers as Lima, Valparaiso, Buenos Aires, and Rio de Janeiro. Although, in 1900, Asunción, La Paz, Quito, Bogotá, and Caracas still stood out as interior citadels of extraction and administration, Central America constituted the chief exception to the huddling of major Latin American cities along the seas, where access to (and from) Europe and North America was easier and more profitable.

Seen from the outside, then, the history of urban North, Central, and South America reflects the hemisphere's changing relations to Europe: first, a more or less autonomous network of peoples centered on the high civilizations that spanned the isthmus; then a zone of European conquest and settlement still pivoting on Central America, a cluster of European colonies exporting both precious metals and food while relying increasingly on slave labor, a growing set of formally independent states dominated by people of European descent, a major zone of immigration from Europe and elsewhere in a period of commercialization and industrialization; and, finally, a differentiated region still deeply attached to Europe but now strongly influenced by North American capital and arms.

By the twentieth century, sharp contrasts between North and South had arisen. Despite such prosperous capitals as Buenos Aires and Santiago, on the average northern urban populations had accumulated much greater wealth than their southern neighbors. Rural landlords weighed more heavily in the politics, commerce, and industry of the South, urban landlords more heavily in the North. The two regions likewise differed in their ethnic-racial composition. North of Mexico, the indigenous populations of 1492 had been destroyed, assimilated, herded into small enclaves, or driven to the peripheries; in the North's cities, they only established a major presence as part of the ancestry of Spanish-speaking immigrants from the South.

By the later twentieth century, descendants of enslaved Africans likewise concentrated in those northern cities, where they encountered European or East Asian immigrants and their descendants in large numbers. Except near Mexico and in the far North, by that time the North's rural populations had become overwhelmingly European in origin. Farther South, on the other hand, rural-urban continua from "Indian" or "African" to "European" prevailed, with concentrations varying in rough correspondence to the nineteenth-century geography of slave, indentured, coerced, and free labor. East Indians complicated the Caribbean's ethnic geography, while elsewhere in Latin America East Asian and European immigrants laid down tangled lineages.

Another contrast came to characterize the Americas: they were the first regions of massive European colonization, then the first European colonial areas to gain substantial political independence of the Continent. Their independent states, however, took rather different forms. Although Latin American states varied greatly in their strength vis-à-vis their resident populations and sometimes adopted formally federal structures, on the whole their segments retained far less autonomy than in the English-speaking states to the north. The subdivisions that became the states and provinces of the United States and Canada held regional and national powers that could make almost any Latin American (or, for that matter, European or East Asian) provincial governor envious. As a corollary, Latin American urban conflicts were likely to involve national authorities more immediately and intensely than did their Anglo-American counterparts.

These vast changes and contrasts constitute the starting point of any attempt to place Latin American urban conflicts in comparative perspective. Only the starting point, to be sure: no one will get very far in such a comparative analysis without considering various staple products such as sugar, coffee, beef, or cotton, such geophysical presences as the Andean *cordillera* and the great river systems, such logistical factors as accessibility to North American ports and military installations, such historical factors as the multiple trajectories of Latin American armies. All the elements that enter into variation in popular politics play their part in the explanation of urban contention.

Popular politics centers on the making of contentious claims in public arenas. Contentious claims are commands, demands, requests, petitions, invitations, applications, and supplications that will, if realized, affect other people's interests. They range from humble expressions of support for one part or another to revolutionary seizures of power. Public authorities, threatened ruling classes, and elite observers commonly condemn popular claim-making as impulsive, irresponsible, destructive, shortsighted, and ignorant. Sometimes they are right, just as ordinary people sometimes justly perceive their rulers as corrupt, contemptuous, covert, crass, and cruel. But popular politics in any particular setting has its own routines and rationale, a set of established means and meanings created and transformed continuously by the very experience of claim-making.

For the purpose of intellectual bookkeeping, we can sort the causes of variation in popular claim-making into three categories: social base, culture, and opportunity structure. The **social base** includes the social relations, everyday routines, resources, and commitments with which potential claimants live their lives, which form the basis of their collective interests and capabilities. Family relations, religious organization, the structure of work, the accumulation of property, the elaboration of friendship networks, the formation of public identities, and the changing web of interpersonal obligations all take their place in the social base, and all affect the occasions on which people make claims as well as the means by which they make those claims.

Culture refers to people's shared understandings, which define the desirable, the likely, and the possible. Culture emphatically includes ideas (often tacit) about what forms of collective action are desirable, likely, or possible, and what consequences they will produce under varying circumstances. Although sometimes people restrict culture to widely shared beliefs, values, and aesthetic patterns or even to the most elaborate and prestigious forms of "high culture," in the explanation of claim-making we must adopt a much broader definition, including the understandings that pervade everyday practices: eating, gossiping, working, defecating, healing, sleeping, washing, making love. Sometimes, likewise, people imagine culture as an autonomously changing power—as in conceptions of Mexican or Argentinian culture "causing" Mexicans and Argentinians to behave differently from each other—but here we must recognize culture as embedded in social relations.

Opportunity structure embraces the estimated advantages and disadvantages of existing, changing, and possible relations of a given actor with all other actors; students of political opportunity structure (POS) often stress the multiplicity of independent centers of power within the polity, the openness of the polity to new actors, the instability of current political alignments, and the availability of influential allies or supporters. Thus, we can think of democratization or the creation of a military dictatorship as changes in all four elements of POS.

In real life, of course, social base, culture, and opportunity structure interweave seamlessly; we sort out their strands as "determinants" of the means and meanings that constitute popular collective action to discipline a causal analysis. For analytic purposes, likewise, we can trace their histories separately: watch transformations of routine social relations, observe shifts in shared understandings, study alterations in POS. Within popular politics itself, for example, the previous history of struggle leaves residues in shared memories, interpersonal solidarities, understandings of what means of action are effective or ineffective, relations with police, allies, enemies, or local authorities. The cumulative histories of social base, culture, and opportunity structure obviously intertwine.

We can reasonably think of popular collective action's means and meanings as grouping into various available **performances**:

the carrying of a popular hero on a crowd's shoulders in one setting, the organization of a solemn procession complete with costumes and religious paraphernalia in another. Each performance links its participants to one or more objects of claims, present or absent, and includes some standard way of articulating those claims. Eighteenth-century Europeans, for example, had available a performance that the English called "pulling down" a dishonored house: breaking its windows, smashing its door, drinking and distributing its wine, sacking its interior, removing its valuables, and destroying them ceremoniously but joyfully (most often by means of bonfires) in the nearby street; in the 1760s and 1770s, Great Britain's North American colonists repeatedly invoked that performance against representatives and collaborators of the British government. In the Quito of 1765, Anthony McFarlane describes a related routine as someone sounded the tocsin (the rapid chiming of church bells, in Europe a standard signal of emergency, and a call for local residents to take action against a shared menace), then crowds gathered to sack the royal excise office and the aguardiente distillery. What is more, he shows us municipal officials vainly invoking a standard counterperformance, illumination and arming by solid citizens.

Performances cluster into **repertoires**, arrays of means available for claim-making among any particular set of actors. Thus, in eighteenth-century western Europe, householders dealt with unjust officials by sending delegations, offering petitions, conducting shivarees or other mocking ceremonies, sacking their residences in the ritual way, or stoning them in the street but not by other means that would have been technically possible but were inconceivable in that time and place: staging marches, holding mass meetings, conducting hunger strikes, creating new political parties, running newspaper advertisements, or organizing recall campaigns. The availability of a limited range of means constrained the claims that people made, and how they made them. That constraint, not incidentally, strongly affected the conditions under which riots were likely to occur.

What is a "riot," after all? Just as the words "mob," "rabble," and "*canaille*" allow authorities, privileged classes, and other hostile observers to deny ordinary people standing as political actors, such words as "riot," "*motín*," "*turba*," or "*tumulto*" constitute deprecatory political labels for some kinds of popular claim-making. Makers of claims in the relevant actions never identify themselves as mob, rabble, or *canaille*, never style their action riot, *motín*, *turba*, or *tumulto*. In European languages, "riot" and similar terms generally refer to gatherings disapproved of by authorities in the course of which some participants not only defy legal summons to disperse but also attack or seize privileged persons, their property, and/or symbols of their position. The actual physical violence in so-called riots often consists chiefly of attacks by police and other armed forces on people who are making illegal claims or refusing to disperse.

Riots, in this sense, often begin with gatherings and claims that are quite legal, even publicly encouraged: parades, public meetings, festivals, entertainments, electoral assemblies. Such occasions turn "riotous" under two main circumstances: when confrontations with enemies or authorities escalate to open attacks of one on the other; and when some participants take advantage of the protection provided by the gathering to attack or seize objects of their disapproval, vengeance, fear, hate, lust, greed, or envy. But "riots" also take the form of actions in which from the moment of gathering some participants set out to perform forbidden actions, seizures, or attacks in the presence of resistance from authorities or the objects of their action.

More generally, we can define a continuum of initial conditions from legal, low-risk, everyday gatherings to the deliberate organization of commandos. Gatherings at one end of the continuum rarely become riotous, while those at the other end often do. At every position along the continuum, nevertheless, actions that turn into violent encounters spring from combinations of established routines, shared understandings, and political opportunity structure, which themselves alter in part as a function of struggles and their outcomes. Although the existence of such a continuum seems obvious, seven crucial conclusions follow immediately from this characterization of riots:

1. Whatever regularities appear in the so-called riots of a given region and period spring from the conjunction of several kinds of social routines: in the public making of claims, in the gathering of substantial numbers of people, in official control of substantial gatherings, in the presence or absence of objects of popular claims;

2. The actual frequency, timing, and geographic distributions of these routines significantly affect the likelihood, character, timing, location, and consequences of riots;

3. Since all of these routines vary greatly among times and places, no single model can conceivably account for all events that authorities and hostile observers call riots;

4. At least two contradictory accounts, those of authorities and those of ordinary participants, emerge from every so-called riot;* in most cases, available records privilege the accounts of authorities, enemies, victors, and survivors. Where available, the confrontation of contradictory accounts itself clarifies what was at issue;

5. Whatever else it involves, the explanation of riots therefore entails both the sorting out of contradictory accounts and the establishment of patterns of popular politics that extend far beyond the world of violent confrontation. "Riots" are therefore in no sense sui generis;

6. Conversely, because of the official action, records, and public reporting they generate, violent events provide precious documentation concerning change and variation in less visible and more routine ways of making claims; and

7. The proper frame for the historical analysis of "riots" is not some general model of social change, conflict, or collective action but an interpretation of routine popular politics, its interruptions, and its changes.

For all their difficult interpretation, then, violent urban confrontations provide an exceptional entrée into popular politics. In the case of European history, these principles (however ill understood) have generated a vast, argumentative literature on urban conflicts. Some of European historiography's most intense disputes have concerned precisely such phenomena: the crowd in the French Revolution, the aspirations of St. Petersburg's workers in 1917, the character of Barcelona's struggles in the 1930s. In the most recent rounds of discussion, the interest- and class-based interpretations of popular collective action that gained popularity in the 1960s have come under assault from aficionados of discourse, mentalities, and political culture, only to generate counteranalyses treating routine social life, shared understandings, collective organization, and po-

---

*Note how Sandra Lauderdale Graham confronts and adjudicates conflicting accounts of Rio's Vintem Riot of 1880.

litical opportunity structure as joint, interacting determinants of popular collective action.

Populist and radical analysts of popular collective action have often applied evolutionary schemes to its forms: prepolitical/political, traditional/modern, and so on. Great Marxist scholars such as E. J. Hobsbawm and George Rudé frequently worked on the assumption (or the explicit argument) that revolutionary consciousness and organization would eventually sweep away spontaneous, ineffectual protest. Beginning my own work on European popular collective action under the influence of work by Hobsbawm, Rudé, and their French counterparts, I myself experimented with such schemes as a division into "primitive," "reactionary," and "modern," then "competitive," "reactive," and "proactive." But I abandoned these schemes for three reasons:

1. They suggest an evolutionary (or even teleological) displacement of inferior by superior forms of action—from spontaneous protest to mass revolution, or from machine-breaking gangs to labor unions—when, in fact, the older forms were often quite effective in their time, and in any case supposedly backward forms long coexisted with their ostensibly superior competitors;

2. They confuse the forms of action (urban rebellion, strike, seizure of grain, occupation of public buildings) with the occasions on which they occur (rivalry among factions, reaction to tax increases, revolutionary bid for power); and

3. They assume a direct functional connection between the means of action available to a given population without regarding the cumulative effect of historical changes in their social bases, culture, and political opportunity structure.

It is crucial to inventory the forms of collective claim-making that are actually available to any historical population. But it is a mistake to classify them in progressive sequences.

How have historians **explained** popular collective action? Schematically, we can array the various positions that historians have taken as in the diagram. In one dimension, historians—and, for that matter, participants, observers, and social scientists as well—disagree over the spontaneity of intentions in popular collective action. The continuum in that dimension runs from 1) **direct impulse** (misery, anger, or the pleasure of mayhem being frequent candidates) to 2) **imposed consciousness** in the form of learned ideologies, creeds, and traditions to 3) **shared understanding** seen as accumulated awareness of interests and opportunities, one extreme version being an interpretation of popular politics as consciously calculating rational collective action. The other dimension concerns the social process that generates popular collective action from 1) **social stress** (for example, famine) to 2) **political mobilization** (for example, top-down recruitment of clients into a political movement) to 3) **continuous struggle** (for example, interaction between employers and workers). In combination, the two dimensions give us standard tales of Disorder (direct impulse encouraged by social stress), Progress (imposed consciousness resulting from political mobilization), and Struggle (shared understanding induced by continuous struggle). Evolutionary schemes commonly portray the forms of popular collective action as moving up the diagonal from spontaneous response to social stress at one extreme toward continuous struggle based on shared understanding at the culmination of a long process of education, organization, or self-realization.

Not all tales of popular collective action, however, lie on the diagonal; if they did, we would only need one dimension to represent them. At times, for example, historians have portrayed continuous struggle as favoring spontaneous responses to rage or righteous indignation at the appearance of an enemy. Advocates of revolutionary parties, on the other hand, have often claimed that effective political mobilization would eventually lead to shared understanding, hence onward to mass revolution. Although prevailing analyses cluster along the disorder-progress-struggle axis, that is not because no logical alternative exists.

Nor must all real instances of popular collective action occupy the same location within the two-dimensional space. On the contrary: part of the historian's challenge is to discover in any particular case the weights and interactions of intentions and social processes. As students of urban conflicts, we must inventory and then explain the actual range of social interactions by which ordinary people make claims, from faction fights to attacks on public buildings to general strikes; not all exhibit the same degree of spontaneity or the same precipitating social process. The diagram therefore has two uses: to identify the terms of competing explanations for popular collective action, and to specify two important regards in which popular collective action does, indeed, vary. Another part of the historian's challenge is to show how and why the conditions

Alternative Accounts of Popular Collective Action

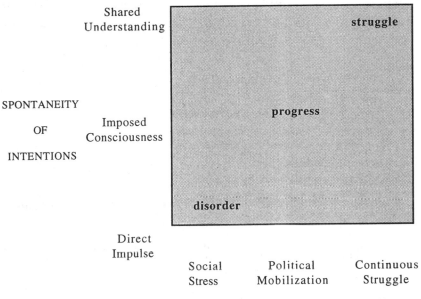

SPONTANEITY

OF

INTENTIONS

Shared
Understanding

Imposed
Consciousness

Direct
Impulse

struggle

progress

disorder

Social   Political   Continuous
Stress   Mobilization   Struggle

PRECIPITATING SOCIAL PROGRESS

generating popular collective action shift from one time and place to another.

Since these observations are commonplaces of European social and political history, it is puzzling for a European historian to find the literature on eighteenth- and nineteenth-century Latin American urban conflicts so thin. One might have thought that historians of Latin America, intuiting the relations between violent and nonviolent popular politics, would have rushed to examine how independence from Spain affected the pattern of urban violence in former Spanish colonies, whether urban violence differed significantly among regions of slave, indentured, coerced, or free labor, whether frontier cities produced different sorts of collective violence from capitals, how the presence or absence of caudillos and effective patron-client systems shaped urban rebellion, to what extent influential models of collective action spread from the United States southward, and so on through large questions of Latin American history prior to the twentieth century.

The essays in this book suggest that the absence of such studies in Latin American history stems from historians' (perhaps unwitting) adoption of two surprising suppositions: Latin America was so rural prior to the twentieth century that only agrarian conflict mattered; and elites so dominated urban politics that popular claim-making made no historical difference. In European perspective, both suppositions look dubious, even shocking. Not the relative or absolute size of cities, but their relation to large-scale social organization, constitutes their political importance in European history. Urban conflicts, furthermore, made enormous differences to European history even when (as was usually the case) plebeian claimants failed to achieve their aims. They made differences for several reasons:

1. Interaction between authorities and ordinary people created repressive routines, bargains, and even rights that constrained both sides;

2. When authorities and ruling classes split, one side or both frequently made popular alliances;

3. In urban areas, third parties such as shopkeepers and militias often became involved in conflicts that did not initially concern them;

4. The public spaces of cities offered wonderful, visible stages for dramatization of current issues; and

5. The threat of popular resistance or rebellion limited the actions available to the powerful.

These features of urban conflicts have drawn European historians to them in droves.

The exceptional papers on Latin America in the present volume address both challenges to the historical analysis of popular collective action: weighing and interweaving intentions and social processes in particular instances as well as reflecting on reasons for variation in the character of popular collective action. McFarlane, for example, deals with both; first, he places the Quito insurrection of May-June 1765 in the politics of its time, opting for a combination of social stress, top-down mobilization, and shared awareness; then he locates it among the various sorts of conflict and rebellion that characterized late colonial Spanish America. He criticizes previous accounts of the Rebellion of the Barrios, in essence, for locating it in our diagram's lower left-hand corner: an impulsive reaction to social stress (poverty induced by economic decline) devoid of ideological content; he then moves the rebellion's analysis up the diagonal, toward shared understanding and continuous struggle.

Examining the popular sacking of Mexico City's Parián Bazaar in December 1828, Silvia Arrom tries somewhat harder than McFarlane to draw from it a reading of popular mentalities, but she also interprets it as evidence about the political situation of the time, not to mention as a spur to subsequent repression and control. Arrom sets up her analysis as an application and critique of the Hobsbawm-Rudé portrayal of popular collective action, which entails rejection of the understanding that authorities of the time formed when they dismissed the participants as an excited rabble. But she also demurs from the cool, purposive picture offered by Hobsbawm and Rudé in favor of a characterization in terms of political mobilization plus direct impulse. She then argues a correspondence between her characterization of the December riot and the continuous characteristics of Mexico's populist politics in the era.

João José Reis traces popular resistance—with yet another call to assembly by tocsin, and another illumination, this time on the side of insurgents—to the government's intervention in Brazilian burial rites. In this case he finds more evidence of formal organization, in the form of religious brotherhoods, and of deliberate organization of a demonstration, in the Salvador of 1836. In one of those evolutionary schemes that Arrom rightly distrusts, we might locate Salvador's cemetery riot halfway to "modern" forms of popular collective action; after all, in 1836 street demonstrations had existed in western Europe for no more than forty years. But then we note the sacking of the cemetery company, the dismantling of the cemetery, and the parading of a mortuary cart to its ostentatious destruction, and we recognize forms of vengeance that had prevailed in Europe for centuries. More so than his colleagues, Reis grounds his analysis of the Cemiterada in mentalities, the mutation of traditional Portuguese and African attitudes toward death by their encounter with Latin American states and capitalism. Thus, he places his events in an unusual position: the upper left-hand corner of our diagram, where shared understandings prevail, but social stress with no more than a touch of political mobilization suffices to create a popular movement.

In the work of Sandra Lauderdale Graham we likewise find an emphasis on shared understandings, this time cast as political culture. Like Reis, she takes for granted that in the Rio de Janeiro of 1880 street demonstrations were available as means of claim-making. But she regards the event as a sort of *prise de conscience* that transformed subsequent understandings, hence subsequent politics. In her discussion we find the clearest expression of one contending view of popular politics: of political culture as an autonomously changing realm that **creates** political behavior and its changes. Even more so than Reis, her implicit conception of our diagram contains causal arrows running from the upper shared understanding to consciousness, impulse, stress, mobilization, and struggle.

David Sowell takes a very different view of the *bogotazo* of 1893, as a "window" onto artisan political activity. Like Graham, he uses competing accounts of the conflict as levers to pry open its mechanism. But he seeks first to single out the artisans' understandings of what they were doing, then to treat those understandings as partial causes of their action, then to set the understandings among other causes, eclectically enumerated, and finally to locate the *bogotazo* in the longer stream of Colombian collective violence. Sowell's pivot lies somewhere around the center of our diagram, at the intersection of political mobilization with imposed consciousness.

Jeffrey Needell's analysis of Rio de Janeiro's Revolta Contra Vacina (1904) resembles Arrom's treatment of Mexican events three-quarters of a century earlier: both of them treat the events in question as weighty, motivated political acts having considerable consequences. To a greater degree than Arrom, Needell places the performances in question within an established repertoire, the "Carioca tradition." Doing so pushes his interpretation toward the upper right-hand corner of our diagram, where previously shared understandings cross continuous struggle; the Revolta becomes one more round in strategic interactions that produced real winners, real losers, and realignments of Brazilian politics.

Finally, the anti-Yankee actions of Guadalajara residents in 1910 impress Avital Bloch and Servando Ortoll as a drama whose meaning emerges from its internal sequence. The highly selective expression of popular hostility to *norteamericanos* and Protestants indicates that, far from blind hate and random destruction, the people knew what they were doing. Both the method and the message resemble those by which four decades ago George Rudé challenged dismissive accounts of crowd action in England and France, right up to the assessment of the crowd's revolutionary potential, or lack thereof.

Note the paradox. So long as we search for invariant general models of popular collective action, we can say nothing useful about these 150 years of Latin American conflict; no general model fits all these varied events. Yet, in examining them, we recognize that we are dealing with very general phenomena, forms of action and causal relationships that extend far beyond Latin America in the eighteenth and nineteenth centuries. How can both be true? The paradox dissolves with this observation: defined broadly as social base, culture, and opportunity structure, the causes of popular contention prevail through all of human history. Social base, culture, and opportunity structure intertwine in so many combinations, and change so significantly as a cumulative consequence of popular contention, that we have no choice but to embed explanations of particular events and changes in their historical settings. That is precisely what we find the authors of these outstanding articles seeking to do.

Suggested Readings

Aya, Rod. *Rethinking Revolutions and Collective Violence: Studies on Concept, Theory, and Method.* Amsterdam: Het Spinhuis, 1990.

Benford, Robert D., and Scott A. Hunt. "Dramaturgy and Social Movements: The Social Construction and Communication of Power." *Sociological Inquiry* 62 (Winter 1992): 35–55.

Birnbaum, Pierre. *States and Collective Action: The European Experience.* Cambridge: Cambridge University Press, 1988.

Boggs, Carl. *Social Movements and Political Power: Emerging Forms of Radicalism in the West.* Philadelphia: Temple University Press, 1986.

Braud, Philippe, ed. *La violence politique dans les démocraties européennes occidentales.* Special issue of *Cultures et Conflits* 9/10 (Spring/Summer 1993).

Brewer, John D., Kathleen Magee, and Richard Jenkins. *The Police, Public Order, and the State: Policing in Great Britain, Northern Ireland, the Irish Republic, the U.S.A., Israel, South Africa, and China.* New York: St. Martin's Press, 1988.

Bright, Charles, and Susan Harding, eds. *Statemaking and Social Movements.* Ann Arbor: University of Michigan Press, 1984.

Brooks, Clem. "Class Consciousness and Politics in Comparative Perspective." *Social Science Research* 2, 23 (1994): 167–95.

Burke, Edmund, III, ed. *Global Crises and Social Movements: Artisans, Peasants, Populists, and the World Economy.* Boulder: Westview, 1988.

Casanova, Julián. *La historia social y los historiadores.* Barcelona: Editorial Crítica, 1991.

Casanova, Julián, Angela Cenarro, Julita Cifuentes, Pilar Maluenda, and Pilar Salomón. *El pasado oculto. Fascismo y violencia en Aragón (1936–1939).* Madrid: Siglo Veintiuno de España, 1992.

Clemens, Elisabeth S. "Organizational Repertoires and Institutional Change: Women's Groups and the Transformation of U.S. Politics,

1890–1920." *American Journal of Sociology* 98 (January 1993): 755–98.

Conell, Carol, and Kim Voss. "Formal Organization and the Fate of Social Movements: Craft Association and Class Alliance in the Knights of Labor." *American Sociological Review* 55 (April 1990): 255–69.

Cruz, Rafael. "Crísis del estado y acción colectiva en el período de entreguerras, 1917–1939." *Historia Social* 15 (1993): 119–38.

Diani, Mario, and Ron Eyerman, eds. *Studying Collective Action*. Newbury Park: Sage, 1992.

Duyvendak, Jan W. *Le poids du politique. Nouveaux mouvements sociaux en France*. Paris: L'Harmattan, 1994.

Favre, Pierre, ed. *La manifestation*. Paris: Presses de la Fondation Nationale des Sciences Politiques, 1990.

Gambrelle, Fabienne, and Michel Trebitsch, eds. *Révolte et société. Actes du Colloque d'Histoire au Présent, Paris mai 1988*. Paris: Histoire au Présent, 1989. 2 vols.

Gamson, William A. *The Strategy of Social Protest*. 2d ed. Belmont, CA: Wadsworth Publishing Co., 1990.

Goodwin, Jeff, and Theda Skocpol. "Explaining Revolutions in the Contemporary Third World." *Politics and Society* 17 (December 1989): 489–509.

Gould, Roger V. "Multiple Networks and Mobilization in the Paris Commune, 1871." *American Sociological Review* 56 (December 1991): 716–29.

———. "Trade Cohesion, Class Unity, and Urban Insurrection: Artisanal Activism in the Paris Commune." *American Journal of Sociology* 98 (January 1993): 721–54.

Hanagan, Michael P. "New Perspectives on Class Formation: Culture, Reproduction, and Agency." *Social Science History* 18 (Spring 1994): 77–94.

Hanagan, Michael P., and Charles Stephenson, eds. *Proletarians and Protest: The Roots of Class Formation in an Industrializing World*. New York: Greenwood, 1986.

———. *Confrontation, Class Consciousness, and the Labor Process: Studies in Proletarian Class Formation*. New York: Greenwood, 1986.

Hirsch, Eric L. *Urban Revolt: Ethnic Politics in the Nineteenth-Century Chicago Labor Movement*. Berkeley: University of California Press, 1990.

Hobsbawm, Eric J. "What is Ethnic Conflict and How Does it Differ from Other Conflicts?" In Anthony McDermott, ed., *Ethnic Conflict and International Security*. Oslo: Norwegian Institute of International Security, 1994.

Kirby, Andrew. *Power/Resistance: Local Politics and the Chaotic State*. Bloomington: Indiana University Press, 1993.

Kitschelt, Herbert. "Political Opportunity Structures and Political Protest: Anti-Nuclear Movements in Four Democracies." *British Journal of Political Science* 16 (January 1986): 57–85.

Klandermans, Bert, Hanspeter Kriesi, and Sidney Tarrow, eds. *From Structure to Action: Comparing Social Movement Research across Cultures.* Greenwich, CT: JAI Press, 1988. International Social Movement Research, vol. 1.

Martínez Dorado, Gloria. "La formación del estado y la acción colectiva en España: 1808–1845." *Historia Social* 15 (1993): 101–18.

McAdam, Doug, John D. McCarthy, and Mayer N. Zald. "Social Movements." In Neil J. Smelser, ed., *Handbook of Sociology.* Newbury Park: Sage, 1988.

McCarthy, John D., David W. Britt, and Mark Wolfson. "The Institutional Channeling of Social Movements by the State in the United States." *Research in Social Movements, Conflicts, and Change* 13 (1991): 45–76.

McPhail, Clark. *The Myth of the Madding Crowd.* New York: Aldine De Gruyter, 1991.

Melucci, Alberto. *Nomads of the Present: Social Movements and Individual Need in Contemporary Society.* Philadelphia: Temple University Press, 1989.

Meyer, David S. "Institutionalizing Dissent: The United States Structure of Political Opportunity and the End of the Nuclear Freeze Movement." *Sociological Forum* 8 (June 1993): 157–79.

Morris, Aldon, and Cedric Herring. "Theory and Research in Social Movements: A Critical Review." *Annual Review of Political Science* 2 (1987): 137–95.

Olzak, Susan. *The Dynamics of Ethnic Competition and Conflict.* Stanford: Stanford University Press, 1992.

Opp, Karl-Dieter. *The Rationality of Political Protest: A Comparative Analysis of Rational Choice Theory.* Boulder: Westview, 1989.

Rasler, Karen. "War, Accommodation, and Violence in the United States, 1890–1970." *American Political Science Review* 80 (September 1986): 921–45.

Roy, Beth. *Some Trouble with Cows: Making Sense of Social Conflict.* Berkeley: University of California Press, 1994.

Roy, William. "Class Conflict and Social Change in Historical Perspective." *Annual Review of Sociology* 10 (1984): 483–506.

Rule, James B. *Theories of Civil Violence.* Berkeley: University of California Press, 1989.

Scott, James. *Weapons of the Weak: Everyday Forms of Peasant Resistance.* New Haven: Yale University Press, 1985.

———. *Domination and the Arts of Resistance: Hidden Transcripts.* New Haven: Yale University Press, 1990.

Silver, Beverly J., Giovanni Arrighi, and Melvyn Dubovsky, eds. "Labor Unrest in the World Economy, 1870–1990." Special issue of *Review* 18 (1995).

Tarrow, Sidney. *Democracy and Disorder: Social Conflict, Political Protest, and Democracy in Italy, 1965–1975.* New York: Oxford University Press, 1989.

————. *Power in Movement*. Cambridge: Cambridge University Press, 1994.

Walton, John. *Western Times and Water Wars: State, Culture, and Rebellion in California*. Berkeley: University of California Press, 1992.

Williams, Robin. "The Sociology of Ethnic Conflicts: Comparative International Perspectives." *Annual Review of Sociology* 20 (1994): 49–79.

Index

Acciavoli, José Ignacio, 106
Acordada revolt (Mexico City), 73, 75
Adamo, Samuel C., 161, 172
Alamán, Lucas, 74, 77, 79, 84, 87
Almeida Rosa, Francisco Otaviano de, 121, 128
Amat, Viceroy (Peru), 57
American Candy Company (Guadalajara): attack on, 205
Anjos, Rita dos, 106
Anti-Americanism: in Guadalajara, 196–215, 238
Anti-Protestantism: in Guadalajara, 196–215
Anti-Spanish feeling: in Quito unrest, 43–44
Araújo, José, 110
Ariès, Philippe, 99
Arrom, Silvia: on Parián riot, 237
Artisans: rioting in Bogotá and, 137–50
Audiencia (Quito): tax reform and, 23–24, 32, 36–37, 39, 43–44, 46, 48–49, 53–54

Bahia, Brazil: African population of, 100; riot in, 97–111
Banditry: relationship of riots to, 4–5
Barragán, Vicente, 207
Barral, Countess, 130
Belle époque: triumph of, in Rio de Janeiro, 183–85
Benchimol, Jaime Larry, 161, 170
Bendix, Richard: on characteristics of riots, 88
Bicalho, Francisco, 163
Bloch, Avital, 238
Bocanegra, José María, 74
Bogotá, Colombia: growth in population of, 138; rioting in, 1–2, 137–50, 238
Borja, Francisco de, 33, 38, 46, 50, 54–55; proposed reforms in Quito and, 22–23, 25–29, 31
Bourbon Reforms, 1

Brazil: political situation in, 161–64; social conditions in, 168–79; societal changes in, 115–16
Brazilian Anti-Slavery Society: formation of, 128
Bustamante, Carlos María de: Parián riot and, 74–81, 87, 90

Cabildo abierto (Quito), 23, 26–28, 30–33, 59
Caicedo, Ignacio B., 142
Calixto de Alarcón, Nicolás, 53
Camacho, José Leocadio, 142, 146–48; on suppression of Philanthropic Society, 144
Campos Sales, Manuel Ferrez de, 162–63, 167, 174
Caracas, Venezuela: rebellion in, 60
Cardoso, Ferro, 125
Cardoso de Castro, Antonio Augusto, 167
Carmo Liberals, 123, 126
Caro, Miguel Antonio, 139, 142, 144, 146
Carothers, Carlos B., 197, 202; Guadalajara rioting and, 205, 207–8; Magill on, 203
Carvalho, Carlos Augusto de, 125
Carvalho, Carlos Leôncio de, 121
Carvalho, José Carlos de, 125; describes Vintem riot, 120
Carvalho, Luiz Pedro de, 101
Cemiterada reform movement (Salvador), 2, 99, 111, 237
Chaunu, Pierre, 99
Chiriboga, Juan de, 22
Cistué, José de, 22, 36, 40, 48, 51, 54–55; opposes tax reform in Quito, 23, 25
Class conflict, 4; in Quito, 19, 57–62
Club dos Diários (Rio de Janeiro), 163
Coatsworth, John: on urban social struggles, 1
Colombia Cristiana, 142, 146; Bogotá riot and, 141

Latin American Silhouettes
Studies in History and Culture

William H. Beezley and
Judith Ewell
Editors

Volumes Published

William H. Beezley and Judith Ewell, eds., *The Human Tradition in Latin America: The Twentieth Century* (1987). Cloth ISBN 0-8420-2283-X Paper ISBN 0-8420-2284-8

Judith Ewell and William H. Beezley, eds., *The Human Tradition in Latin America: The Nineteenth Century* (1989). Cloth ISBN 0-8420-2331-3 Paper ISBN 0-8420-2332-1

David G. LaFrance, *The Mexican Revolution in Puebla, 1908–1913: The Maderista Movement and the Failure of Liberal Reform* (1989). ISBN 0-8420-2293-7

Mark A. Burkholder, *Politics of a Colonial Career: José Baquíjano and the Audiencia of Lima*, 2d ed. (1990). Cloth ISBN 0-8420-2353-4 Paper ISBN 0-8420-2352-6

Kenneth M. Coleman and George C. Herring, eds. (with Foreword by Daniel Oduber), *Understanding the Central American Crisis: Sources of Conflict, U.S. Policy, and Options for Peace* (1991). Cloth ISBN 0-8420-2382-8 Paper ISBN 0-8420-2383-6

Carlos B. Gil, ed., *Hope and Frustration: Interviews with Leaders of Mexico's Political Opposition* (1992). Cloth ISBN 0-8420-2395-X Paper ISBN 0-8420-2396-8

Charles Bergquist, Ricardo Peñaranda, and Gonzalo Sánchez, eds., *Violence in Colombia: The Contemporary Crisis in Historical Perspective* (1992). Cloth ISBN 0-8420-2369-0 Paper ISBN 0-8420-2376-3

Heidi Zogbaum, *B. Traven: A Vision of Mexico* (1992). ISBN 0-8420-2392-5

Jaime E. Rodríguez O., ed., *Patterns of Contention in Mexican History* (1992). ISBN 0-8420-2399-2

Louis A. Pérez, Jr., ed., *Slaves, Sugar, and Colonial Society: Travel Accounts of Cuba, 1801–1899* (1992). Cloth ISBN 0-8420-2354-2 Paper ISBN 0-8420-2415-8

Peter Blanchard, *Slavery and Abolition in Early Republican Peru* (1992). Cloth ISBN 0-8420-2400-X   Paper ISBN 0-8420-2429-8

Paul J. Vanderwood, *Disorder and Progress: Bandits, Police, and Mexican Development*. Revised and Enlarged Edition (1992). Cloth ISBN 0-8420-2438-7   Paper ISBN 0-8420-2439-5

Sandra McGee Deutsch and Ronald H. Dolkart, eds., *The Argentine Right: Its History and Intellectual Origins, 1910 to the Present* (1993). Cloth ISBN 0-8420-2418-2   Paper ISBN 0-8420-2419-0

Jaime E. Rodríguez O., ed., *The Evolution of the Mexican Political System* (1993). ISBN 0-8420-2448-4

Steve Ellner, *Organized Labor in Venezuela, 1958–1991: Behavior and Concerns in a Democratic Setting* (1993). ISBN 0-8420-2443-3

Paul J. Dosal, *Doing Business with the Dictators: A Political History of United Fruit in Guatemala, 1899–1944* (1993). Cloth ISBN 0-8420-2475-1   Paper ISBN 0-8420-2590-1

Marquis James, *Merchant Adventurer: The Story of W. R. Grace* (1993). ISBN 0-8420-2444-1

John Charles Chasteen and Joseph S. Tulchin, eds., *Problems in Modern Latin American History: A Reader* (1994). Cloth ISBN 0-8420-2327-5 Paper ISBN 0-8420-2328-3

Marguerite Guzmán Bouvard, *Revolutionizing Motherhood: The Mothers of the Plaza de Mayo* (1994). Cloth ISBN 0-8420-2486-7 Paper ISBN 0-8420-2487-5

William H. Beezley, Cheryl English Martin, and William E. French, eds., *Rituals of Rule, Rituals of Resistance: Public Celebrations and Popular Culture in Mexico* (1994). Cloth ISBN 0-8420-2416-6 Paper ISBN 0-8420-2417-4

Stephen R. Niblo, *War, Diplomacy, and Development: The United States and Mexico, 1938–1954* (1995). ISBN 0-8420-2550-2

G. Harvey Summ, ed., *Brazilian Mosaic: Portraits of a Diverse People and Culture* (1995). Cloth ISBN 0-8420-2491-3 Paper ISBN 0-8420-2492-1

N. Patrick Peritore and Ana Karina Galve-Peritore, eds., *Biotechnology in Latin America: Politics, Impacts, and Risks* (1995). Cloth ISBN 0-8420-2556-1   Paper ISBN 0-8420-2557-X

Silvia Marina Arrom and Servando Ortoll, eds., *Riots in the Cities: Popular Politics and the Urban Poor in Latin America, 1765–1910* (1996). Cloth ISBN 0-8420-2580-4   Paper ISBN 0-8420-2581-2

Roderic Ai Camp, ed., *Polling for Democracy: Public Opinion and Political Liberalization in Mexico* (1996). Cloth ISBN 0-8420-2583-9